IMAGES
of America

DEER ISLE AND STONINGTON

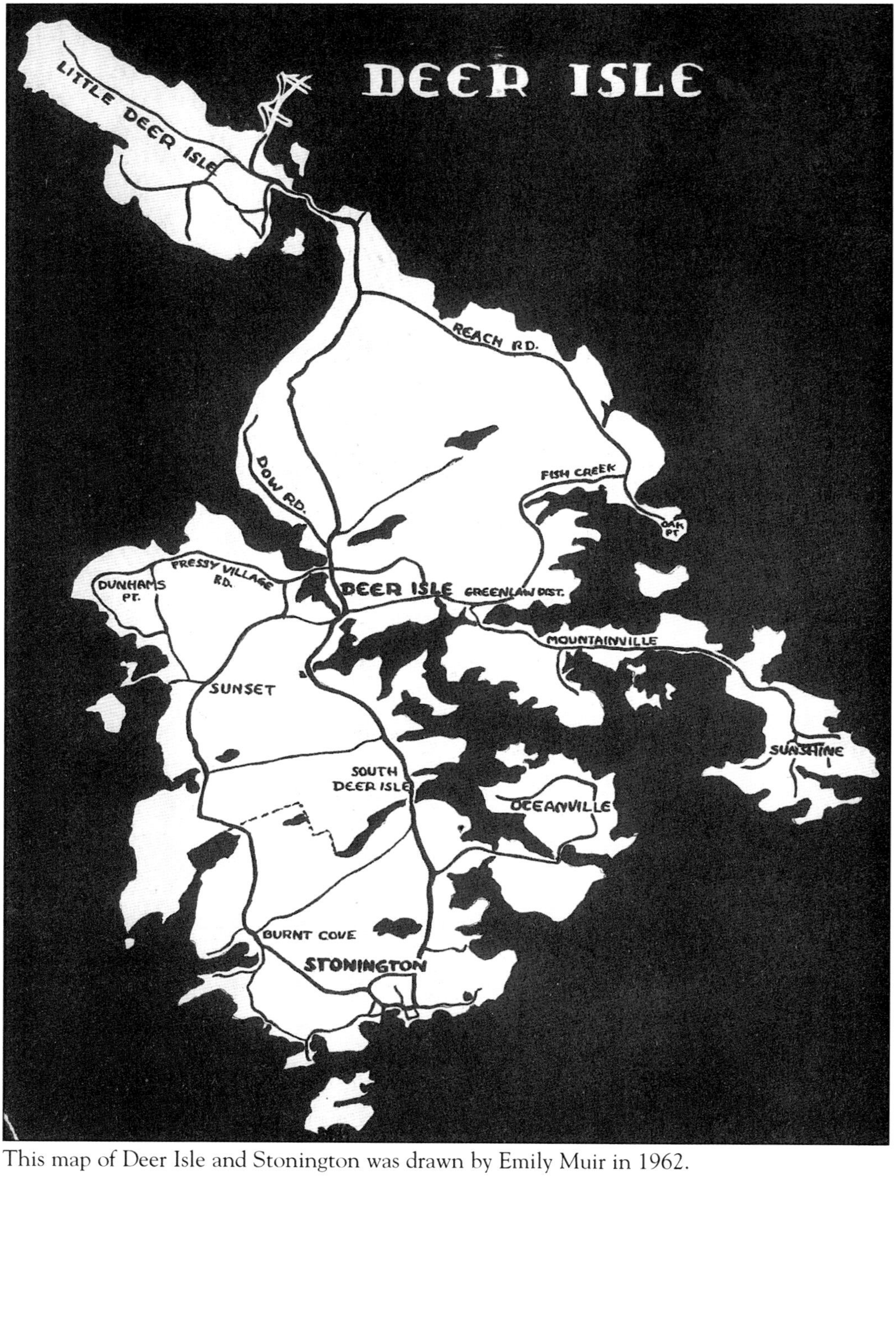

This map of Deer Isle and Stonington was drawn by Emily Muir in 1962.

IMAGES of America
DEER ISLE AND STONINGTON

The Deer Isle-Stonington Historical Society

ARCADIA PUBLISHING

ISBN 978-0-7385-3566-1

Published by Arcadia Publishing
Charleston, South Carolina

Printed in the United States of America

Library of Congress Catalog Card Number: 2004101332

For all general information contact Arcadia Publishing at:
Telephone 843-853-2070
Fax 843-853-0044
E-mail sales@arcadiapublishing.com
For customer service and orders:
Toll-Free 1-888-313-2665

Visit us on the Internet at www.arcadiapublishing.com

On the cover: This Stonington image was captured in 1937.

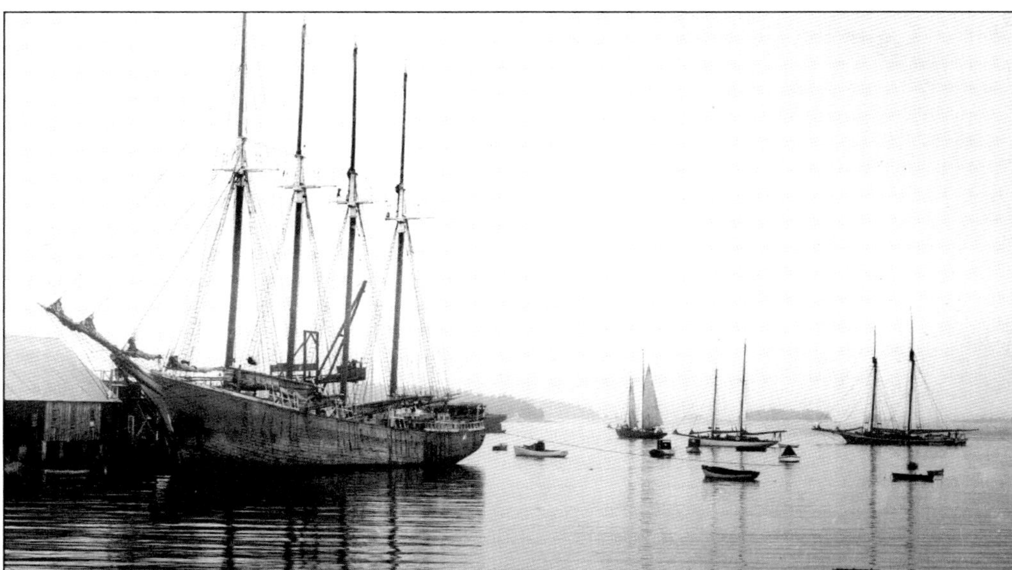

In this Stonington Harbor scene, the four-masted schooner *Theoline* unloads coal at the R. K. Barter Company dock in the late 1930s. Note the men on the upper unloading ramp. Accompanying them is a coal cart, which they will load and haul to a building, where they will dump its contents into coal bins. In the harbor at anchor, another schooner waits to deliver its cargo. Two schooner yachts are also at anchor.

Contents

ACKNOWLEDGMENTS

The following people made this book possible by sharing their photographs, knowledge, time, and writing and computer skills: Neva Beck, Paul Blanchette, Lloyd Brimigion, Barbara Britton, Carol Billings, Hubert Billings, Tinker Crouch, Rena Day, Aimee Eaton, Denise Hardy, Myron Hardy, William Haviland, Judy Hill, Mayotta Kendrick, Marjorie Loberg, Edith Marshall, Caroline Rittenhouse, Paul Stubing, Sylvia Tate, Becke Thompson, Marvel Torrey, Connie Wiberg, and Bob Williams.

We also want to acknowledge the following photographers, who created and saved these historical records of the island: Burton Ames, Walter Fowler, Thomas P. Haviland, Dr. B. Lake Noyes, and the Penobscot Bay Studio (Sally Gilliland).

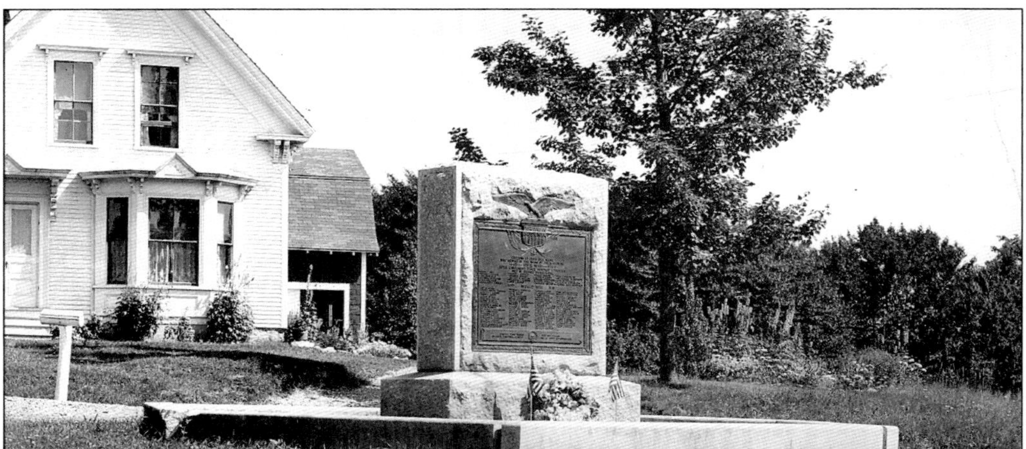

The Veterans Monument, made of granite from Stonington, is located on Route 15 just outside Deer Isle Village. It was dedicated in 1921, funded by $500 from the town of Deer Isle, with the balance (and subsequent additions) paid for by individual contributions. One side shows the names of those from Deer Isle who died in the Civil War and World War I Deer Isle veterans. At a later date, the names of Deer Isle World War II and Korean War veterans were added to the other side. For many years , it was the site of Memorial Day ceremonies.

INTRODUCTION

Deer Isle lies in Penobscot Bay, separated from the mainland by Eggemoggin Reach. A bridge over the Reach connects Little Deer Isle to the mainland. A causeway connects Little Deer Isle to Deer Isle, which is home to two towns—Deer Isle and Stonington—and several villages—Sunset, Sunshine, Mountainville, and Oceanville.

The first people to live on Deer Isle were American Indians, and they were here as early as 6,100 years ago. Their descendants were known to early French explorers as *Etchemins*; some continued to frequent the island long after Anglo-Americans established their settlements.

The first European to venture into the region was Estevan Gomez. On a voyage of exploration for the king of Spain, he sailed up the Reach between Deer Isle and the mainland. But it was the French who became the most active, establishing a fort at Castine and trading and intermarrying with the American Indians. It was likely a Frenchman who was found buried in full armor on Campbell's Island off Oak Point, Deer Isle. Accompanying his body were those of two American Indian companions.

Deer Isle was settled by English-speaking colonists from New England near the end of the French and Indian War, c. 1760. Men from the island eventually became known for their skills as mariners; this was reflected in the selection of Deer Isle crews for defenders of the America's Cup, both before and after the famous victories in 1895 and 1899. Their ancestors, however, did not come here to follow the sea. Indeed, some came to leave seafaring behind. They were interested in establishing farms, and their first cabins were built on the northern portion of the island, where the best soils for raising crops were found. The southern part of the island was not settled until after 1800, and then only sparsely. This situation did not change until the granite boom of the late 19th century.

At first farming did well on Deer Isle, but over time heavy reliance on fire to clear and maintain fields led to a decline in fertility of the soil. Faced with declining productivity of their farms, islanders were forced to find economic alternatives. Given their insular location and reliance on water transportation, it was natural that they should turn to seafaring. This happened just as maritime commerce was undergoing a boom all along the coast, so Deer Isle men became active in shipbuilding, seafaring, and fishing, especially in South Deer Isle and Oceanville. Deer Isle sailors, like other merchant seamen of New England, became goodwill ambassadors for America in seaports all over the world. Unfortunately, the boom time did not last, as seagoing commerce was periodically affected by depression. Thus, family farming remained important as a cushion against hard times. A labor pool sufficient to tend the farm while at the same time furnishing officers, crew, or both for locally owned vessels was satisfied by the practice of a newly married couple settling on the farm owned by either the bride's or groom's parents. Most people spent their lives cooperating on a day-to-day basis in economic activities with close relatives, all of whom lived together (even if in separate houses) on the same farm.

Limited mining—for silver, zinc, serpentine, and lime—took place on Deer Isle in the late 19th and early 20th centuries, but these enterprises did not last long and never became "big business," as granite quarrying did in Stonington. In the 1880s, a few "summer people" began coming to the island, establishing small colonies at Eggemoggin (the north end of Little Deer Isle) and Dunham's Point. The mainstays of economic activity continued to be farming and seafaring. This unique mix of activities served islanders well, even after the decline of commercial sailing in the first half of the 20th century. Deer Isle men adapted to this change, serving as officers and crew on private yachts; for years, several hundred men left the island every summer to "go yachting." As a consequence, the distinctive pattern of large family residence continued, especially in the northern part of the island, until midway through the 20th century. In the early 1950s, although farming had all but disappeared as a significant occupation, many people were still living on parts of farms established by their ancestors in the late 1700s.

For Stonington, what had been a sparsely settled fishing village underwent a boom in the late 19th century, when quarrying became the major occupation. In 1897, what had been known as Green's Landing separated from the town of Deer Isle to become the new town of Stonington. Many Europeans, mostly from Italy, were imported as stone cutters. Some were housed in barracks at Crotch Island, but most lived in the hotels and large boardinghouses constructed in Stonington, as close to the steamboat landing as possible. Family homes were built in the same area.

Life on the island changed forever when automobiles brought a demand for a bridge. The Deer Isle-Sedgwick Bridge was completed in 1939. In 1941, when the United States joined World War II, island people left in large numbers to serve in the armed forces and to work in munitions plants. One of the major occupations of island men came to an end; yachts and steamships were taken over for a variety of military purposes. When the war ended, many of the people who had left returned, but some did not. New construction materials were developed, and steel, glass, and concrete began to take the place of granite. Quarrying, as a major industry, came to an end shortly after the war.

Maritime employment was affected by the same force that brought the occupation of seafaring virtually to an end in the United States: the merchant marine gradually employed sailors from other countries. By the beginning of the 21st century, the last yachtsman had come ashore, and only two engineering officers still sailed commercially.

The bridge brought increasing numbers of people who wanted to own land. By the end of the 1950s, fishing and tourism had become the mainstays of the economy, and few of the old families were to be found living on farms. In Stonington, residential patterns changed when the quarries fell on hard times. Since then, much land in both towns has passed to "people from away," and there are continuing concerns about access to the shore and the ability to maintain working waterfronts. At the same time, the end of the 20th century saw a rise in efforts to provide trails, preserves, beaches, and other open spaces to the public.

One

TRANSPORTATION

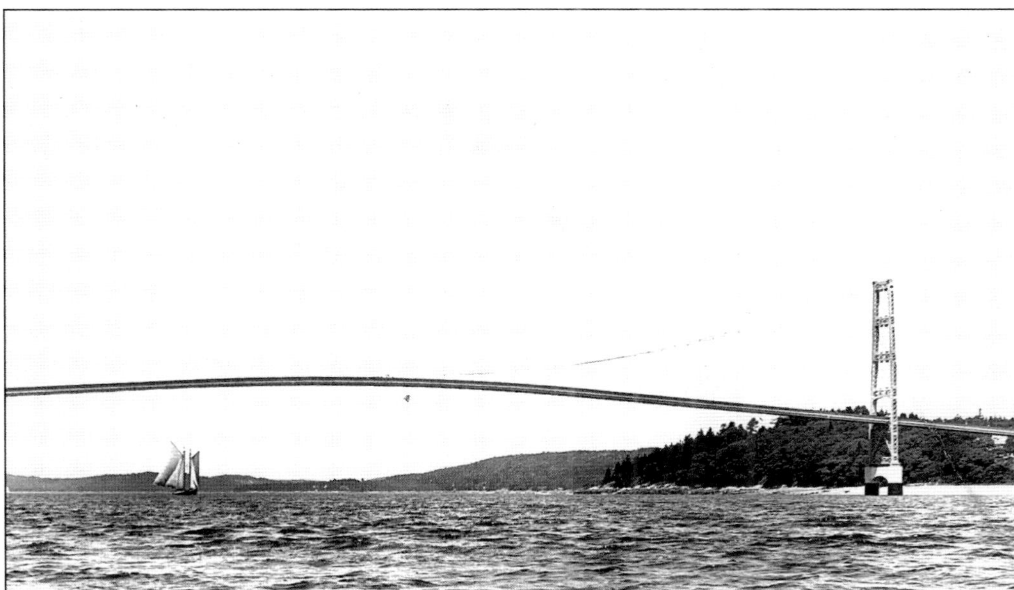

The past and the present meet in this photograph, taken c. 1942, as a schooner sails wing and wing toward the Deer Isle-Sedgwick Bridge. Bound eastward on Eggemoggin Reach, it is one of the last of the coasters, likely the *Mercantile*, loaded with coal. The same scene is frequent today, although the *Mercantile*, like many other old schooners, is now a windjammer carrying tourists.

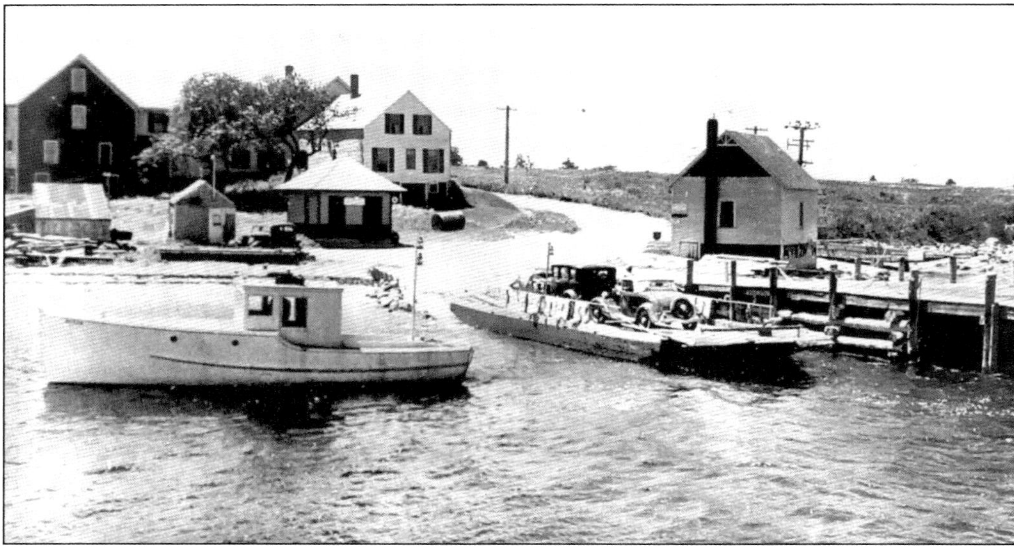

From the early settlement of the island, ferry service of one kind or another has always been provided by the Scott family, descendants of Nathaniel Scott, who came here near the time of the Revolutionary War. Nathaniel's son John provided the first service, which was formalized in 1807, when the town voted to hire him "to build ferryways" for the purpose of crossing Eggemoggin Reach to Sedgwick. The original landing was situated near where the Little Deer Isle Causeway is now.

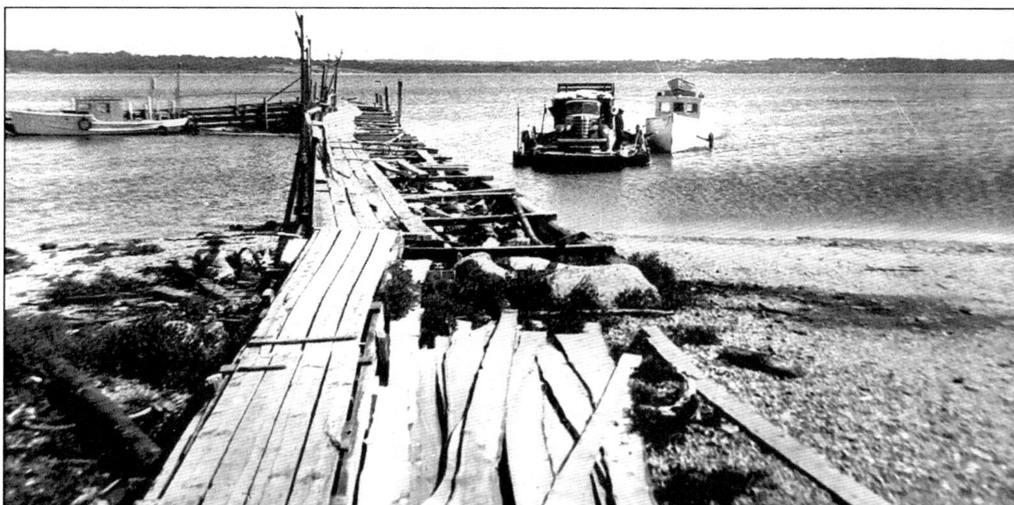

With the coming of steamships, Scott's Landing was established at its North Deer Isle location at the end of Ferry Landing Road. A wharf held an express office and a waiting room. A breakwater, shown here, protected it. In 1910, John Scott built a small scow, which held two automobiles. By 1936, there were two more scows, one carrying six cars and the other three. Both were towed by powerboats. The ferry ran daily at half-hour intervals from 6 a.m. to 9 p.m. Fares were 25¢ for passengers, $1.50 for automobiles, and $2 for trucks. Ferry service ended on June 26, 1939.

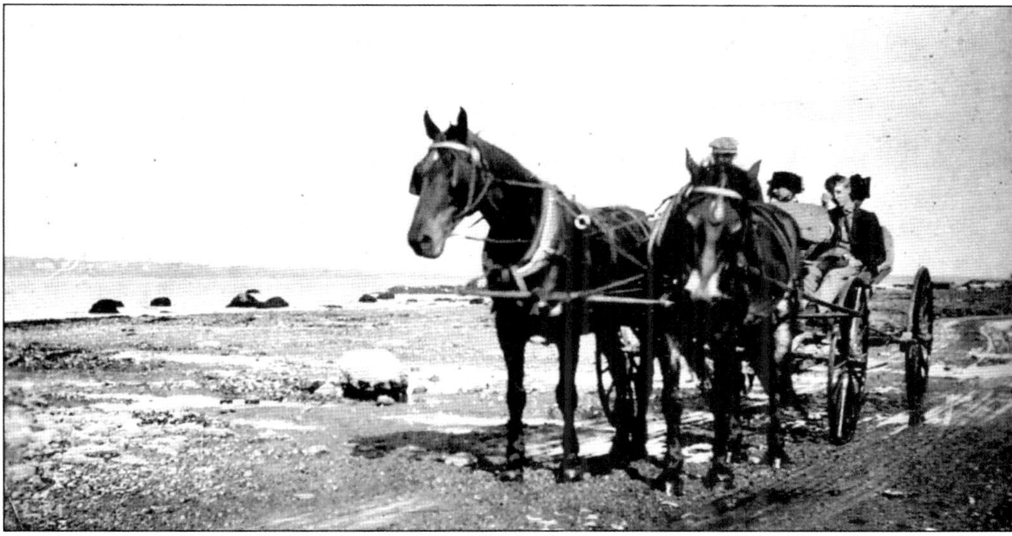

Prior to 1927, passage from Little Deer Isle to North Deer Isle was made on a line of hard clay clam flats by horse and buggy, by foot, and later by automobile. That same year, George E. Snowman of Little Deer Isle, a representative in the legislature, was able to get $15,000 in state funds to start construction of the causeway. In this c. 1910 photograph, a wagon is "crossing the bar" at low tide, headed toward Little Deer Isle.

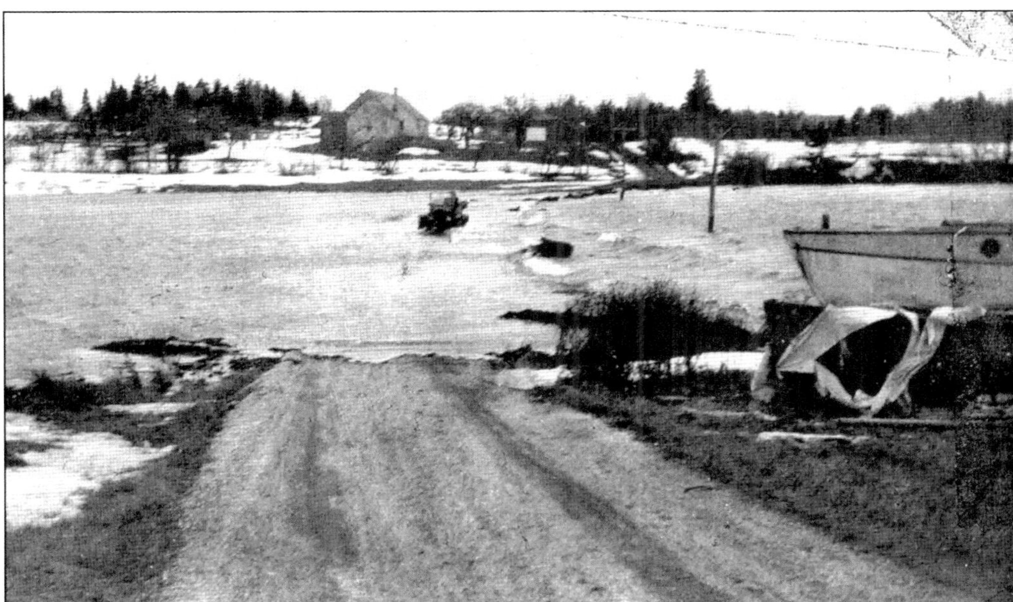

An automobile crosses the Little Deer Isle bar before construction of the causeway. Existence of the causeway helped justify the building of the Deer Isle-Sedgwick Bridge a decade later.

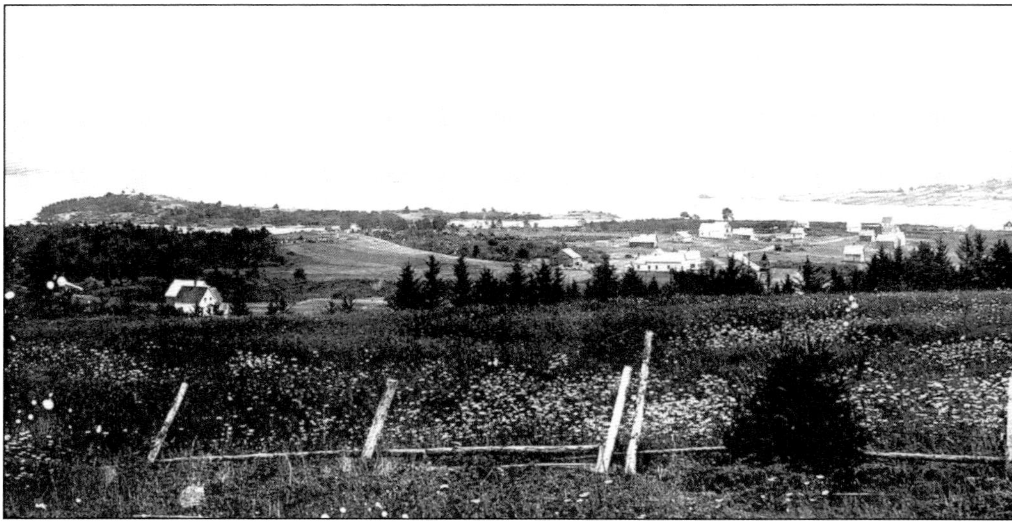

This postcard shows the view from Pine Hill, Little Deer Isle. To the right, the road from North Deer Isle is visible; the causeway was built to meet it. Capt. Walter Scott, in one of his letters to the editor of the *Island Ad-Vantages*, said that flounder used to bed in the mud flats there. In March, people could spear the fish as they pushed their heads up out of the mud.

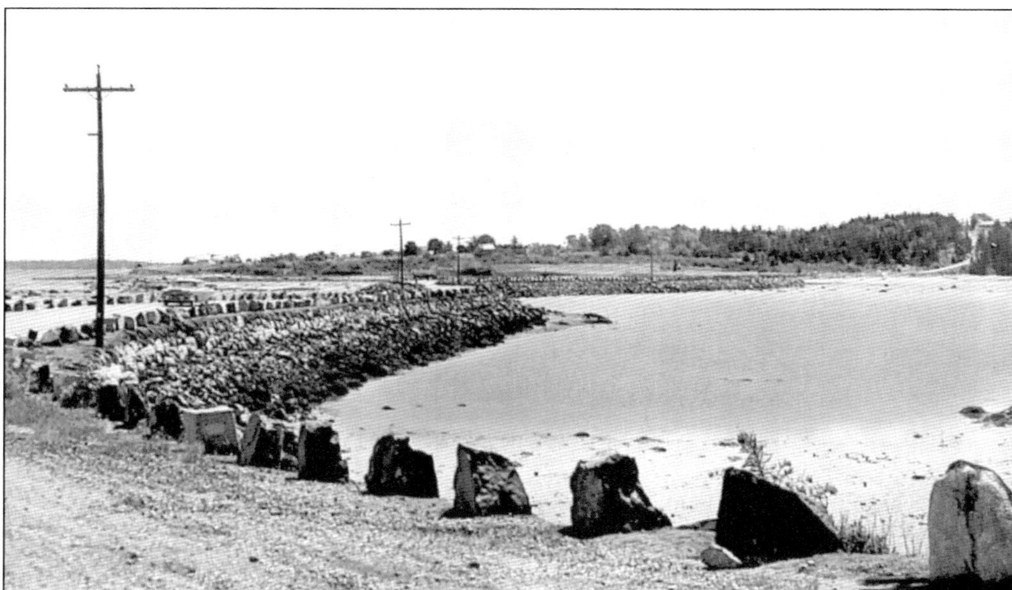

The Little Deer Isle causeway looks very much the same now as it appeared in this 1940s postcard. The area used to be known as "the Bow Cat," after a whaleboat rigged as a schooner ran aground there in 1859. It washed up on the beach in a storm and was badly damaged. Notices were posted in local stores asking for people to go "up to the *Bow Cat*." Ships carpenters repaired her, and two yoke of oxen hauled her to where she could float. Until the early 1900s, the area was still called the Bow Cat.

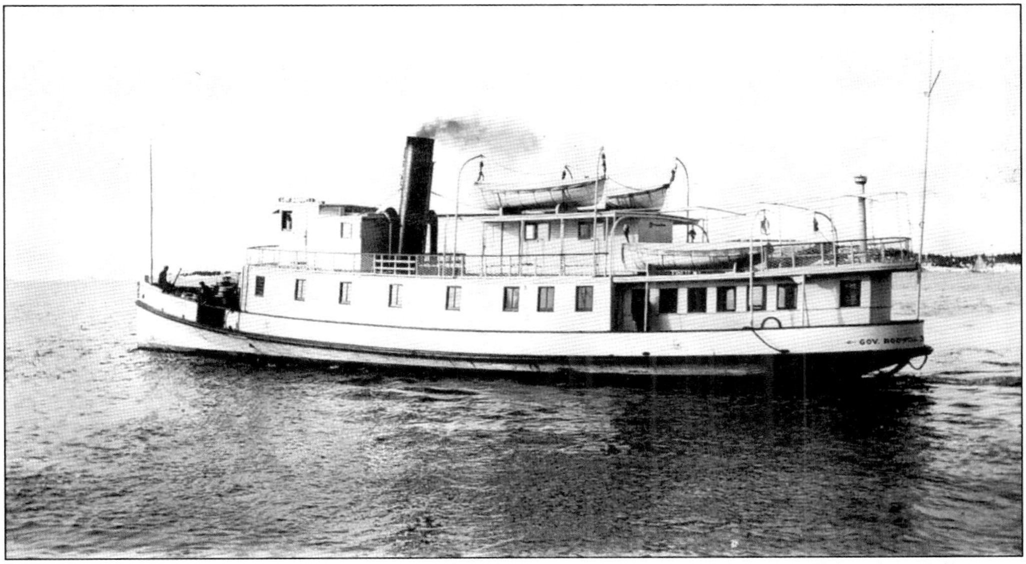

Weather notwithstanding, the *Governor Bodwell* provided service between Rockland, Vinalhaven, North Haven, Stonington, and Swan's Island. On January 26, 1924, she was entering Burnt Coat Harbor on Swan's Island in a blinding snowstorm with sub-zero temperatures when she struck hard on Spindle Ledge. Local fishermen who heard her distress signals came out and rescued her passengers and the first-class mail. While being repaired in Rockland, the *Governor Bodwell* burned to the waterline at her dock.

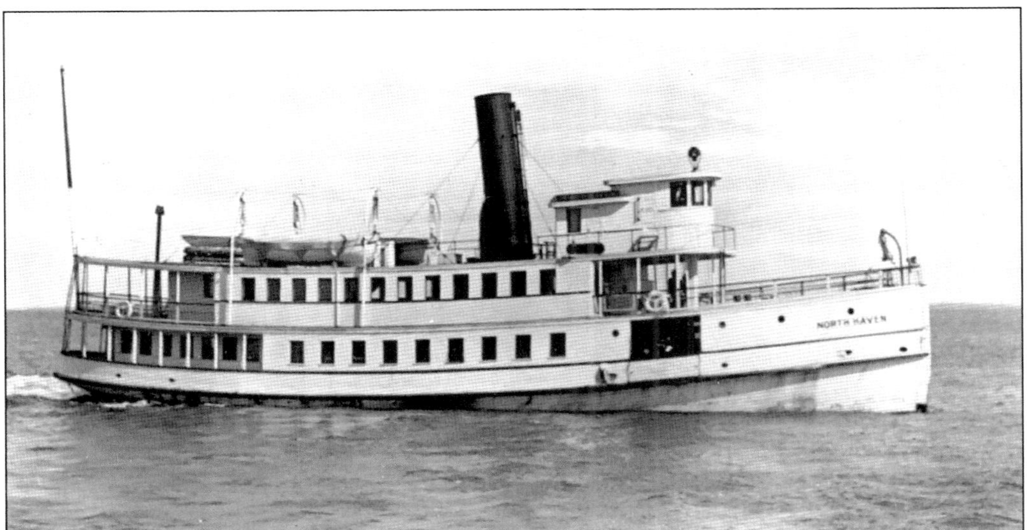

The steamer *North Haven* replaced the *Governor Bodwell* in 1931, providing service between Rockland and Stonington. Under the command of Capt. Roscoe Kent of Swan's Island, the *North Haven* was well known for her ice-breaking capabilities and, on one occasion, broke the Coast Guard cutter *Kickapoo* out of the ice. This photograph shows her final departure from Stonington in 1942.

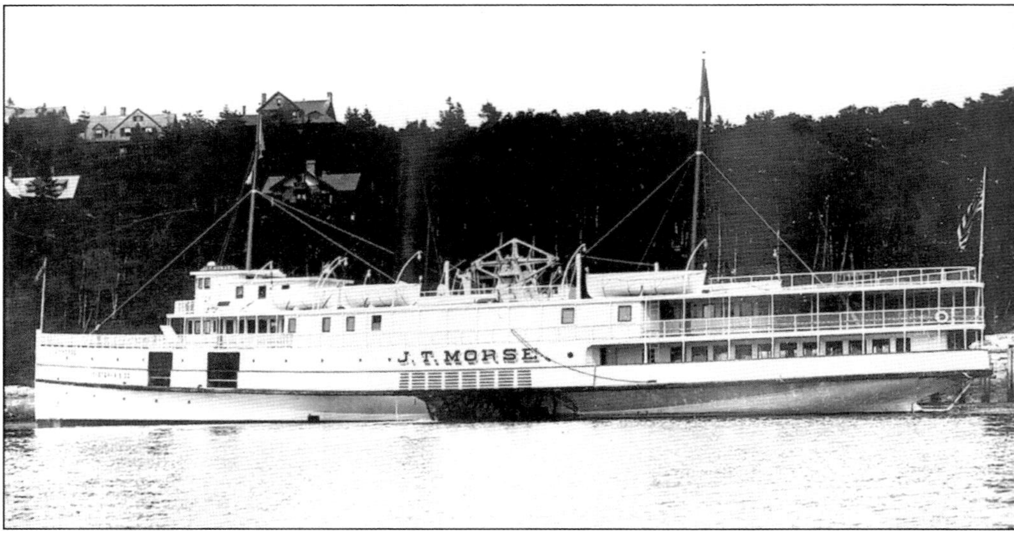

Launched in East Boston in 1904, the *J. T. Morse* was the last side-wheel steamer of her size to be built in New England. She carried a combination of passengers and freight and was one of the largest steamers ever to run regularly through the waters of eastern Maine. In Rockland, she connected with overnight steamers from Boston and ran to North Haven, Stonington, Eggemoggin, North Deer Isle, and Bar Harbor, making several stops on Mount Desert Island. A model of the *Morse* is on display at the Deer Isle-Stonington Historical Society.

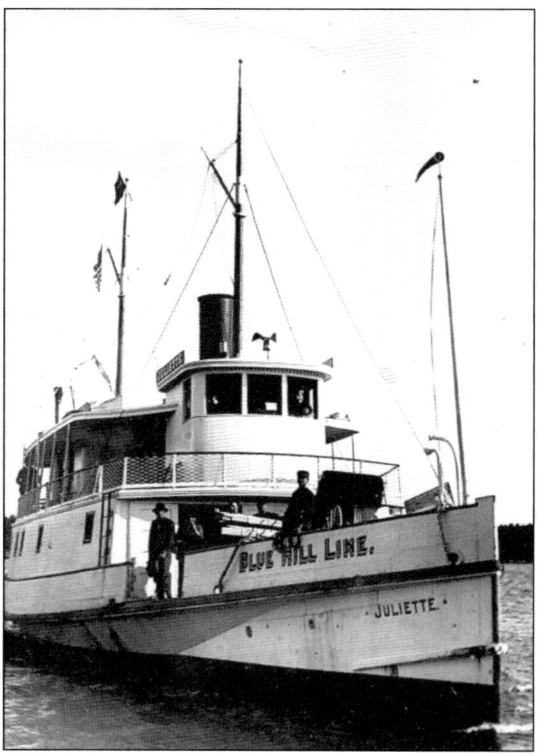

The *Juliette* was built in 1892 for Capt. Oscar Crockett's Blue Hill Lines. In his column "Steamboat Days," John Richardson quotes an admirer of the *Juliette* who remembered her whistle as a "deep, mellow chime, one of the most musical and pleasing whistles ever heard in Rockland."

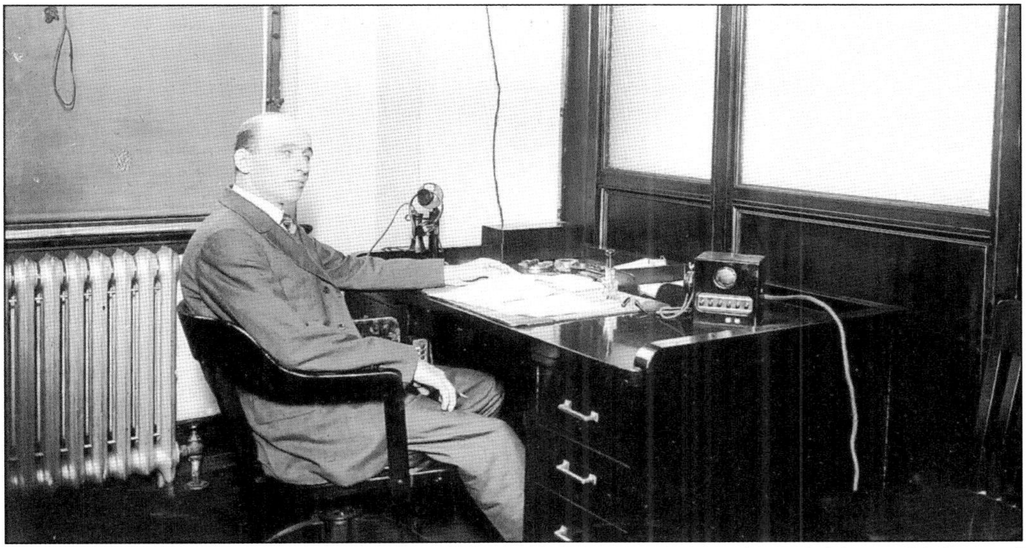

Capt. Walter Scott was born in Deer Isle in 1887, the youngest of 21 children of John and Frances Dow Scott. He went to sea at age 14 and received his master's license at 21. Starting out on sailing vessels, he eventually went to the Eastern Steamship Company, where he became port mate for Boston. This photograph shows him in his Boston office. Throughout his career, Captain Scott wrote letters to the island papers and published articles in several magazines. His first book of poetry, *Poems of Coastal New England*, was published in 1940. He died in 1965.

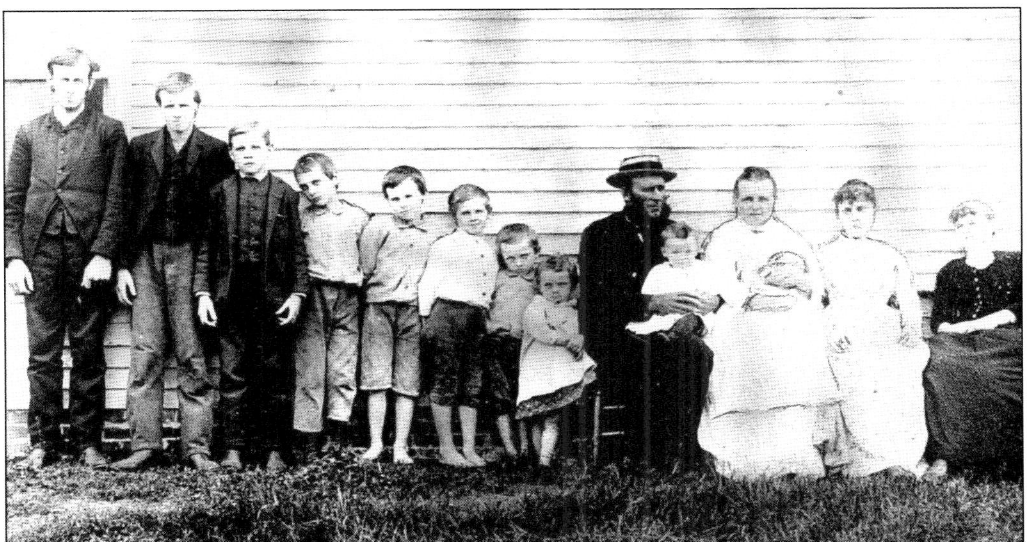

When Walter Scott was an infant, his family moved to Pickering's Island, where this photograph was taken. The family included two girls and 19 boys, 8 of whom died in infancy or childhood. In this photograph, Walter is in his father's arms. As an adult, Captain Scott wrote about the hardships of life on Pickering's and his life at sea. His writings were one of the incentives for starting the Deer Isle-Stonington Historical Society, where he served from the start as vice president.

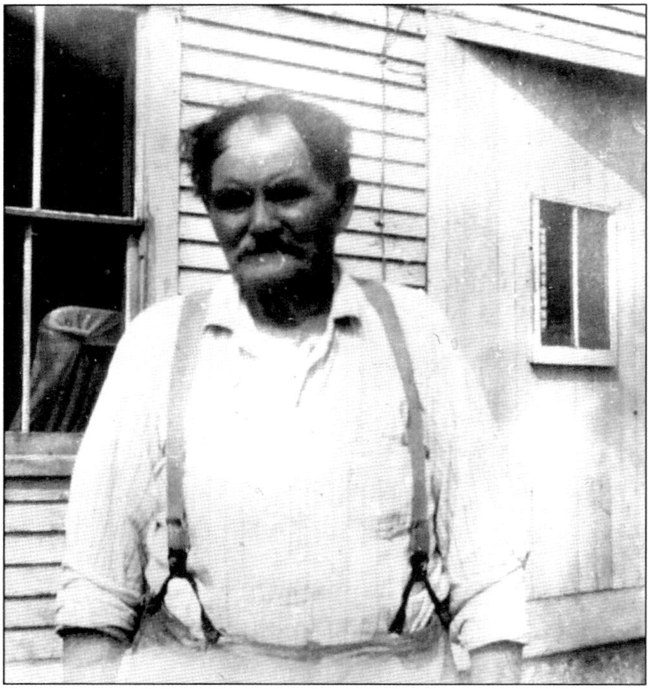

Capt. George R. Sylvester (1840–1921) began his career on the sea at age 10, on a fishing voyage with his father. Eventually, he became owner and master of several coasting vessels, carrying freight mostly form Maine to Virginia but also going as far as Prince Edward Island and Jamaica. He was described as a mild-mannered, quick-motioned man with a grand mustache and a twinkling eye who was respected by all.

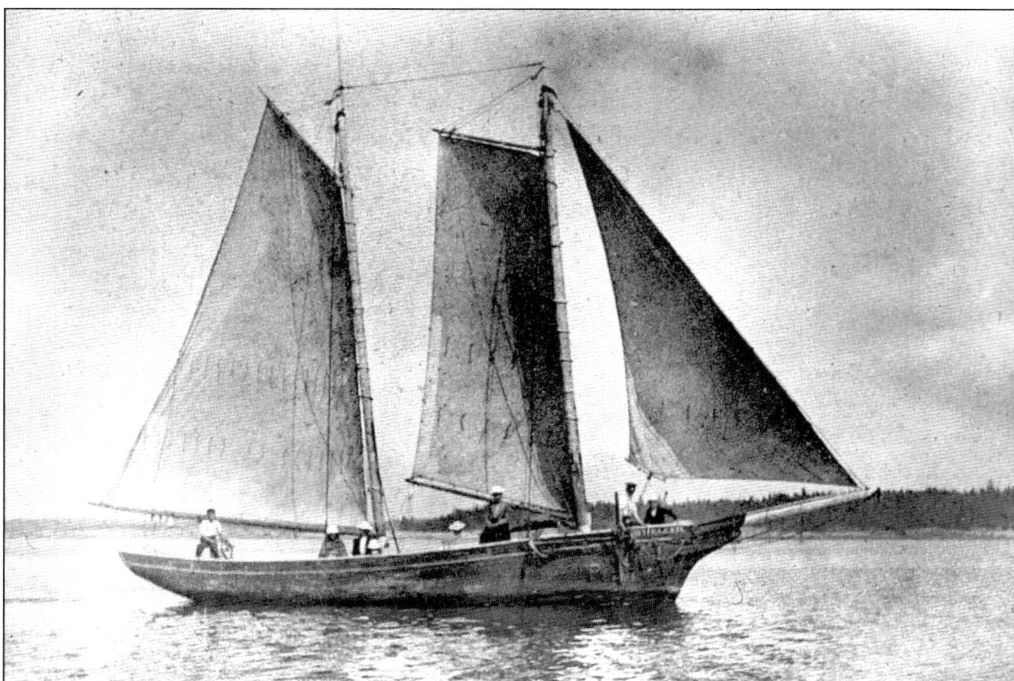

In later years, Captain Sylvester chose smaller schooners that could get into Sylvester's Cove. He established a packet service between there and Rockland, which carried both freight and passengers. He took orders from merchants and individuals, filled them, and returned the following day. The *Hattie L. Gray*, shown here, was one of the last vessels he owned.

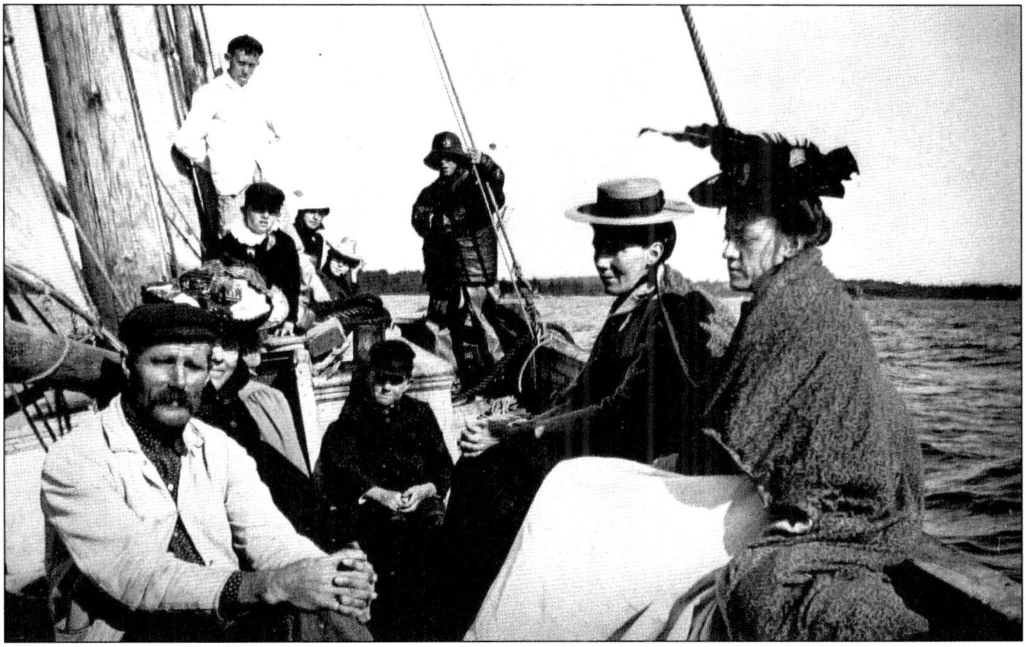

In addition to the coasting trade, Captain Sylvester used the *Hattie L. Gray* for pleasure cruises. On a family outing, from left to right, are Fred Sylvester, Alberta McCormick, Ida Birnie, two Birnie boys, Frank McVeigh (at mast), three unidentified women, Eliza Sylvester, and Emily Sylvester.

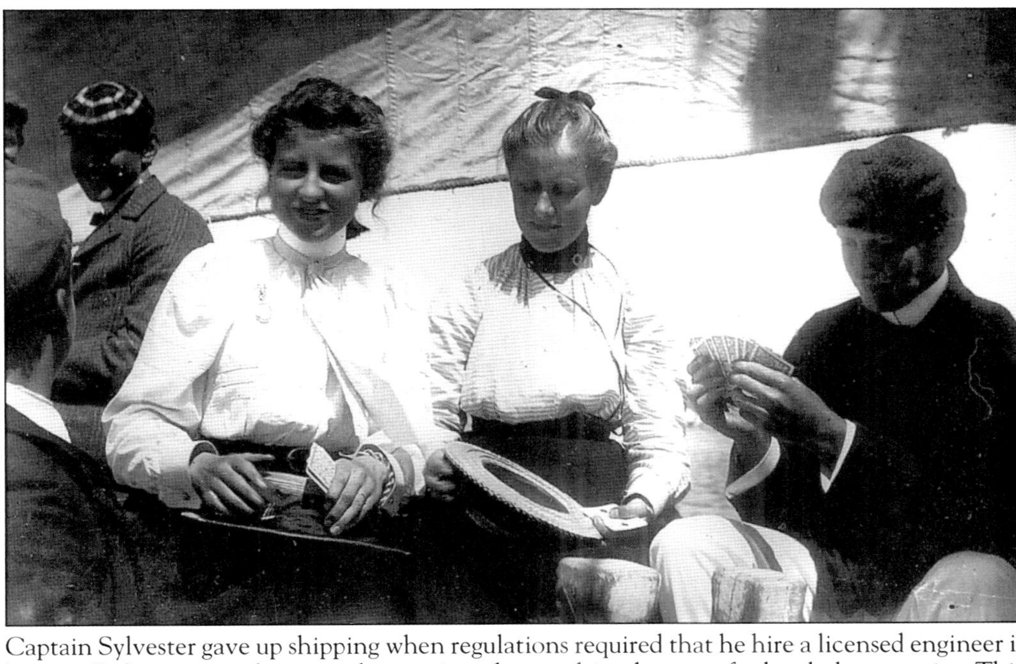

Captain Sylvester gave up shipping when regulations required that he hire a licensed engineer if he installed an engine; however, he continued to use his schooners for local pleasure trips. This photograph shows, from left to right, Edward Southworth, an unidentified friend, and Elizabeth and Melvin Southworth on the *Hattie L. Gray*.

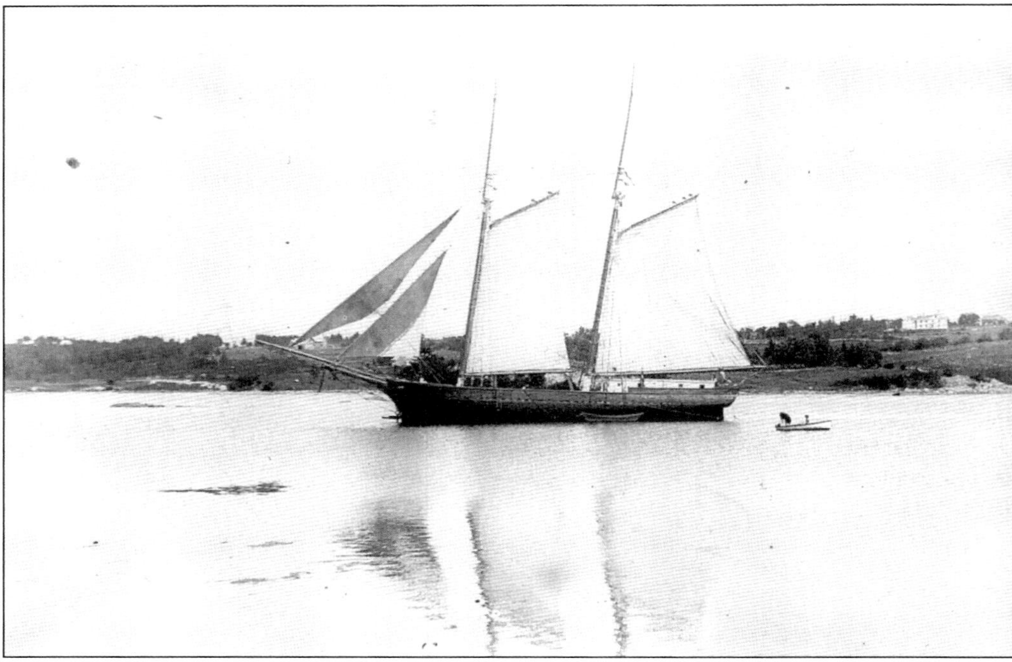

The *N. Curtis* was built in Harrington, Maine, in 1850. She was the last vessel under sail to work out of Northwest Harbor in Deer Isle, from whence she carried firewood to Mount Desert Island. In the end, she leaked so badly that her owners gave up on her, and she was hauled up off Dow Road.

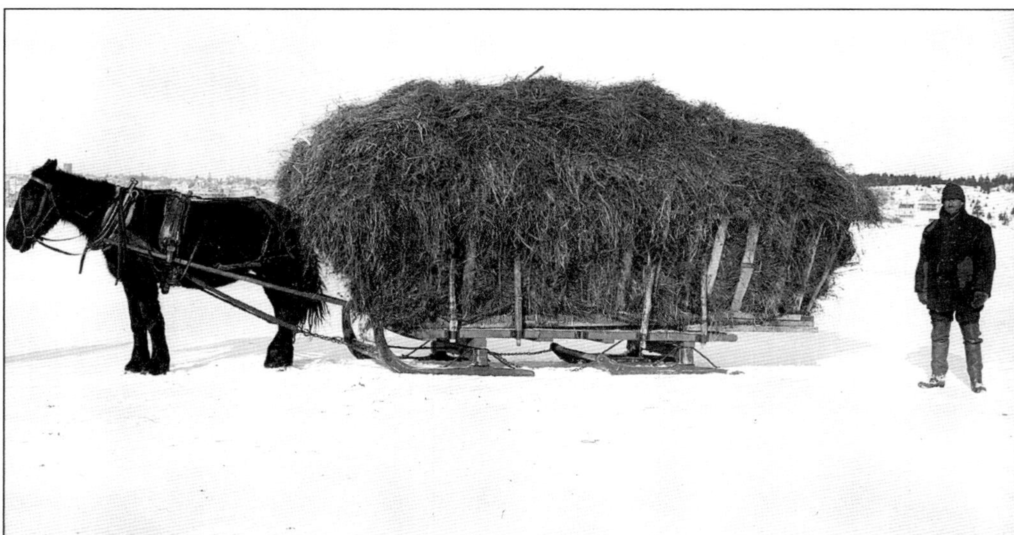

It has been a long time since an "ice embargo" froze the Reach and Stonington Harbor, but some people remember driving on the Reach during the winter of 1934–1935. This photograph was taken during the week-long freeze-up of 1918. At that time, the practice of keeping sheep and some cattle on the small islands was common. Here, an unidentified man takes hay to his sheep. There was such a shortage of hay and fodder that winter that one man had to buy Quaker Oat Flakes to feed his horse.

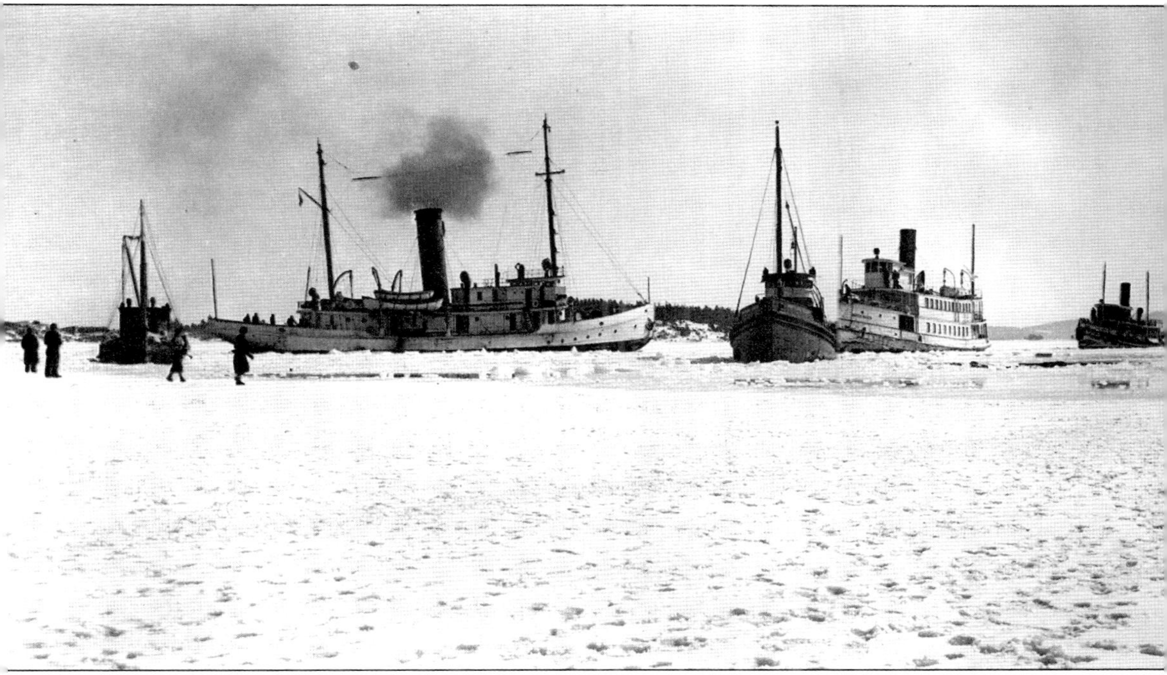

This famous photograph, taken in the Thorofare during the winter of 1934–1935, shows the Coast Guard icebreaker *Kickapoo* frozen in between two oil tankers. The steamer is the *North Haven;* to her right is the *Eugenie Spofford.* This freeze provided one impetus for the construction of the Deer Isle-Sedgwick Bridge. The Thorofare is a sheltered shipping lane separating Stonington from the outlying islands.

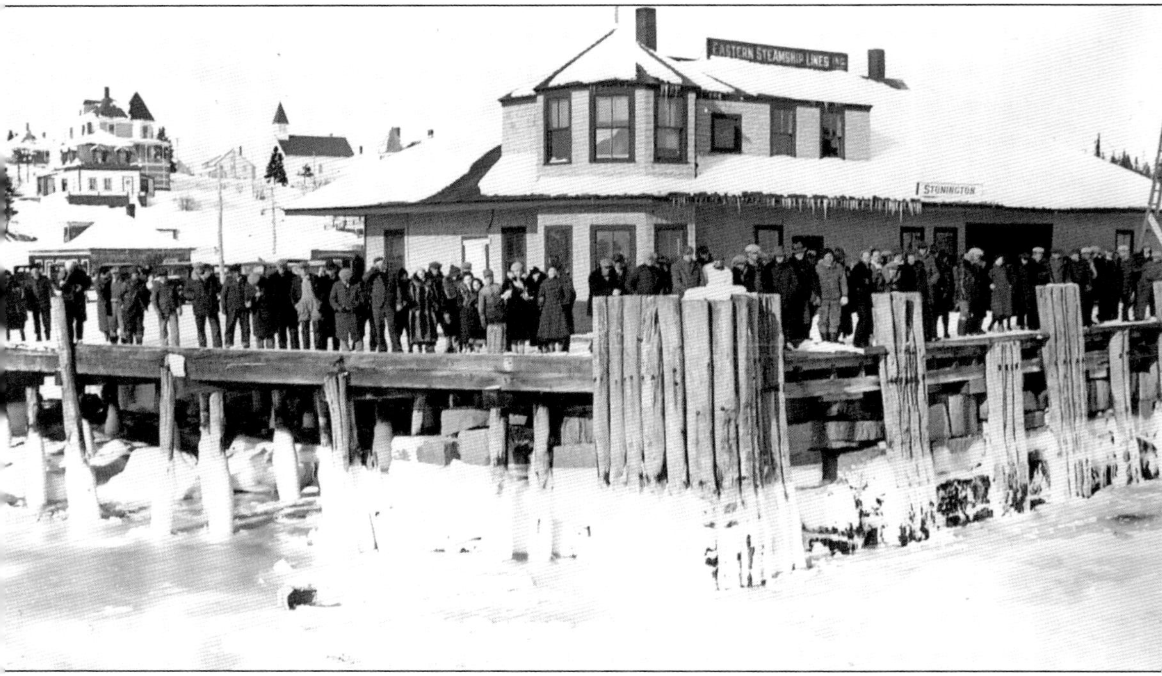

These people, gathered on the Eastern Steamship Lines wharf in Stonington, have probably come to watch the ships that are frozen in and the ice-breaking efforts of the *Kickapoo* and the *North Haven*.

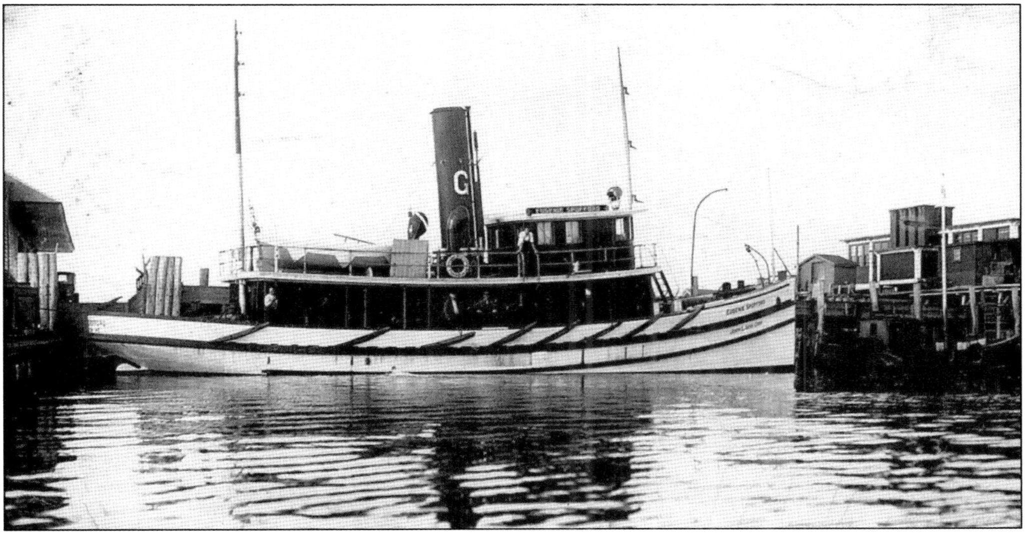

A 1935 account in the *Boston Post* reveals that, during the freeze, the lighthouse keeper at Mark Island was "struck with heart disease." He lit flares for three hours before attracting the attention of people in Stonington. The *Eugenie Spofford*, with Dr. Noyes aboard, "battered her way through the ice for three hours" to bring him ashore. The *Eugenie Spofford*, a towboat, was built in Camden in 1924 for the John L. Goss Granite Corporation of Stonington. A familiar sight in Stonington waters for two decades, she was licensed to operate from Eastport to Sandy Hook. A scale model is on exhibit at the Deer Isle-Stonington Historical Society.

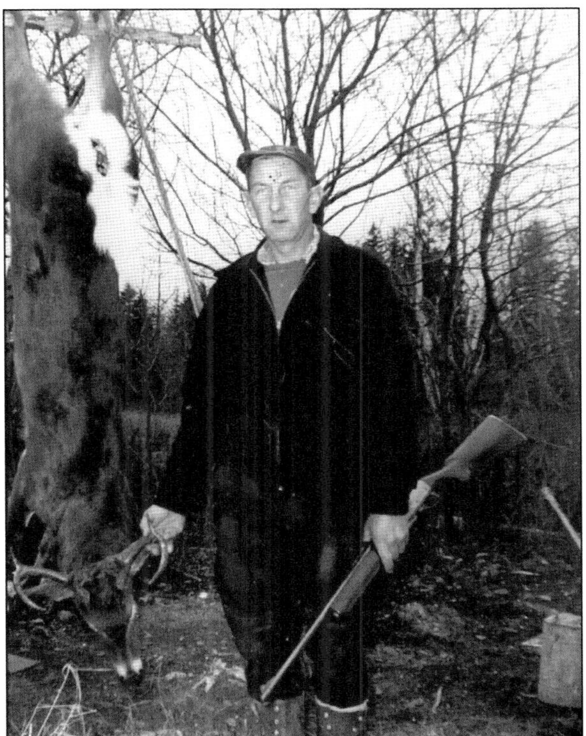

The same 1935 edition of the *Boston Post* reports that the next day, Clyde Snowman of Little Deer Isle carried the 65-year-old Dr. Noyes "piggy back" across the ice from North Deer to Little Deer Isle to care for an 86-year-old woman who had cholera. Although they traveled at half tide, "cold salt water reached nearly to the top of Snowman's hip-high sea boots." An automobile met Dr. Noyes and delivered him to the woman's home. Soon after this, further construction completed an all-tides causeway.

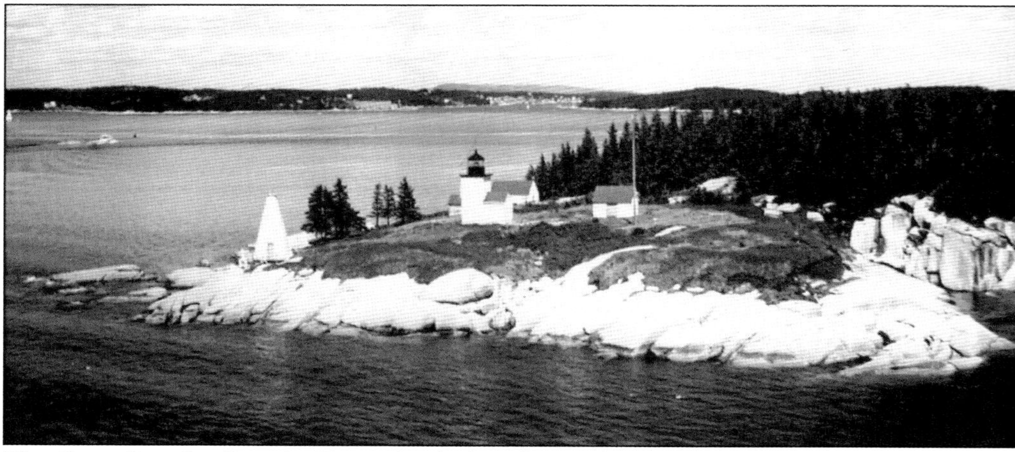

The Coast Guard calls it the Deer Island Thorofare Light, but locally it is known as "the Mark Island Light." Lit for the first time on New Year's Day in 1858, it marks the western entrance to the Thorofare. The lighthouse tower is 25 feet tall, and its light can be seen for 12.5 miles. It was manned until 1959, when the keeper's house burned down and the Coast Guard automated the light. Under the Maine Island Lights Program, and with a lot of local help, Mark Island is now the property of the Island Heritage Trust, which provides stewardship for the island and the lighthouse, while the Coast Guard maintains the light and the foghorn. Because of the fragile nature of the island and its wildlife, the public is discouraged from visiting.

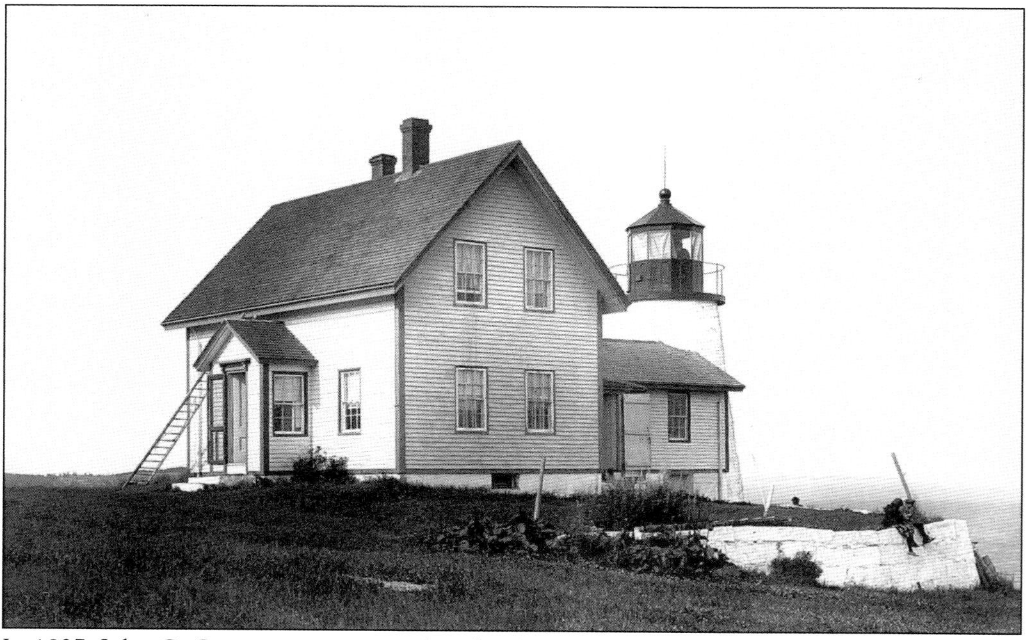

In 1837, John C. Gray gave six acres of Eagle Island to the United States government as a site for a lighthouse. The lighthouse was built in 1839, rebuilt in 1858, and automated in 1959. In 1963, the Coast Guard burned down the keeper's house and demolished all other structures except the bell tower and light. When the Coast Guard attempted to save the bell, it slipped over the cliff into the ocean. It was later retrieved by a lobsterman and sold to photographer Eliot Porter. The lighthouse is now privately owned.

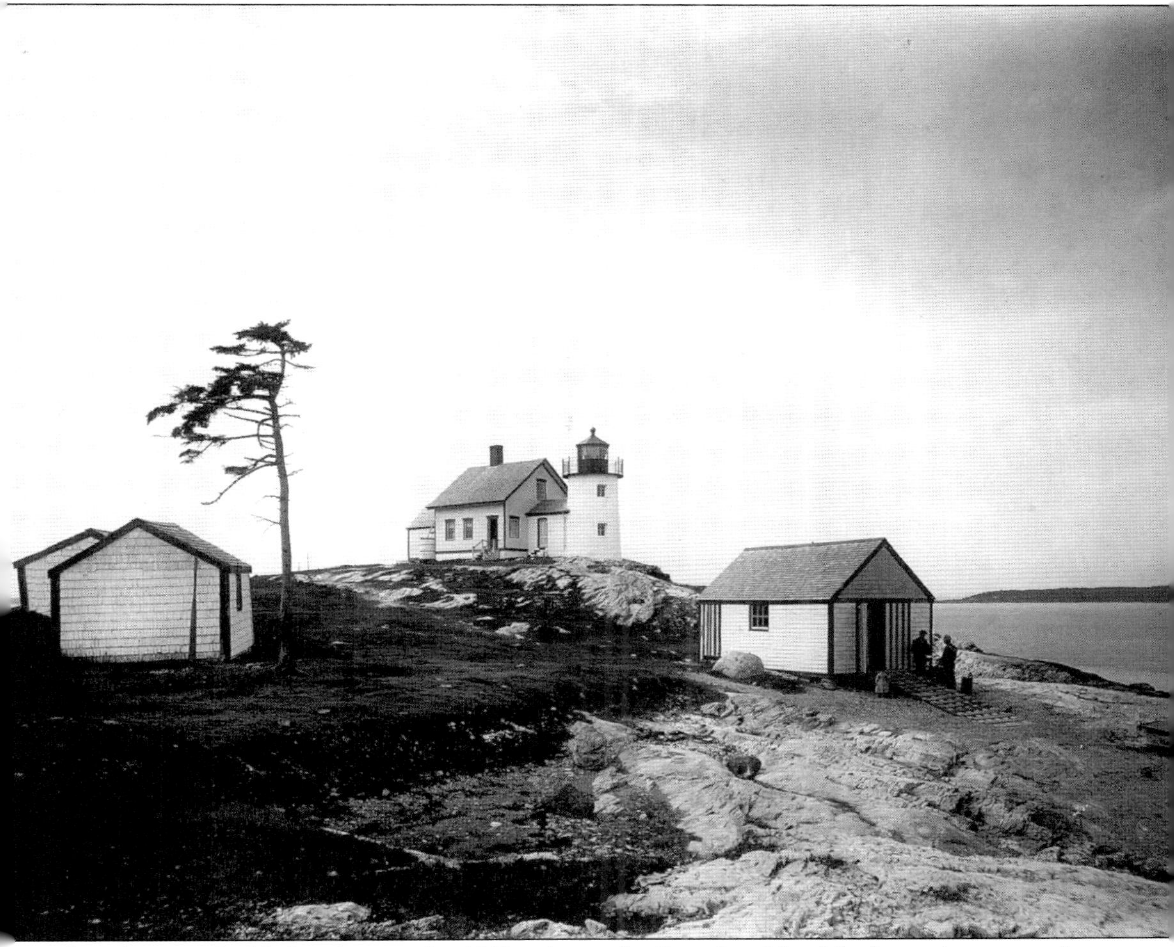

This photograph, likely taken in the 1890s, shows the Pumpkin Island Light at the east end of Eggemoggin Reach, which separates Deer Isle from the mainland. The lighthouse is a 25-foot-high brick tower, with a lantern that brings it to 28 feet. It was first put into use in 1854, automated in 1930, and discontinued in 1934, when it was sold by the government. The lighthouse has changed owners several times since then and remains in private hands. It can be seen in the distance from Caterpillar Hill in Sedgwick or from the Eggemoggin area of Little Deer Isle.

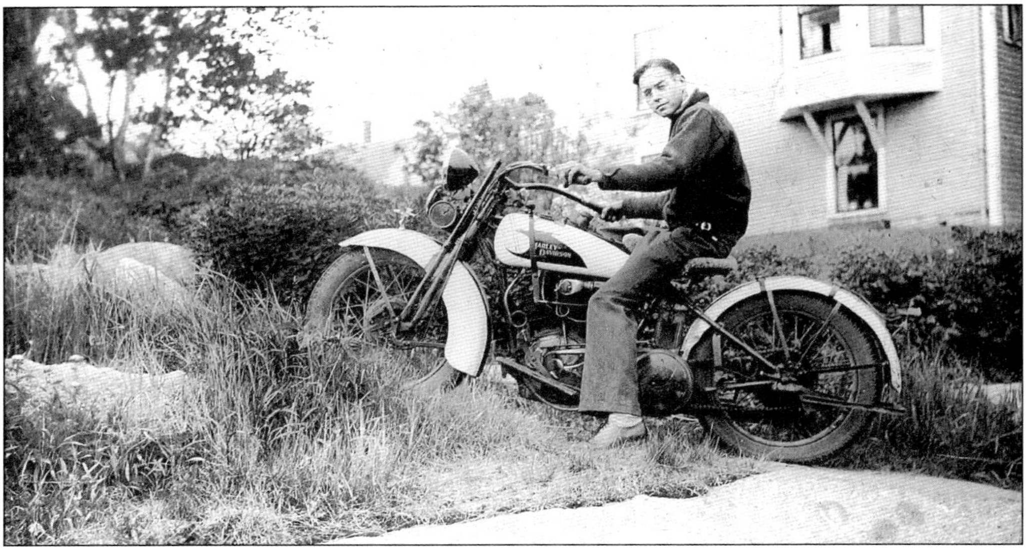

Francis "Babe" Gross sits on *White Elephant,* his Harley Davidson, *c.* 1930. Once, crossing the Little Deer Isle causeway, he failed to negotiate a curve and he and *White Elephant* ended up in the mud flats.

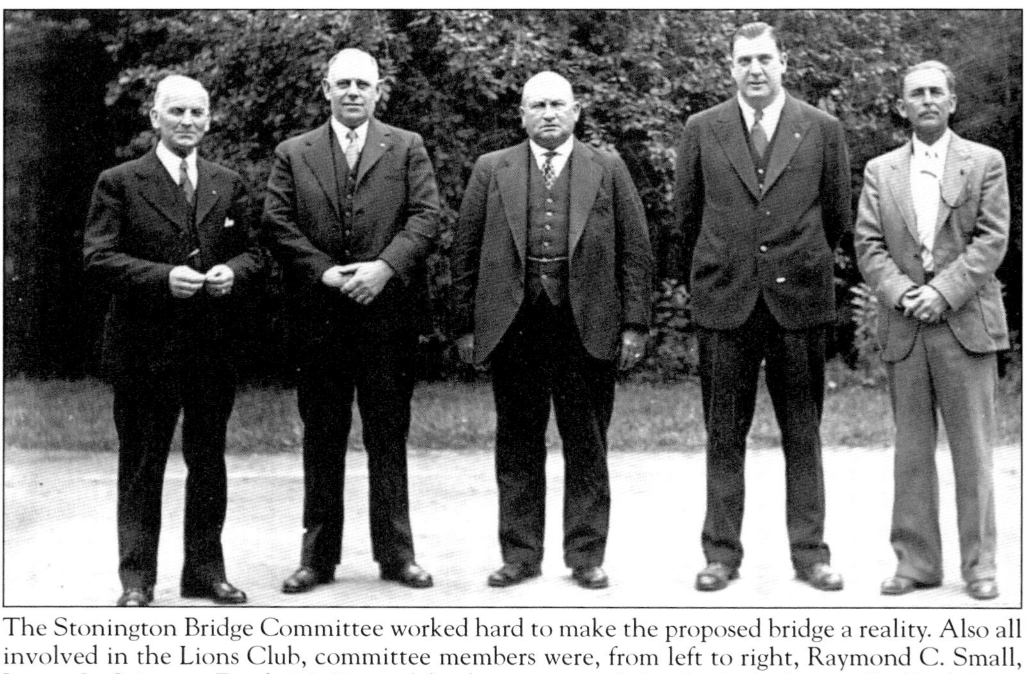

The Stonington Bridge Committee worked hard to make the proposed bridge a reality. Also all involved in the Lions Club, committee members were, from left to right, Raymond C. Small, James I. Stinson, Frank McGuire (chief promoter of the bridge), Lewis G. Tewksbury, and Harry Buxton.

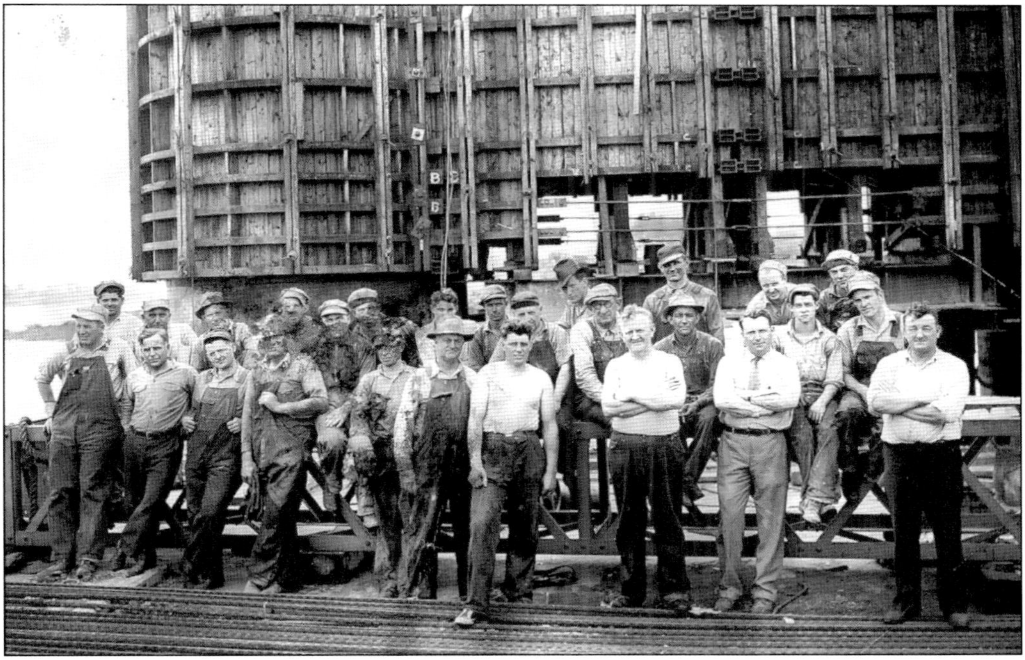

Bridge construction began in 1938, with a crew of 50 working in two shifts. Since most of the work required special training and experience, few jobs were available for local people, a disappointment to many. As construction went on, however, 30 to 50 local people were employed. This photograph shows the crew in 1938.

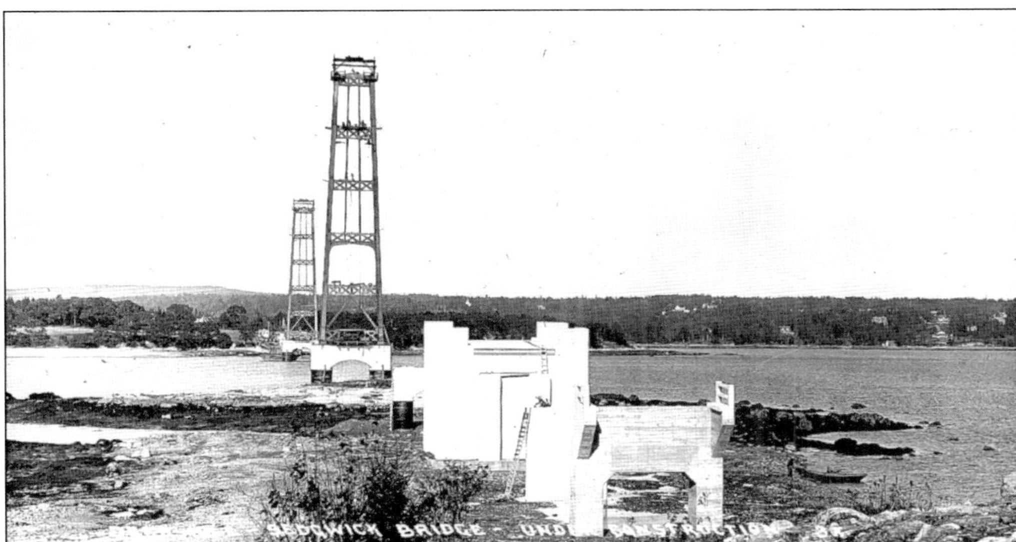

This *c.* 1938 photograph shows the bridge under construction. Clayton Gross, in his book *Steel Over Eggemoggin* (1989), writes of construction on the bridge: "No other event has wrought so many changes in our lives, brought us so many benefits, and created so many new problems."

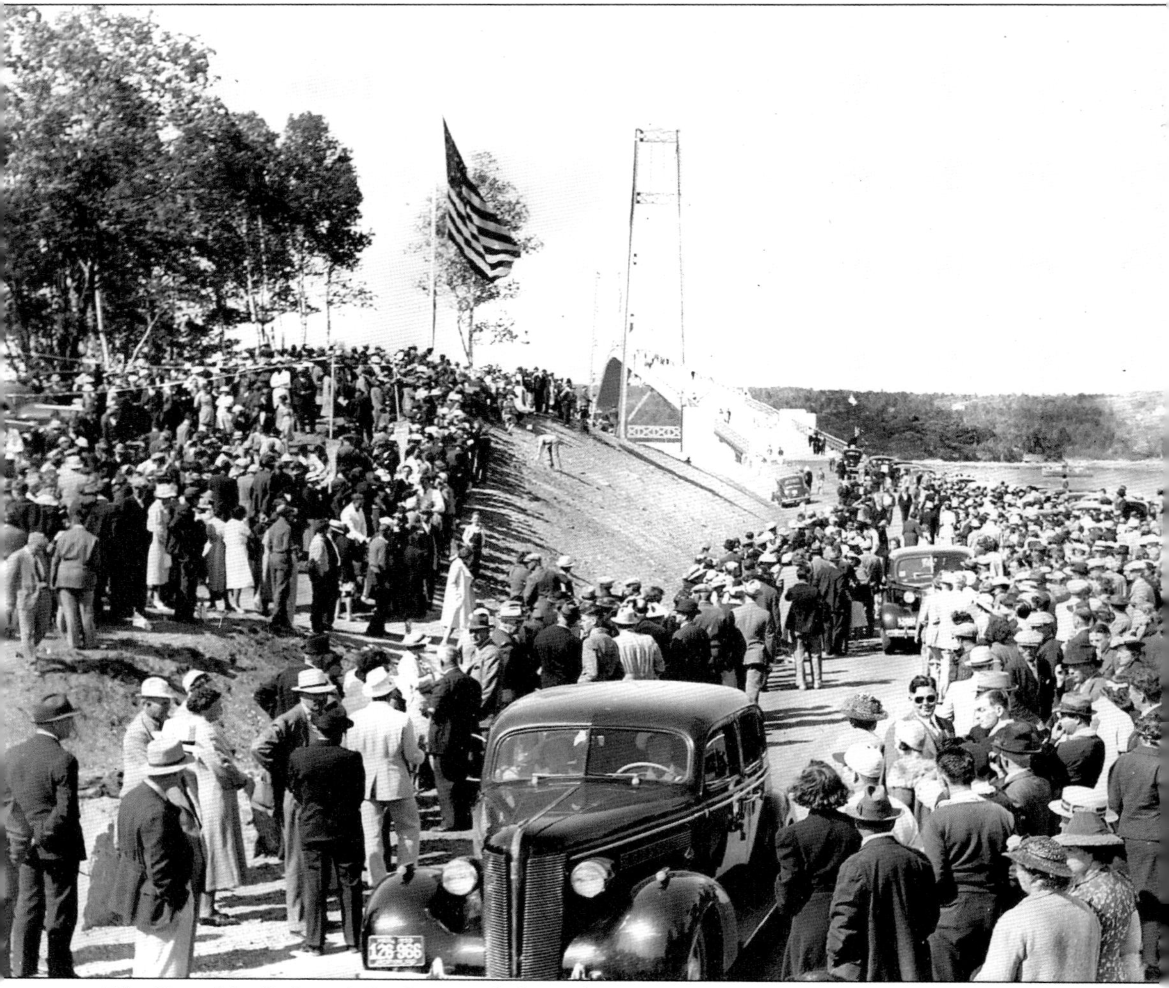

The Deer Isle-Sedgwick Bridge was dedicated on June 19, 1939, a warm and lovely day. A crowd of 5,000 gathered for the event and heard addresses by Gov. Lewis O. Barrows and others. Both the Stonington and Deer Isle High School bands played, and fireworks were displayed in the evening. Three days later, the *Deer Isle Messenger* reported that one or more enterprising pickpockets (unheard of on Deer Isle) had joined the crowd, and that several people lost their wallets. Tolls were not charged on the bridge that day. Lieutenant Wardwell, in the tollhouse, reported that he saw one shabby car driving back and forth all day. Curious, he finally asked the driver why; the man stated that he was poor and did not expect to be able to pay a dollar to cross the bridge again, so "if you don't mind, I want to get in as many rides as I can today, while it's free." The toll was completely removed in 1961.

Two

Island Towns

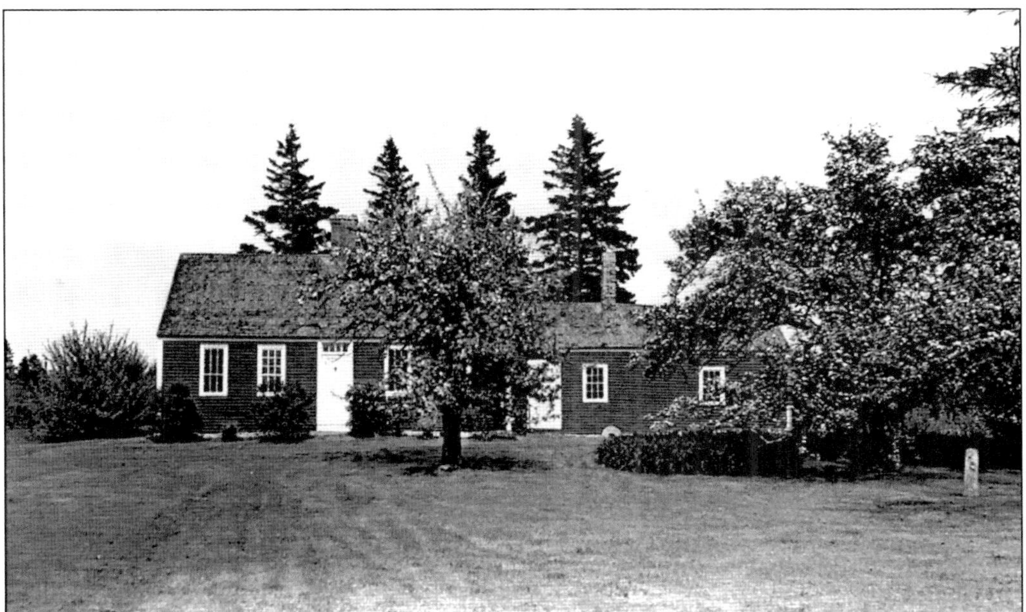

The Sellers House, the museum and headquarters of the Deer Isle-Stonington Historical Society, was built in 1830 by Joseph Sellers for his wife, Salome. The house was restored in the early 1960s by the newly formed historical society and, most recently, was extensively restored in 2002. Some of the furnishings belonged to Salome; others have been contributed from many island homes.

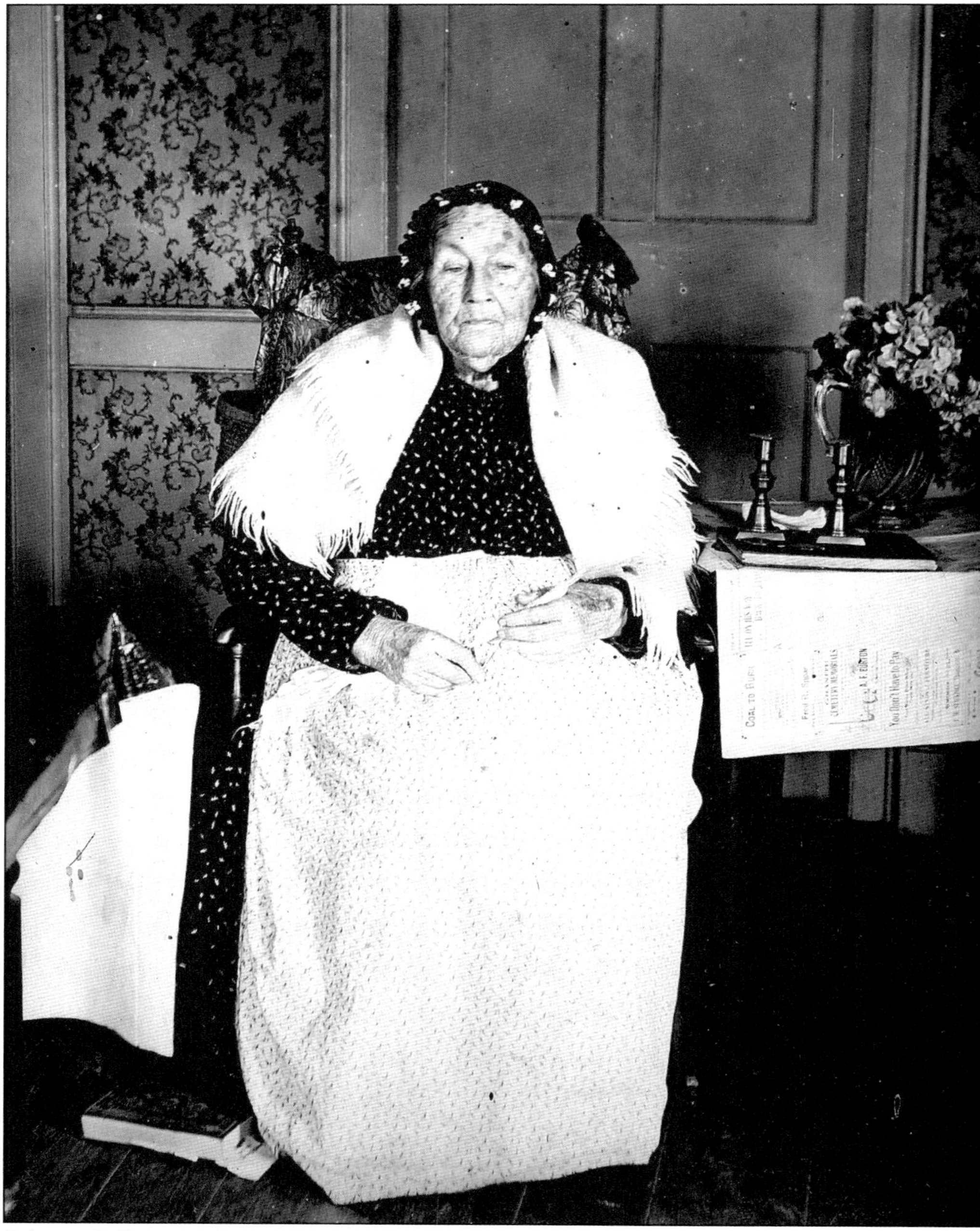

Salome Sellers was born in 1800, the daughter of Capt. Edward and Deborah (Cushman) Sylvester. Her mother was descended from Mayflower stock; her father served in the American Revolution. Joseph and Salome had six children, four of whom died. She was a member of the Martha Washington Benevolent Society and was active in the Temperance movement. After Joseph Sellers died at home during the Civil War, Salome continued to keep house for her youngest son. Sailors felt it was good luck to visit Salome before going to sea. Salome lived into the 20th century, dying at age 108 as the oldest woman in Maine. When this picture was taken, she was 106.

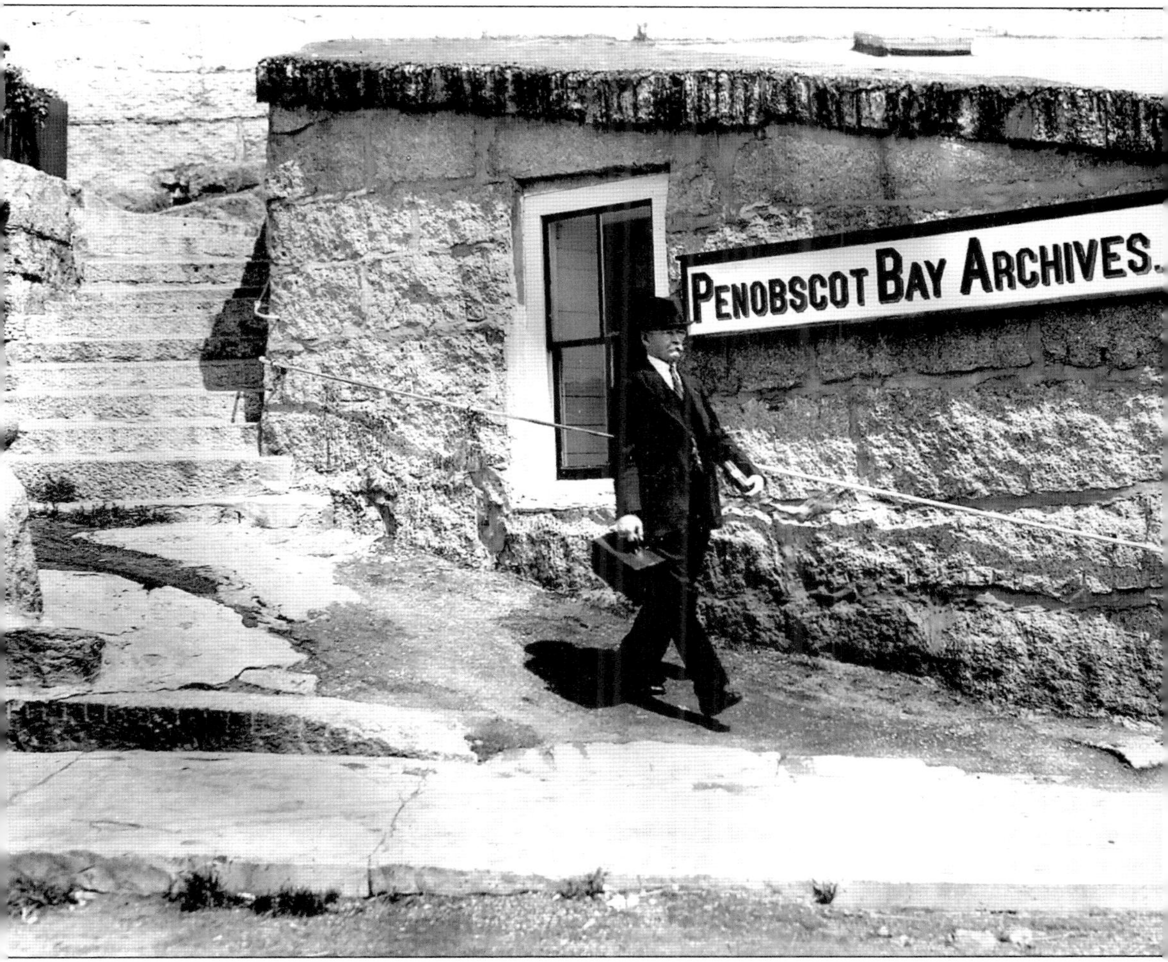

Dr. Benjamin Lake Noyes came to Stonington in 1895 and practiced as a physician for the island until his death in 1945. He built a very imposing house in Stonington, adding a granite vault to secure his extensive collection of history and genealogical records of island families. Much of this information was obtained while he made house visits to island homes. His collection of more than 70 volumes, now housed in the archives of the Deer Isle-Stonington Historical Society, is in constant use by people doing research. In this 1940 photograph, Dr. Noyes is on his way to take his brother's blood pressure. Dr. Noyes was a pharmacist, a photographer, an artist, an inventor, a civic activist, and an innovator, both in medicine and the community.

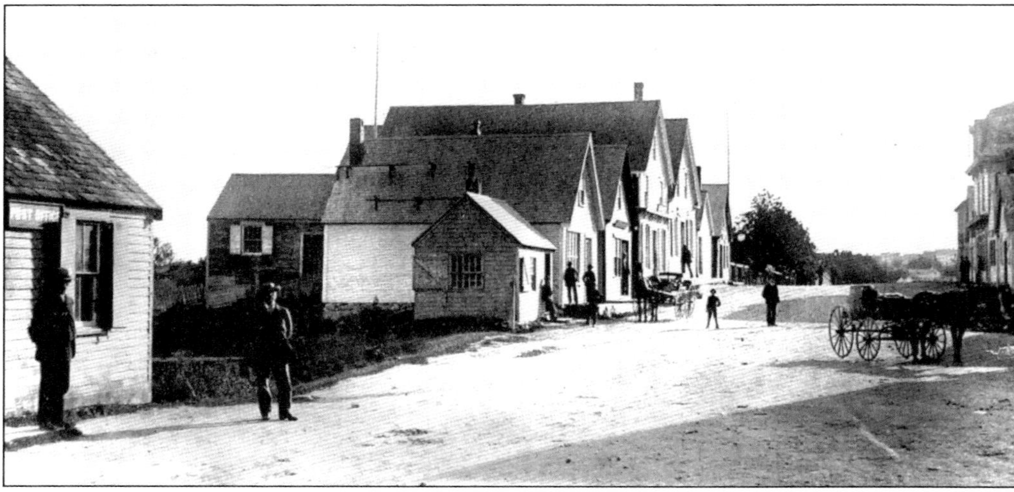

This photograph of the main street in Deer Isle was taken in the 1890s. From left to right, the buildings are the post office; Michael Carman, shoemaker; Dr. Ferguson; Fred Beck's Market; Hudson Pressey, general store, undertaker, and house furnishings; Sam Pickering, groceries, dry goods, and hardware; Sam Pickering, harness repair and leather work; and George Higgins, jeweler. On the right side of street are Levi Scott's house; A. O. Gross building, dry goods, boots, shoes, hardware, and clothing; and Julia Lufkin, millinery.

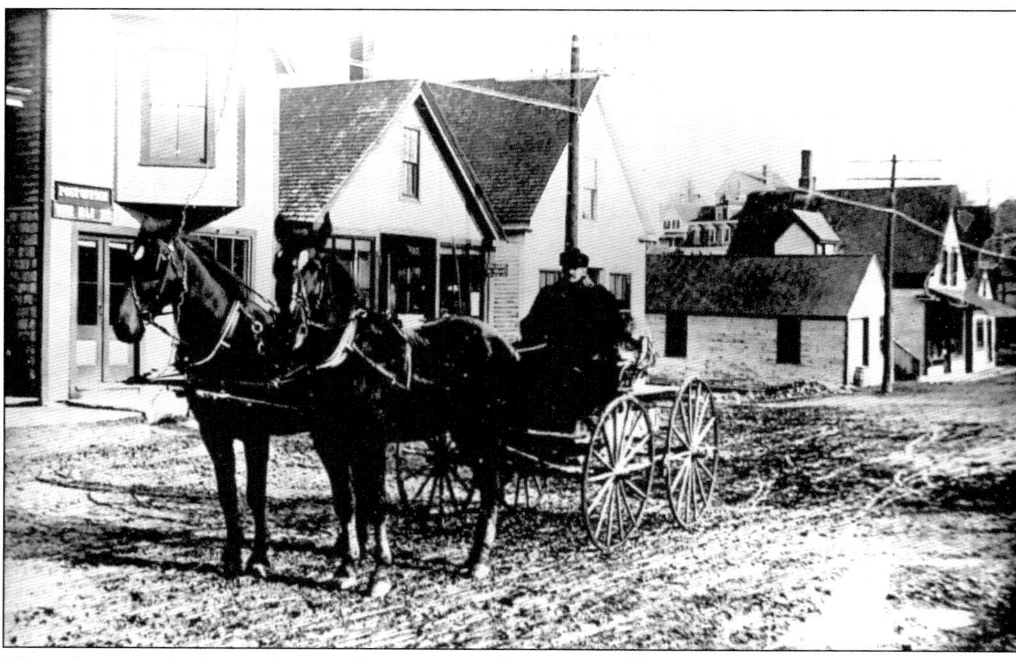

This photograph shows Arthur Greenlaw and his team of horses in Deer Isle Village, in front of the following, from left to right: the Deer Isle Post Office; Isaac Woodworth's plumbing and jewelry store; Cora Beck Torrey's millinery and yard goods store; a blacksmith shop; Ned Haskell's merchandise and barber shop; and William Sellers's Store.

The Deer Isle Town Hall was built in 1893. The first floor held the selectmen's office, a hall where town meetings were held, and a cage, purchased for $100 in 1894 and used as a jail (now housed at the Deer Isle-Stonington Historical Society). The second floor held a stage, home to many local theatrical events, and was used as a basketball court and dance floor. The building burned to the ground in 1972, taking most of the town records with it. Note the boardwalk, which continued across the Mill Dam and up the hill on what is now Bridge Street.

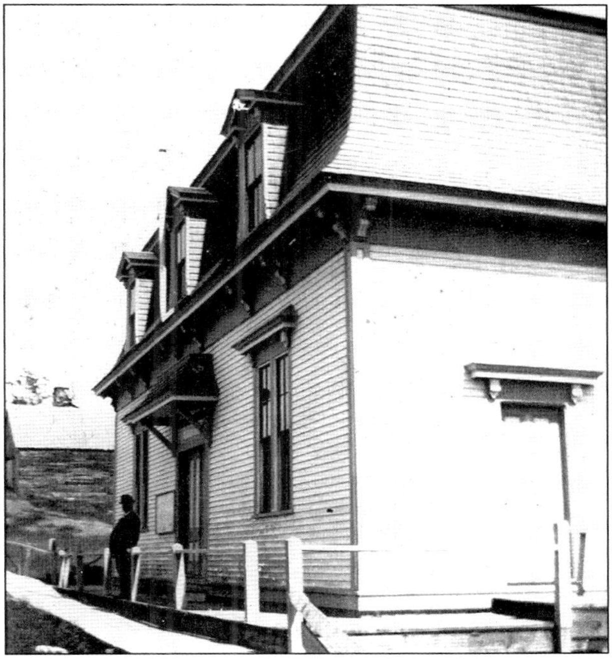

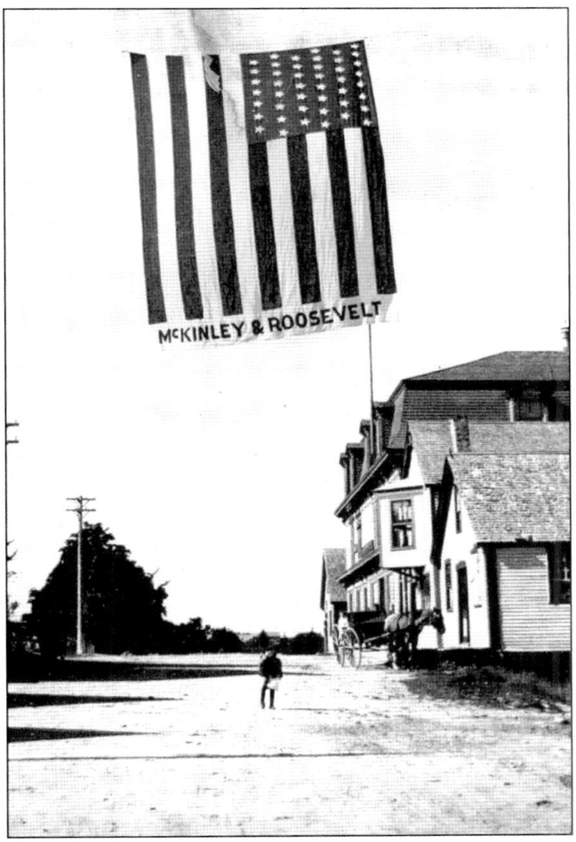

A McKinley and Roosevelt banner flies above an almost deserted main street in Deer Isle Village. This was likely 1897, the first year of McKinley's term, when the nearby McKinley High School was built. After Roosevelt became president, Violet Goss, a Stonington woman, decided to take a group of Stonington High School students to Washington, D.C., and made an appointment to see the president. On the way, they stopped to see someone who had a greenhouse and received an armload of lilies. The group did not have time to take the flowers back to the hotel, so Goss carried them. President Roosevelt, assuming the flowers were for him, stretched out both arms to take them. "You may have *just one*," Goss said. The President looked over the large assortment and at length carefully selected one. "Thank you *very* much," he said.

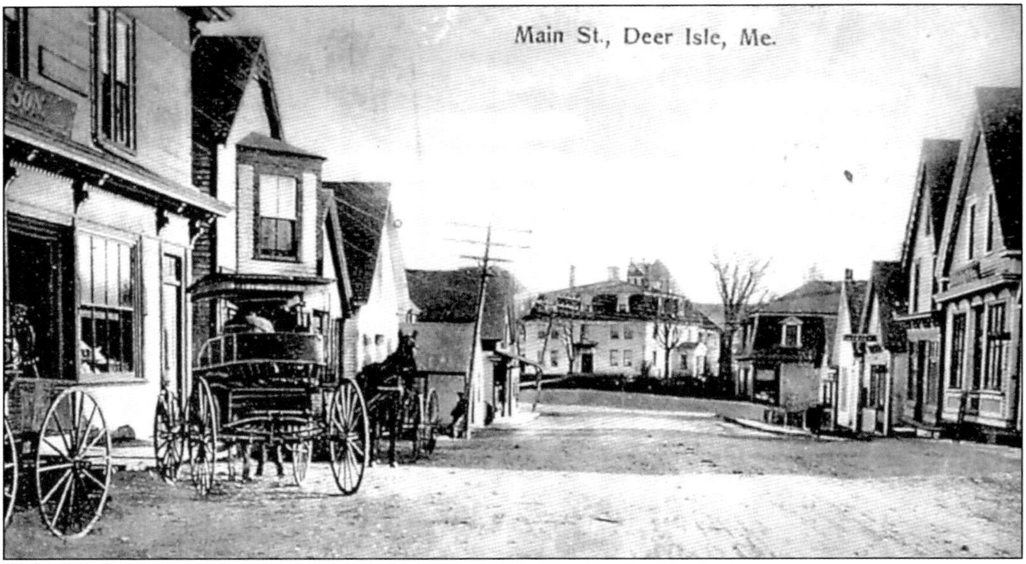

This *c.* 1900 postcard photograph of Main Street in Deer Isle shows, from left to right, A. O. Gross & Son; the post office; Greenlaw livery stable; Cora Beck, millinery; Charles Lufkin, blacksmith; Ned Haskell, barber shop and dry goods; the Lynnmore Hotel and Boarding House; H. P. A. Spofford, dry goods, candy, and ice cream; Michael Carman, shoemaker; Dr. Benjamin F. Ferguson; Fred Beck, meats and groceries; M. D. Joyce and George Beck, hardware and caskets; and T. B. Pickering, groceries and dry goods.

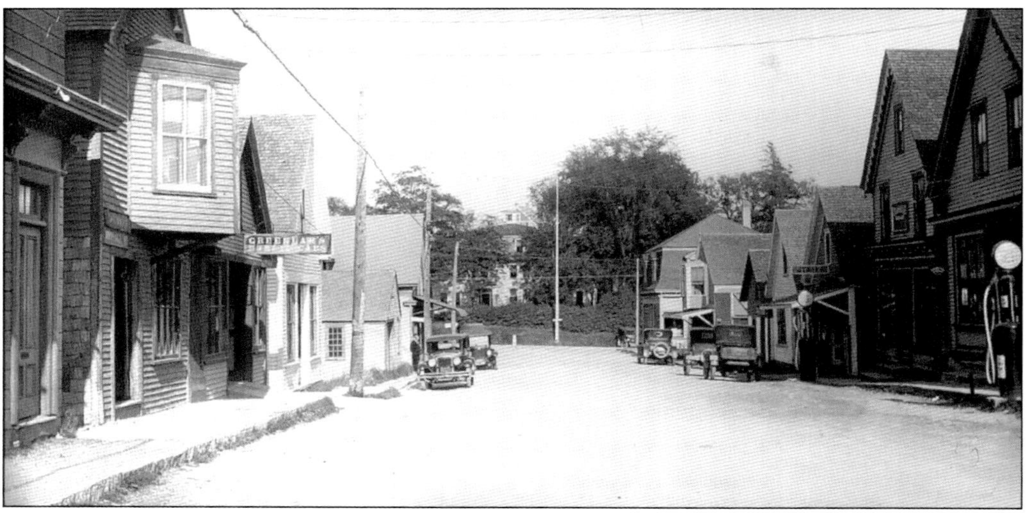

This postcard reveals the main street of Deer Isle *c.* 1926. From left to right, the buildings are the three-story Gross block, with the Beacon Theater downstairs and the town treasurer and tax collector (Paul Scott) upstairs; the Deer Isle post office; Greenlaw Public Cars; Cora Beck's home; Charles Lufkin's building; Ned Haskell, barber shop and dry goods; the Lynnmore Hotel; Dodie Spofford, candy and school supplies; Maurice Greenlaw's Store, with the telephone office upstairs; Frank Carman, shoe repair; the Ferguson building, storage; Beck's Market, meat and groceries; M. D. Joyce, hardware and gas; and S. Pickering & Son, groceries, dry goods, and gas.

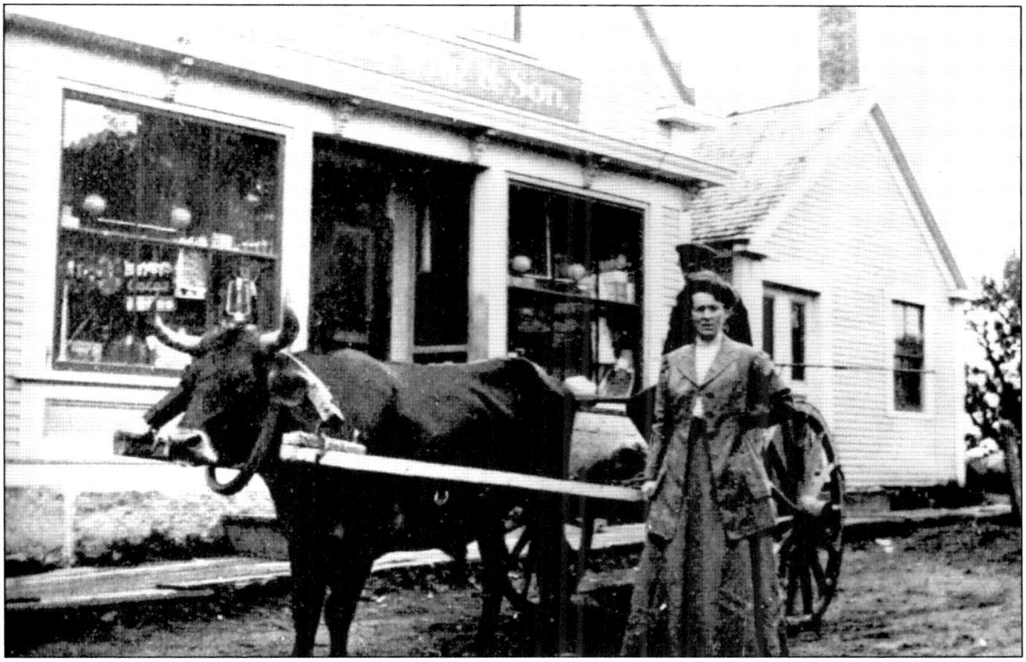

Elsie Rines stands in front of the S. Pickering & Son Store in Deer Isle Village. The man with the ox may have been a member of the Howard family of Beech Hill.

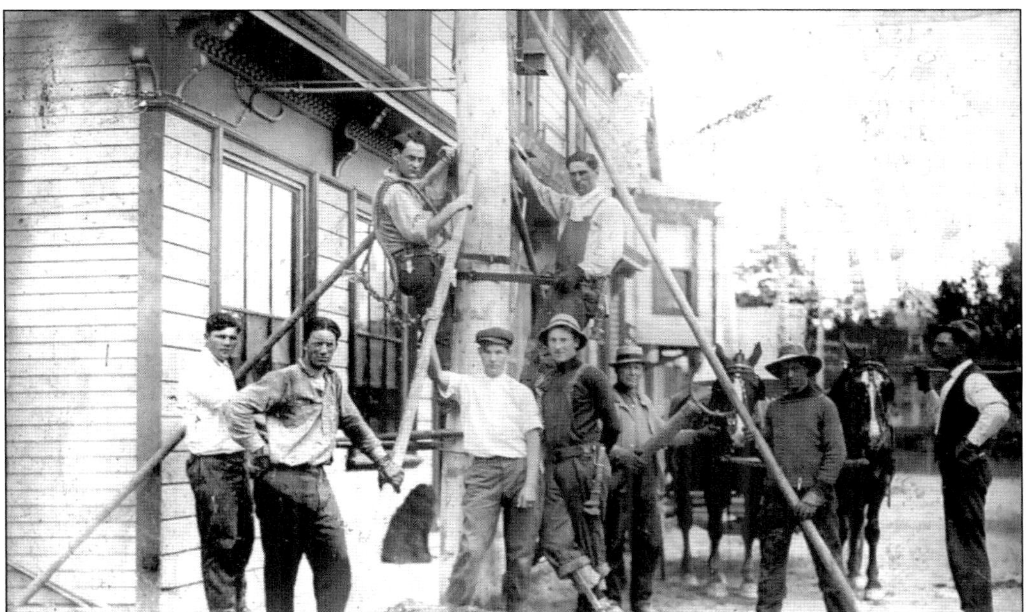

A telephone pole is installed in front of the Gross & Spofford building in Deer Isle Village c. 1911. The windows protruding beyond the building are from Julia Etta Lufkin's apartment over the Deer Isle post office, where she was postmistress. The slanting roof of Beck's Store and the roof of Ned Haskell's Store are beyond it. Seen between the horse's head and the man with the axe slung over his shoulder is the Lynnmore Hotel, later the site of Arthur Barter's home.

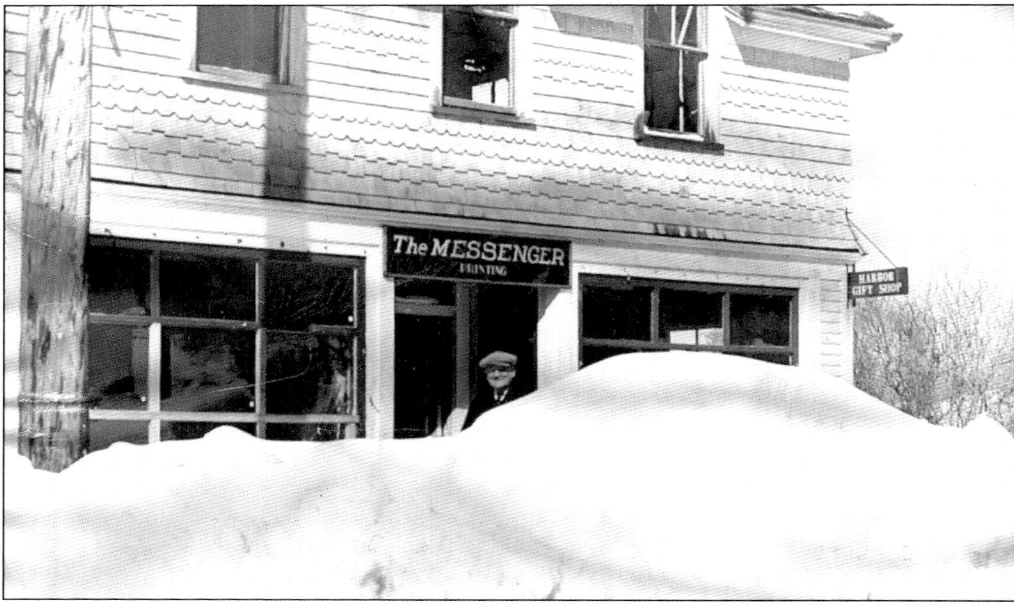

William Robbins stands in front of the office of the weekly *Deer Isle Messenger,* which he edited for a decade starting in the mid-1930s. His wife, Maude, ran the Harbor Gift Shop on the right side of the building, which is now a private home.

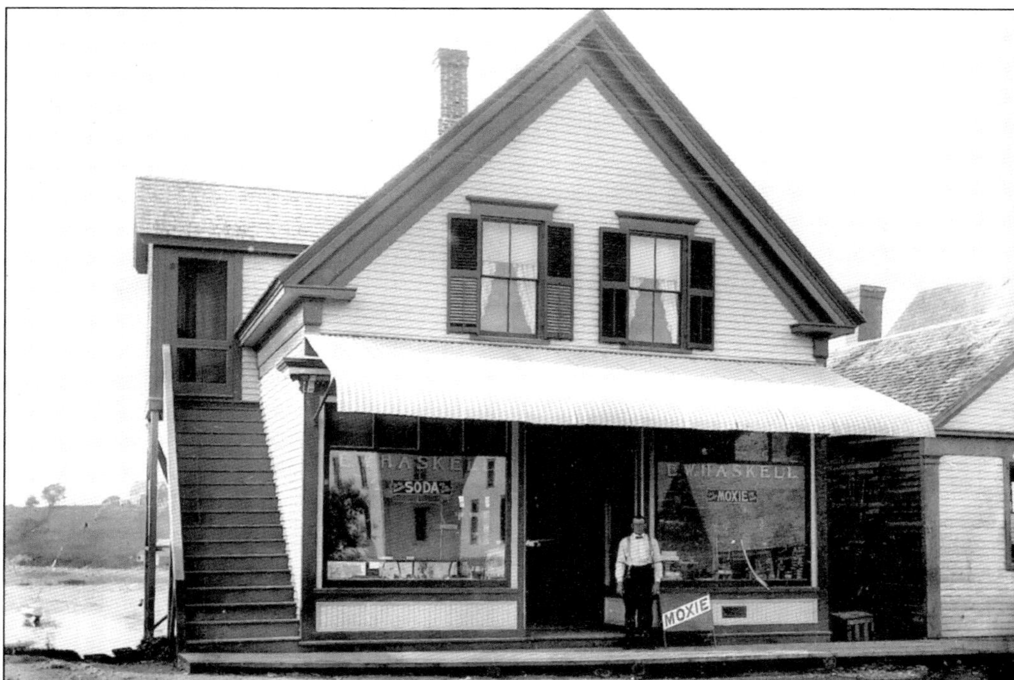

E. W. "Neddie" Haskell was born in 1876 and went to sea at an early age. After some years, he bought a store on the main street of Deer Isle, stocked it with boots, shoes, drugs, and tobacco, and ran it in conjunction with his barber shop. His wife, Harriet, worked there with him. Dr. George Wheeler rented the upper floor during the summer months for his dental practice.

Julia Etta Haskell (later married to Charles Lufkin) stands at the door of her millinery shop in Deer Isle Village; she was one of three milliners on the island at that time. Later, the building became the post office, with Julia as postmistress, and Cora Beck started a millinery shop nearby.

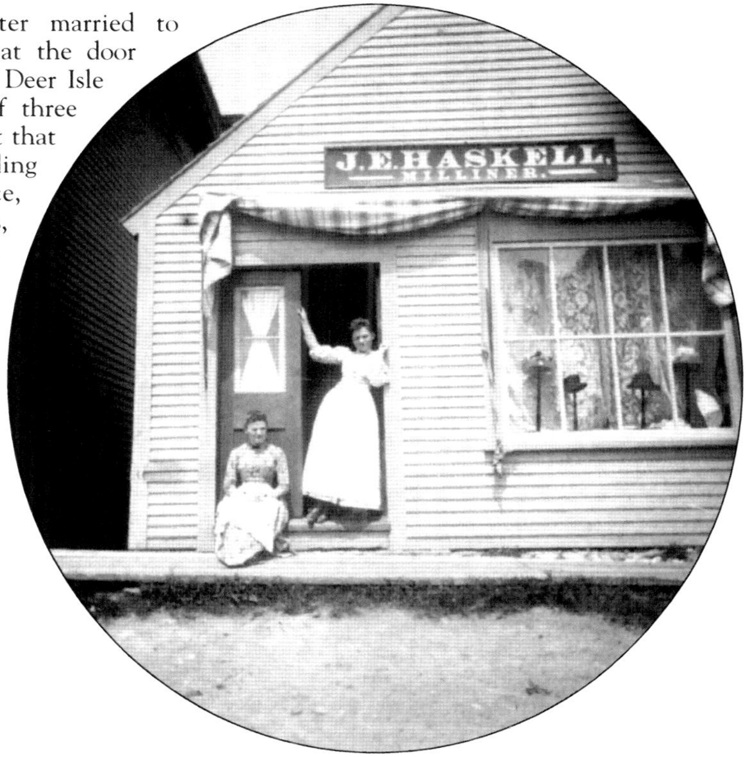

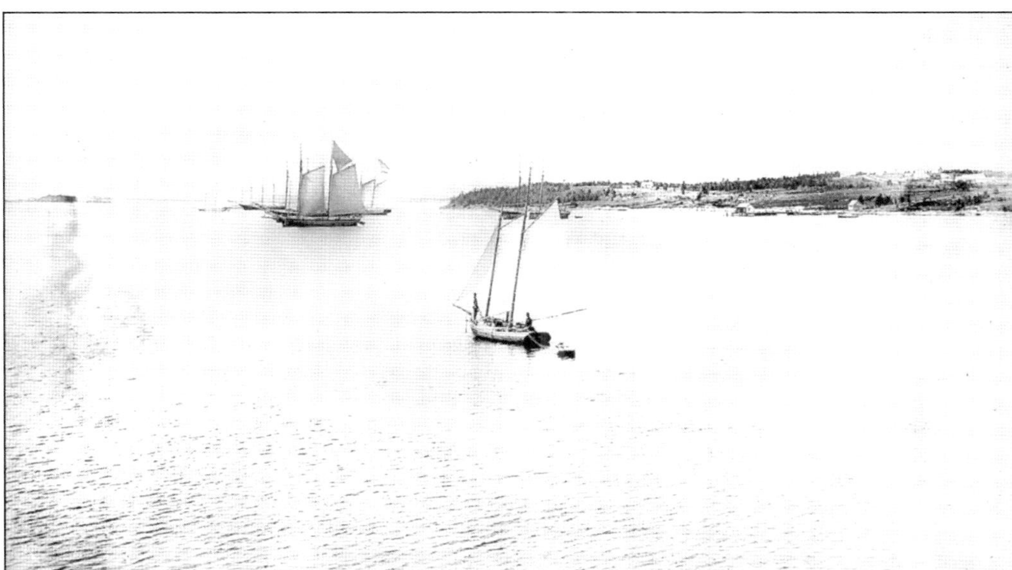

This photograph of North West Harbor was taken c. 1892. The steamboat landing on Dow Road appears on the right. Perhaps these ships await new suits of sails being made at the Haskell Sail Loft.

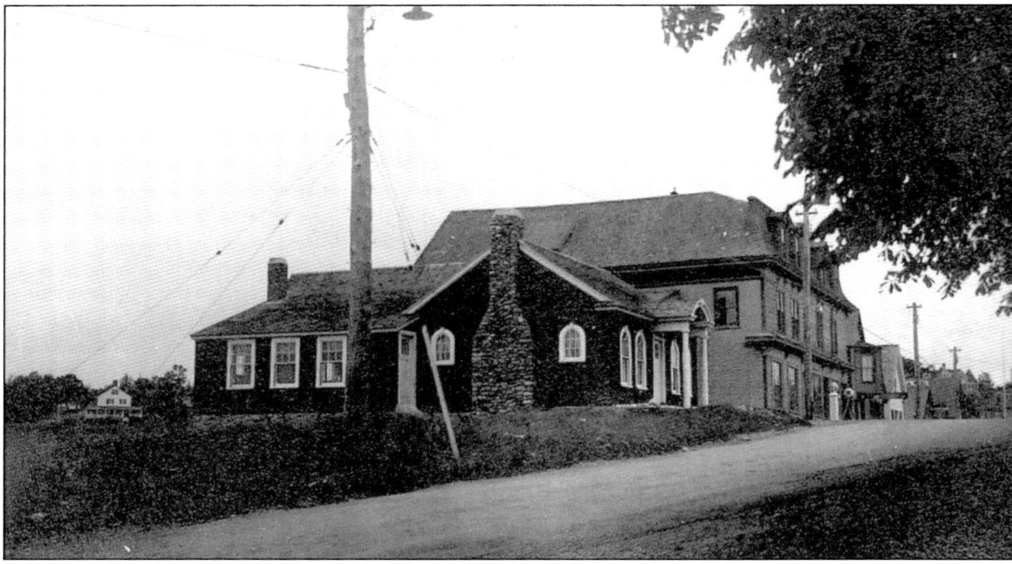

Seen here is the Chase Emerson Memorial Library, located in Deer Isle. The building was originally located across the street and was a jewelry store. Moved to its present site, it became the men's Aquamarine Club. It later became a boys' club and, in 1929, the town library. Behind the library in this 1930s photograph is the Gross block, which burned to the ground in 1988.

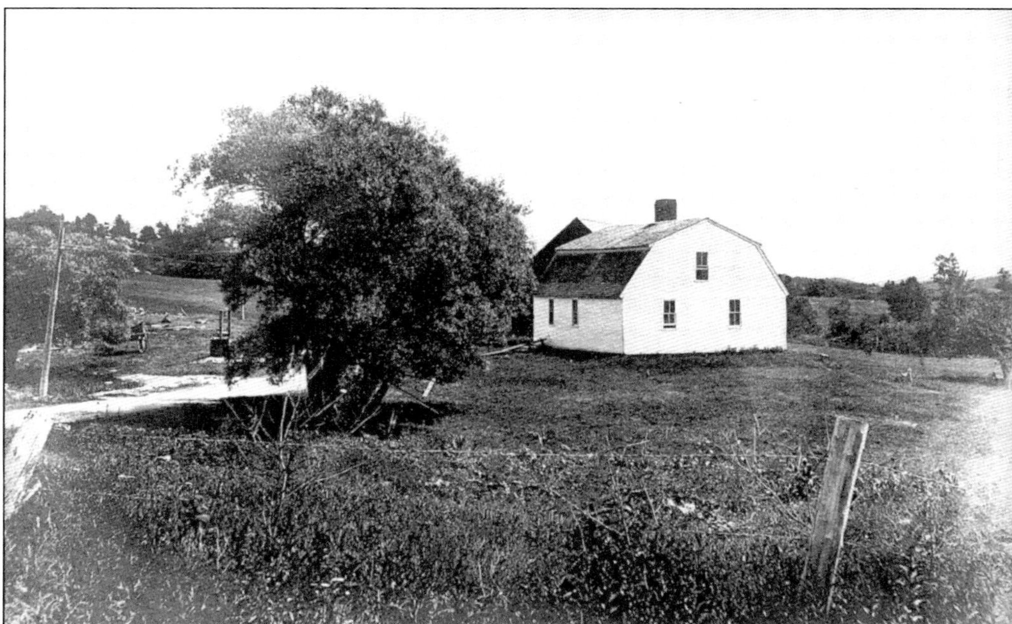

The Peter Powers House, thought to be the oldest house standing on the island, is seen here in 1910. Built in 1791 for Rev. Peter Powers, the first minister on the island, it was part of the town's contribution to the "settlement and support of a gospel minister among us." It included a parcel of 100 acres, given to Reverend Powers and his heirs. The house is near the site of the first church. It has had several owners, but the exterior remains virtually unchanged.

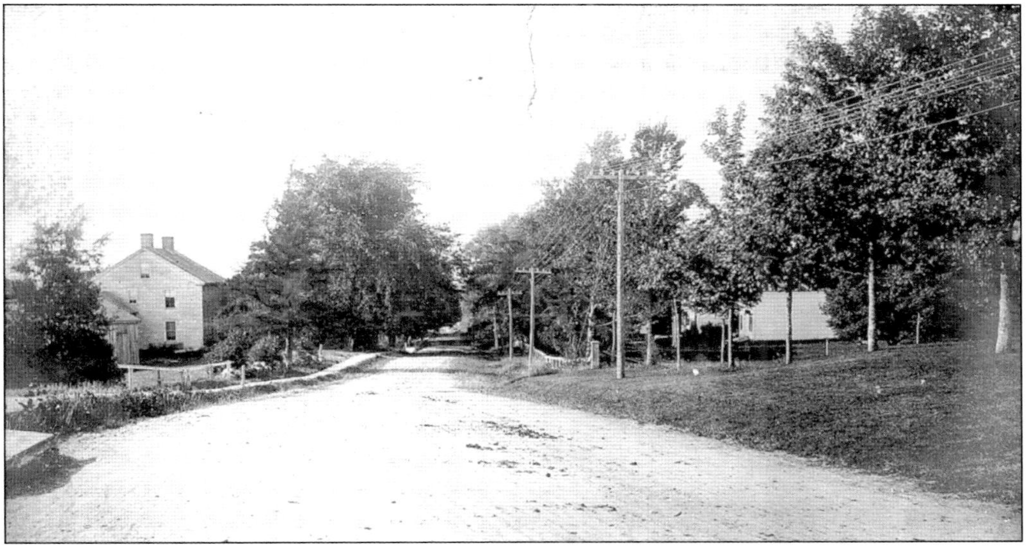

The Haskell House on Church Street was built c. 1793. In 1804, Reuben Rhode Island, likely the first black man on Deer Isle, purchased the site. After his death in 1825, the house passed to Solomon Haskell; it was later occupied by his son Eben, a proprietor of the tannery in Deer Isle Village. Later, the house fell into disrepair, and it was finally torn down by Eben's son Ralph. A house was moved onto the site from the location now occupied by Bar Harbor Banking and Trust; that house is now the Island Star Café.

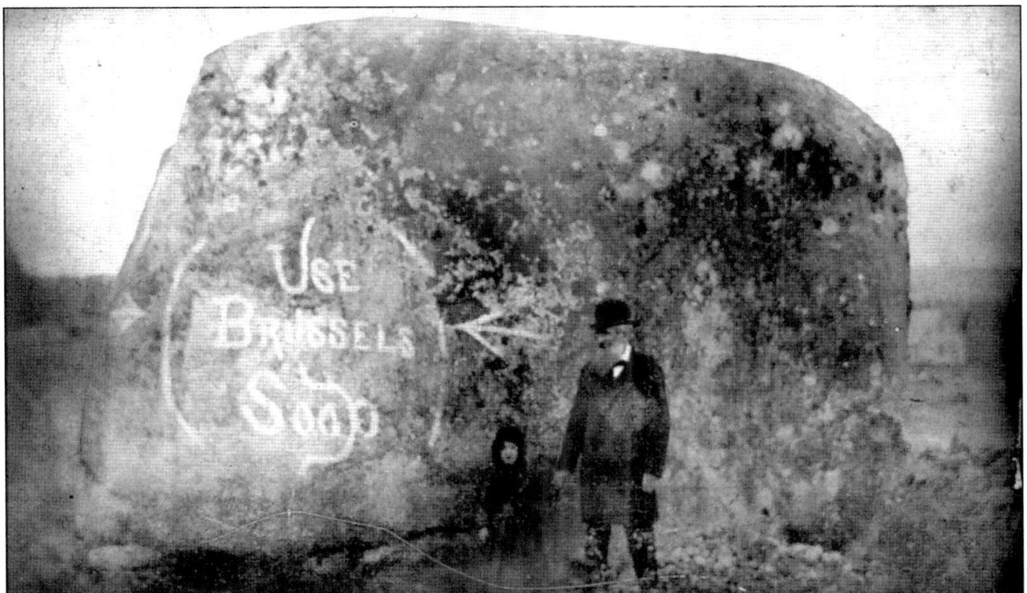

Carman's Rock is a familiar landmark in North Deer Isle. Here, Charles W. Bryant stands in front of it with Breta Haskell, his granddaughter, in the 1890s. Bryant was a geologist who opened and operated the marble quarry at the Reach and organized the Deer Isle Silver Mining Company. He also served one term as superintendent of schools. Carman's Rock was traditionally used for advertising. It is now repainted each year to show the names of the seniors graduating from Deer Isle-Stonington High School.

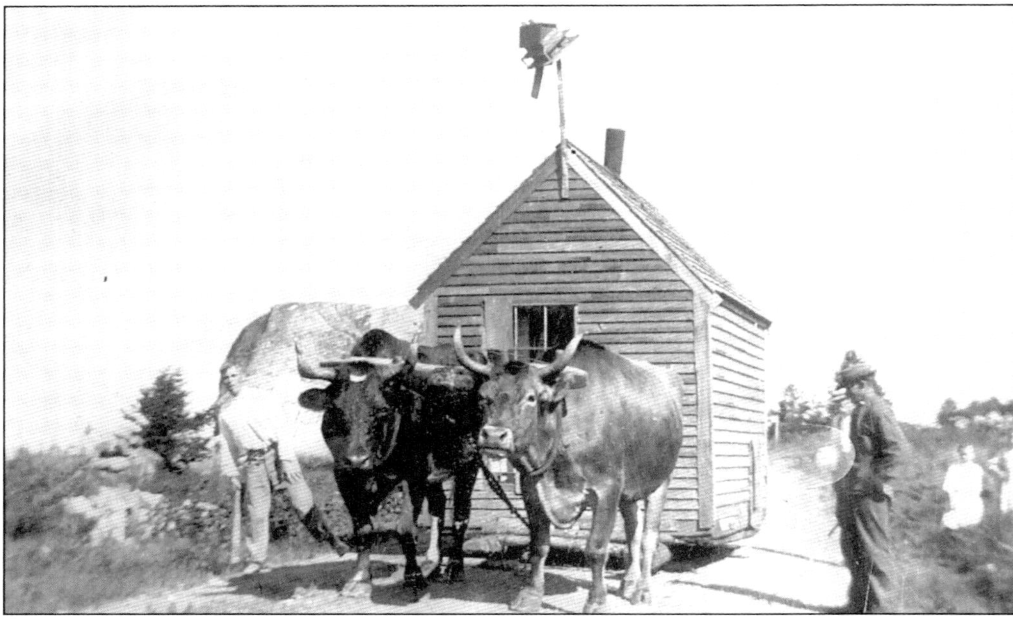

A house is moved in North Deer Isle. The oxen belonged to Charles Eaton. Buildings were frequently moved on the island.

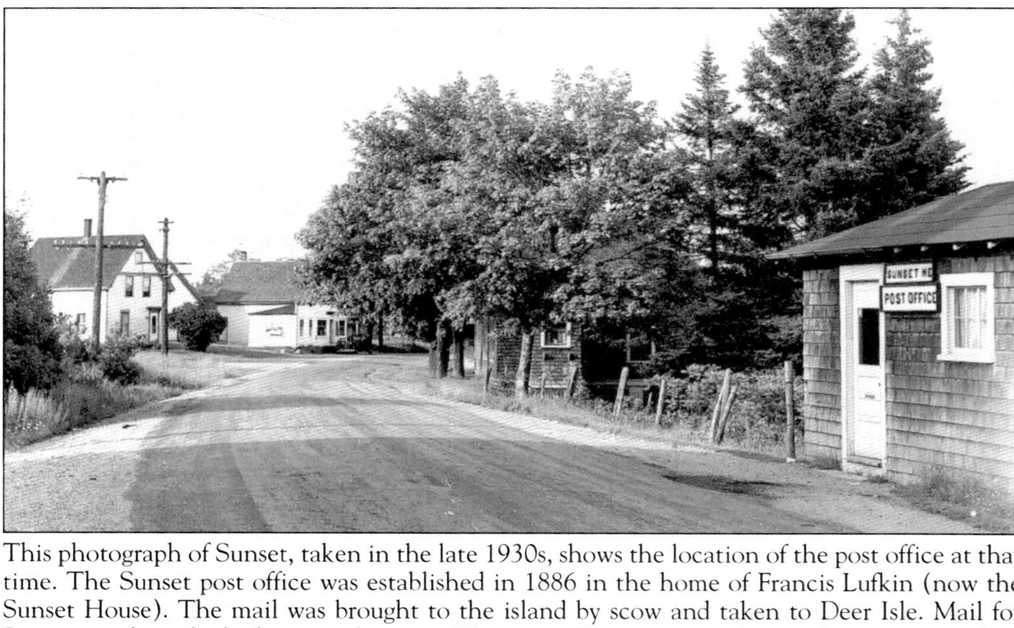

This photograph of Sunset, taken in the late 1930s, shows the location of the post office at that time. The Sunset post office was established in 1886 in the home of Francis Lufkin (now the Sunset House). The mail was brought to the island by scow and taken to Deer Isle. Mail for Sunset was brought by horse and wagon. The post office was moved several times, depending on who was postmaster. In 1936, Dudley Sellers became postmaster and built a post office across from the Sunset Church. Marion Billings then had it moved to the west side of the street, and the building was enlarged in 1949. When the new Sunset post office opened in 1990, the Village Green Association acquired the former building and gave it to the Deer Isle-Stonington Historical Society, where it may be seen today at the roadside.

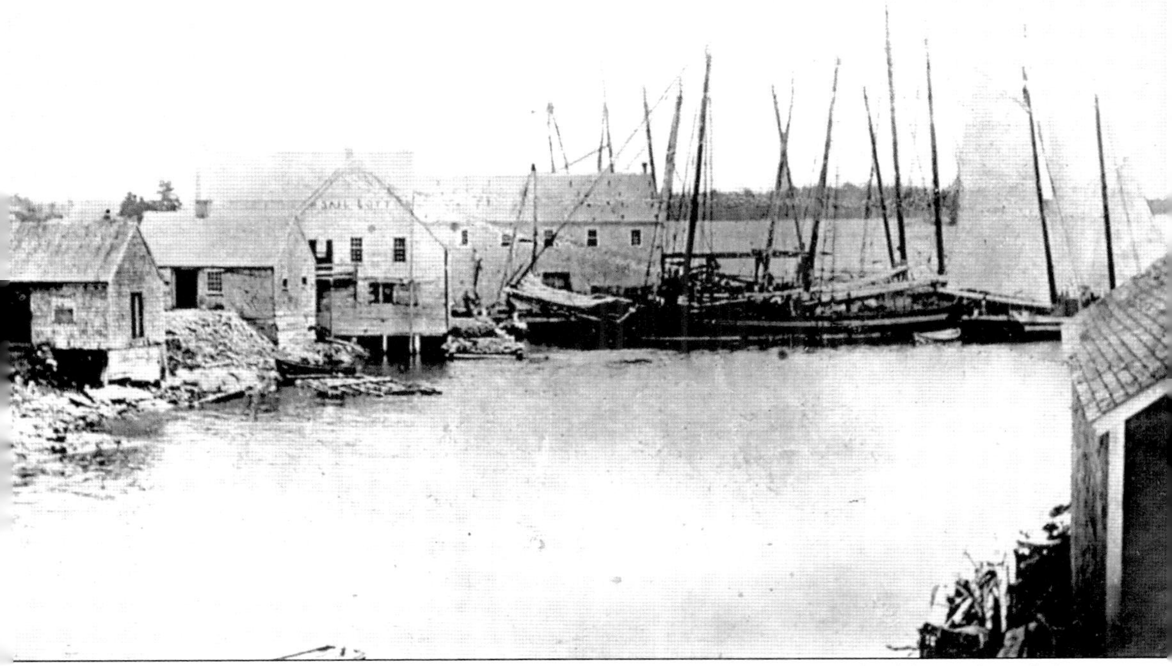

This photograph shows South Deer Isle at the time of the Civil War. The buildings, from left to right, are a store, a hall with dancing facilities, the customs house, a packing factory, and fish houses. Lafayette Collins has just hoisted his sails and is starting off on a fishing trip, probably for mackerel. In her memoirs of growing up in South Deer Isle, Phenie Bray (1883–1974) recalled her grandfather's description of the scene, "[One could see] those stone foundations all along the north shore on which stood the cooper shops, fish-houses, sail-lofts, salt-houses, and shops used for various purposes when ship-building and mackerel fishing was the way folks made their living." There was enough business conducted in South Deer Isle to warrant a customs house separate from the one in Deer Isle. "Salt for the mackerel was brought direct from Spain, and mackerel fishing was important there from 1830 to 1870. My beloved village reached the peak of its activities just before the Civil War."

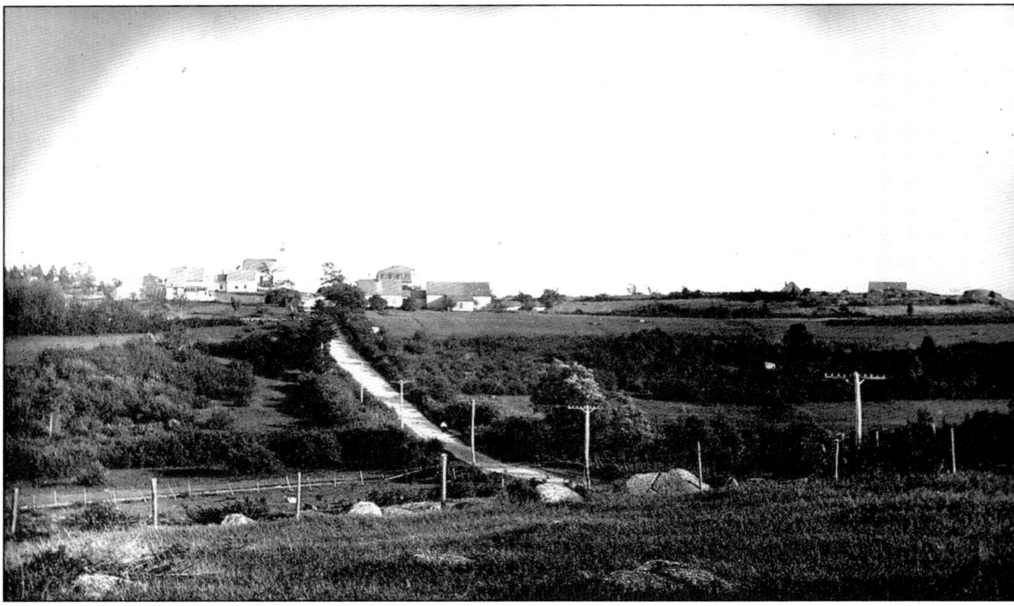

This photograph of South Deer Isle was taken from the beginning of the Sunset crossroad. In 1918, Austin Smith, while burning grass, lost control of the fire. A combination of strong winds, dry conditions, and lack of water and equipment resulted in the loss of the school, church, and three of the homes in South Deer Isle.

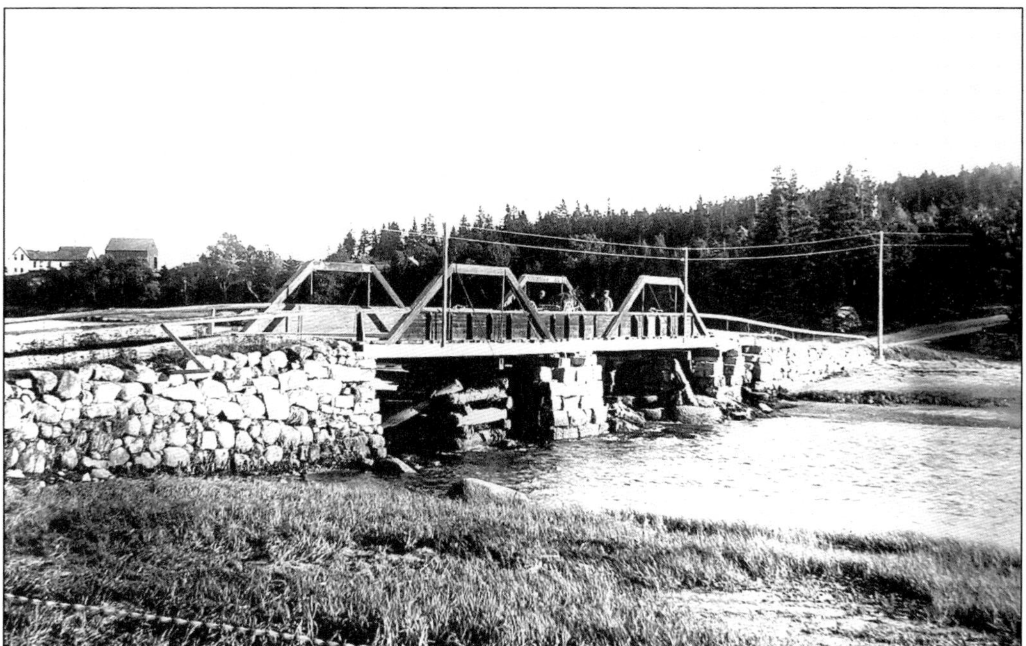

The first bridge to Oceanville was built c. 1846 and was financed by individuals. It was accepted as a public way c. 1859. This photograph shows the second bridge, built in 1910 and replaced in the 1930s by the Works Progress Administration. The house in the upper left belonged to William Buckminster.

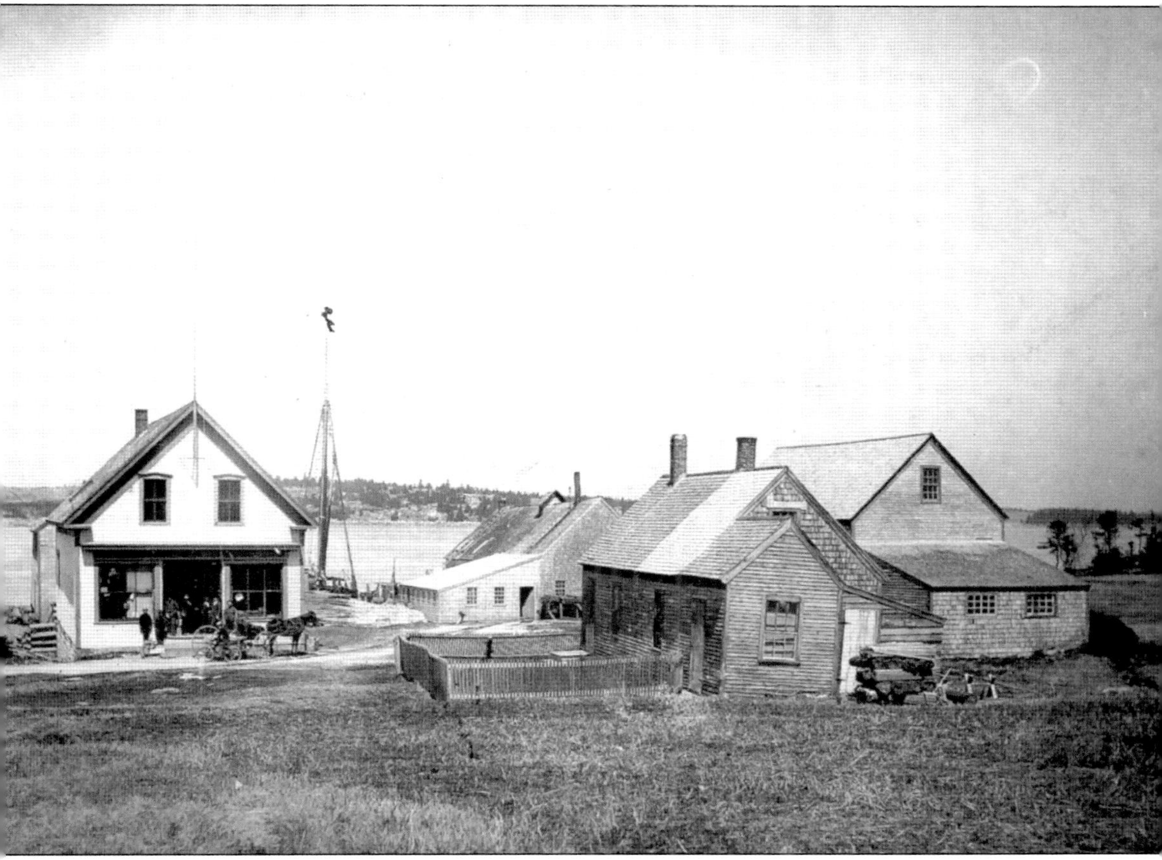

This turn-of-the-century photograph shows the shore at Oceanville. The store belonged to C. H. S. Webb; directly behind it and just visible to the left of it, a salt shed stands. To the right of the store is a clam-canning factory. One of the buildings also contained a cooper shop. The small house in the foreground was the first home of Fred and Jen (Buckminster) Webb. The store was later moved to Main Street in Stonington, where it became the Webb Brothers Store (now the granite museum).

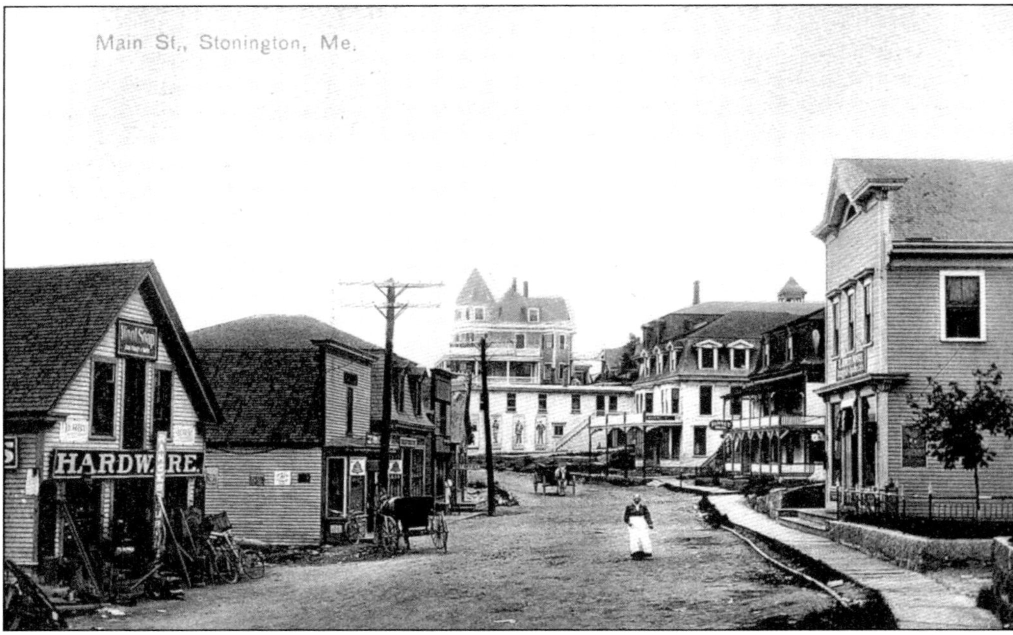

This postcard view looks west down Main Street, Stonington, *c.* 1908.

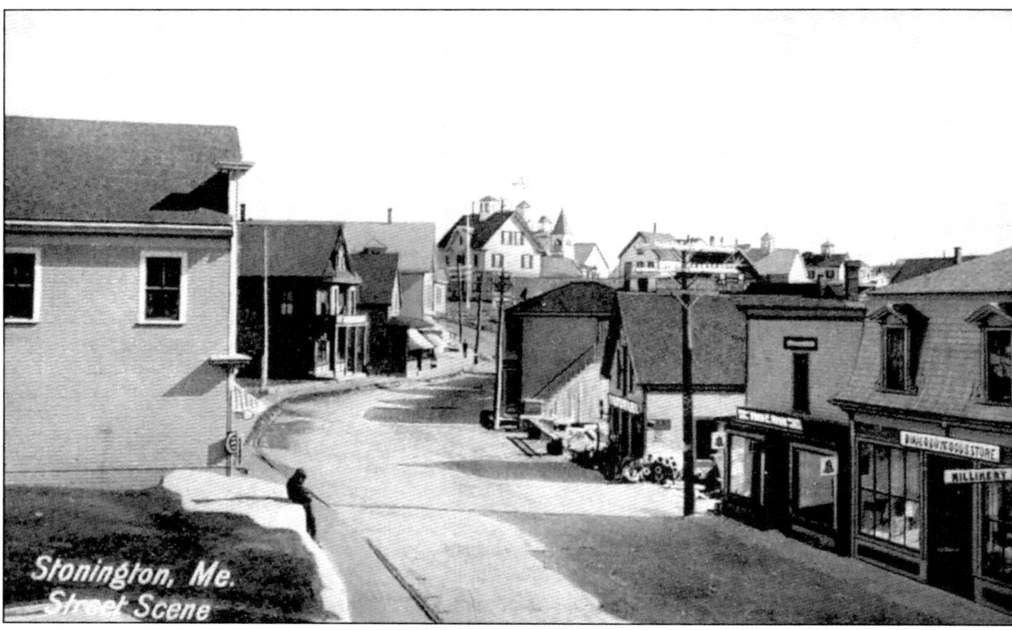

This postcard view looks east down Main Street, Stonington, *c.* 1908.

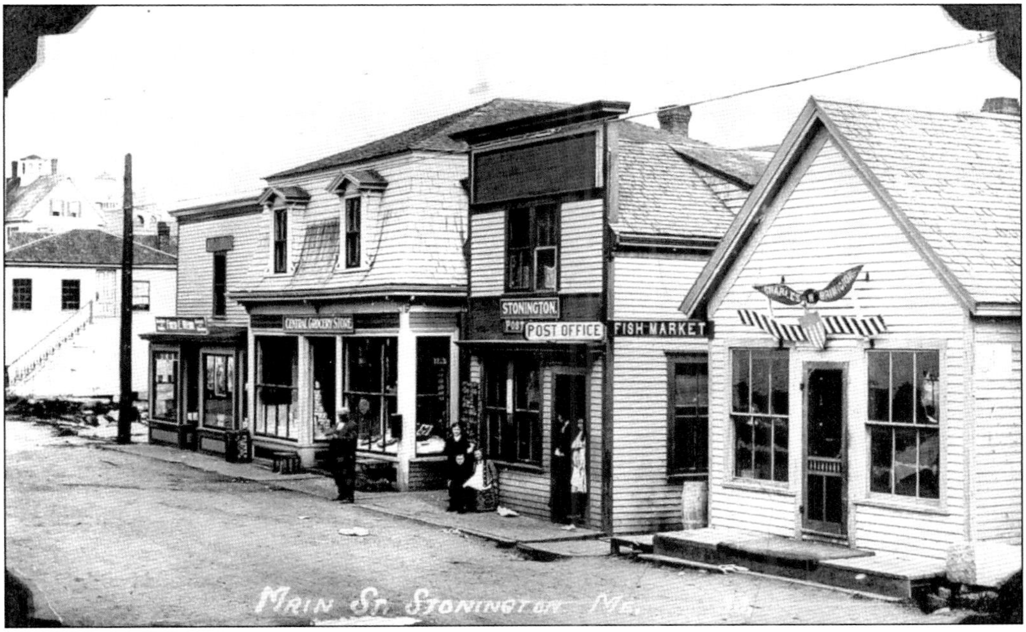

In this early 1900s photograph of Main Street in Stonington, the cupola on the left is atop the Ocean View Hotel. The buildings beside it, from left to right, are a water tower, the steeple of the Methodist church, the Brown House (formerly the Thurlow Carriage House), Webb's Store, the Central Grocery Store, the post office with a fish market behind it, and Charles Brimigion's Barber Shop.

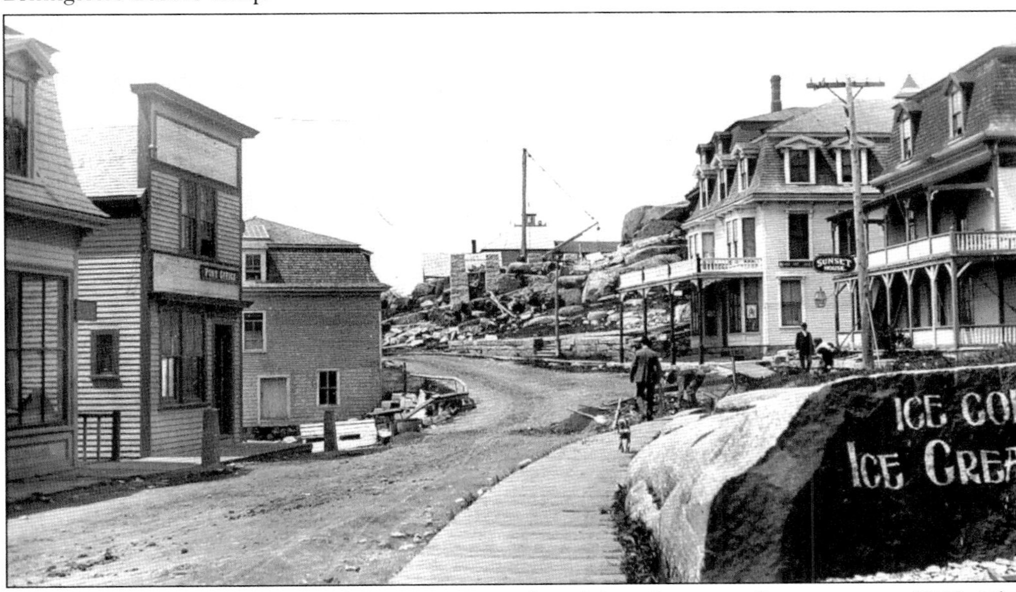

Dr. Benjamin Noyes's house is being constructed on Main Street in Stonington c. 1902. The roof of the music hall appears just behind it. Note the practice of painting advertisements on stone, and the use of boardwalks. The boardwalks were often slippery—from ice or rain in the winter and from oil applied as a wood preservative in the summer. They were eventually removed due to maintenance costs.

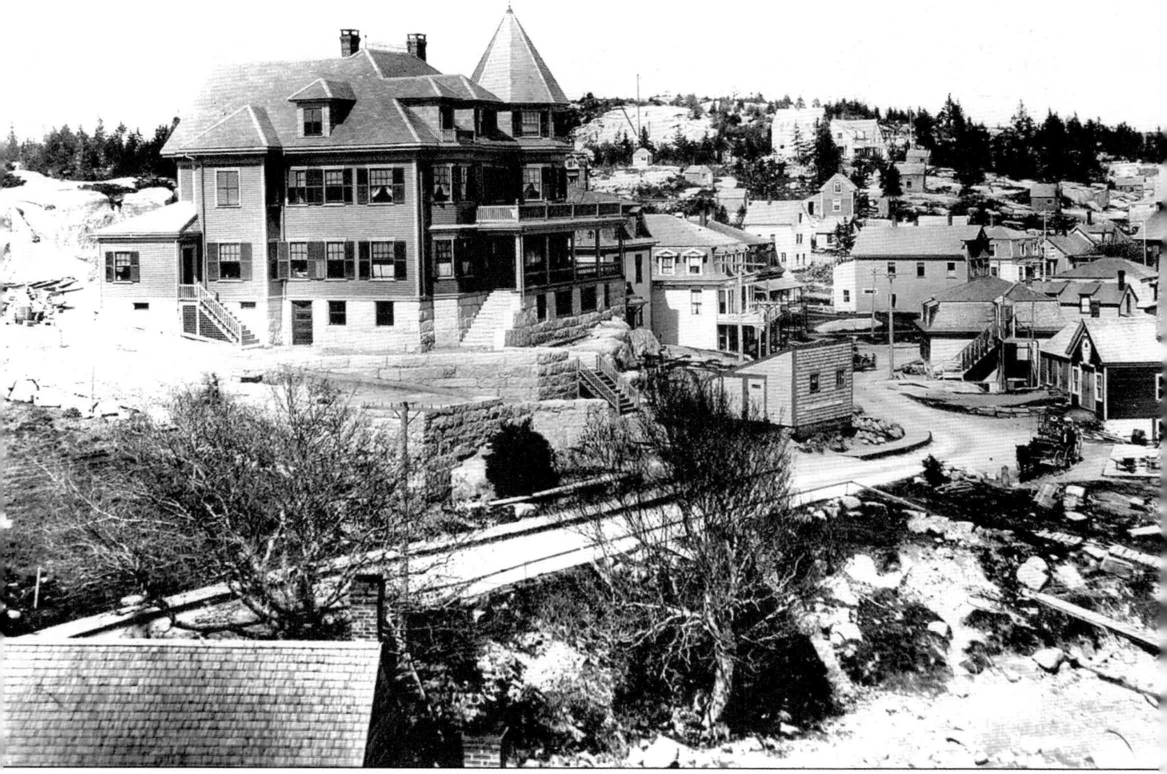

Dr. Benjamin Lake Noyes, newly graduated from Bowdoin College Medical School, came to Green's Landing in 1895. In 1899, he married Linnie Howard, and when they started a family, they built a large house. Their house, in the upper left of this photograph, was situated on a granite ledge overlooking the busy harbor. It contained 22 rooms, including a fine cupola. The inside was finished in cypress, hard pine, and quarter-sawed oak. The house was completed in 1903 at an estimated cost of $20,000. It burned to the ground in 1981.

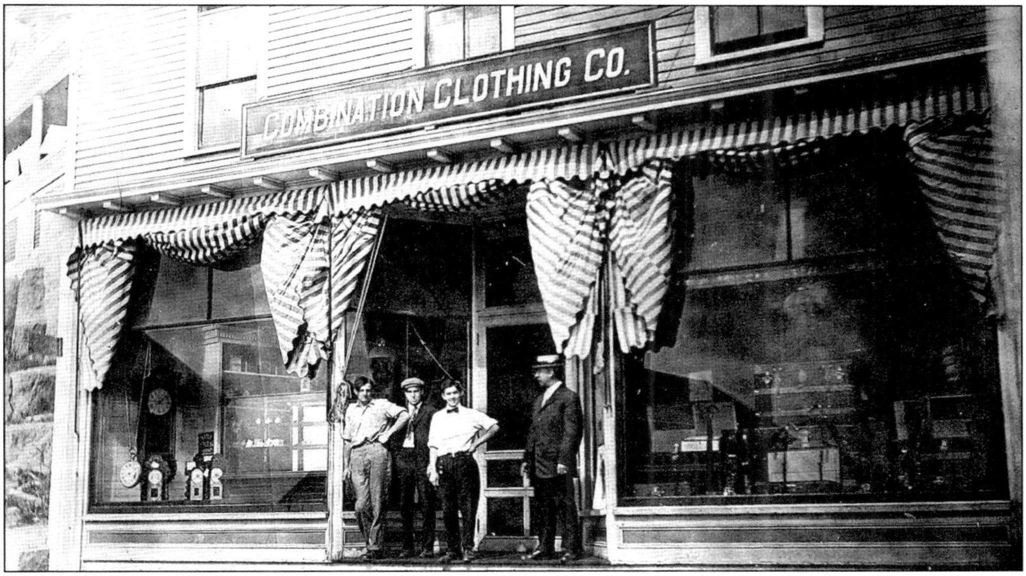

The Combination Clothing Company is shown here on Main Street in Stonington in 1905. Located on the site of a former cemetery, it later housed a number of businesses until becoming the state liquor store in the 1960s. By the end of the 19th century, the population of Stonington was growing so fast and the demand for building sites was so great, that it was no longer economically feasible to use the property as a cemetery. Among those buried there is Stephen Wells, the first part-time postmaster in town. Clayton Gross, writing in the *Island Ad-Vantages* in 1991, described what happened to the cemetery: "The families of those buried there moved [them] to the present cemetery, all except Wells, who had no one to move him. So he remains, the only unbottled spirit in the liquor store."

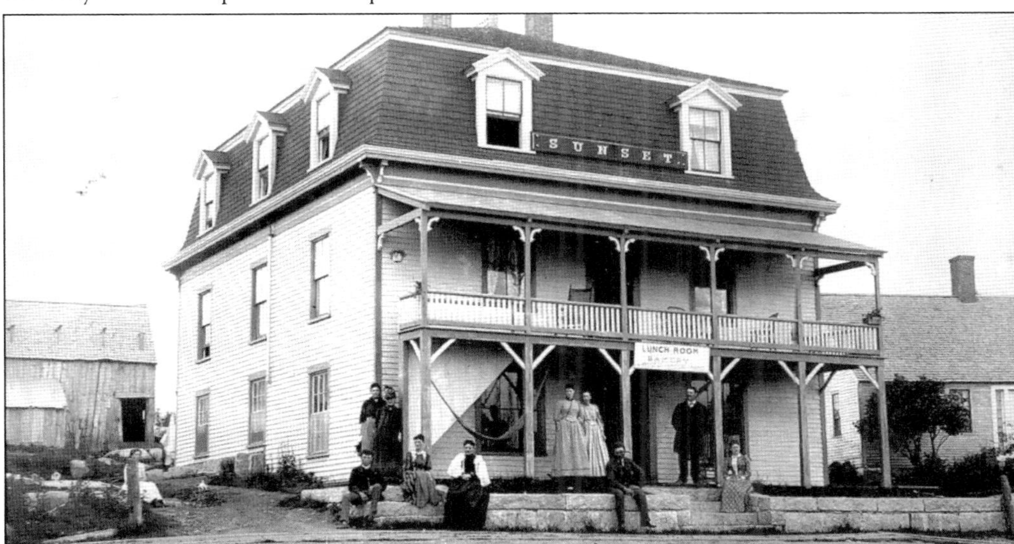

The Sunset House, a boardinghouse on Main Street in Stonington, was operated by Mollie and Stephen Brown. It later became the Knights of Pythias hall and then the post office. It now houses a real estate office and the American Legion. The building seen to the right is Ted Boyce's Grocery Store.

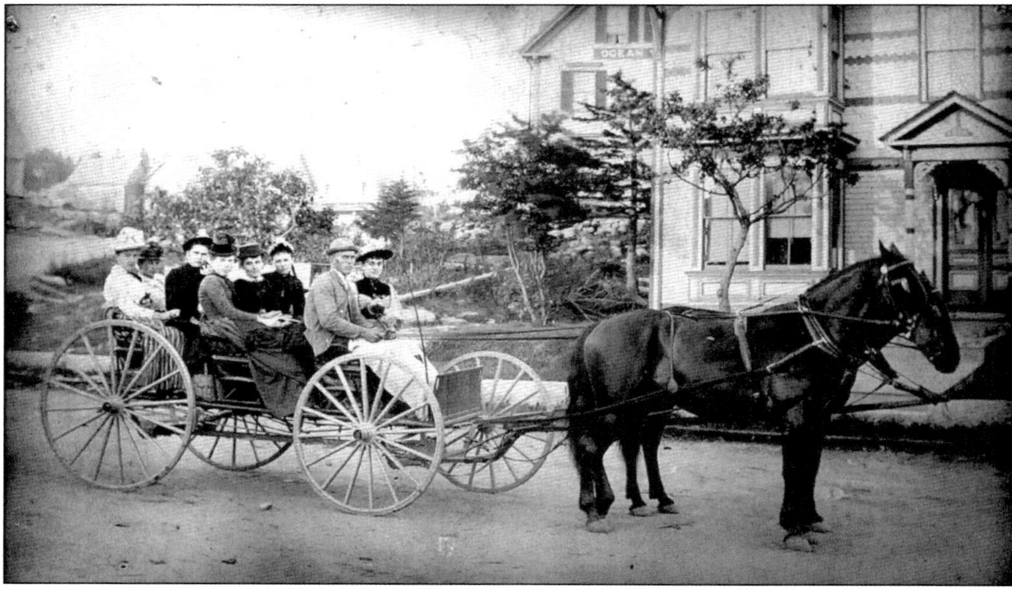

This photograph, taken in Stonington, includes the Ocean View Hotel in the background and the Rockbound Boarding House in the foreground, at what is now the site of the Union Trust Bank, which was built in 1954. The Rockbound was torn down *c.* 1920.

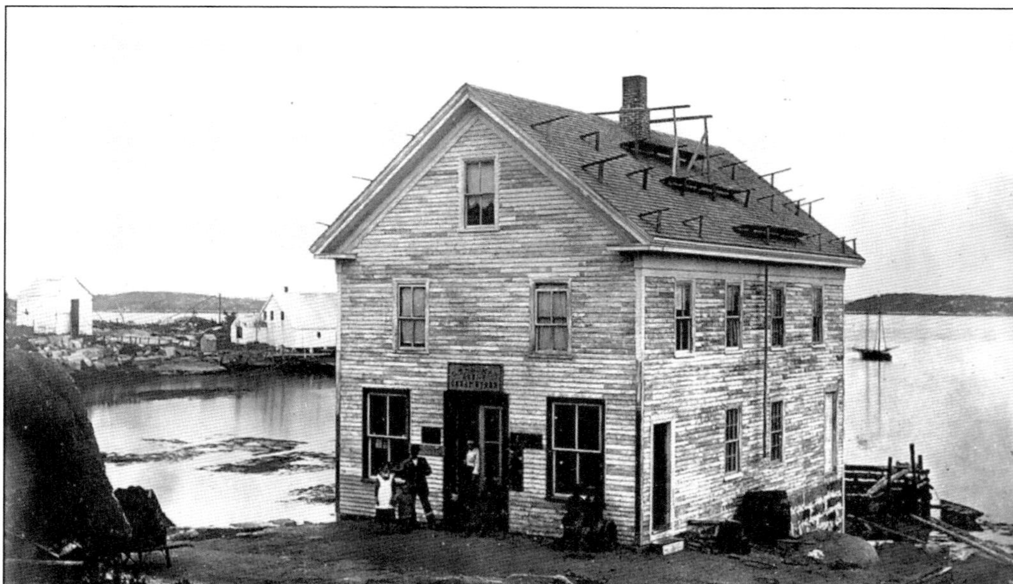

This building, originally in South Deer Isle, was owned by Amaziah Billings. George Redman bought it in 1885, had it taken down in sections, and brought it to Green's Landing to be used as a store and home. Redman added to it and built a wharf beside it; deliveries came by water and were passed up into the store by a trap door. It was a general store, selling furniture, drugs, hardware, and groceries. A sign over the door read, "Cheap Store." The Odd Fellows bought the building from the Redman estate for $1,800 and held their first meeting there in February 1922. It is still their meeting hall.

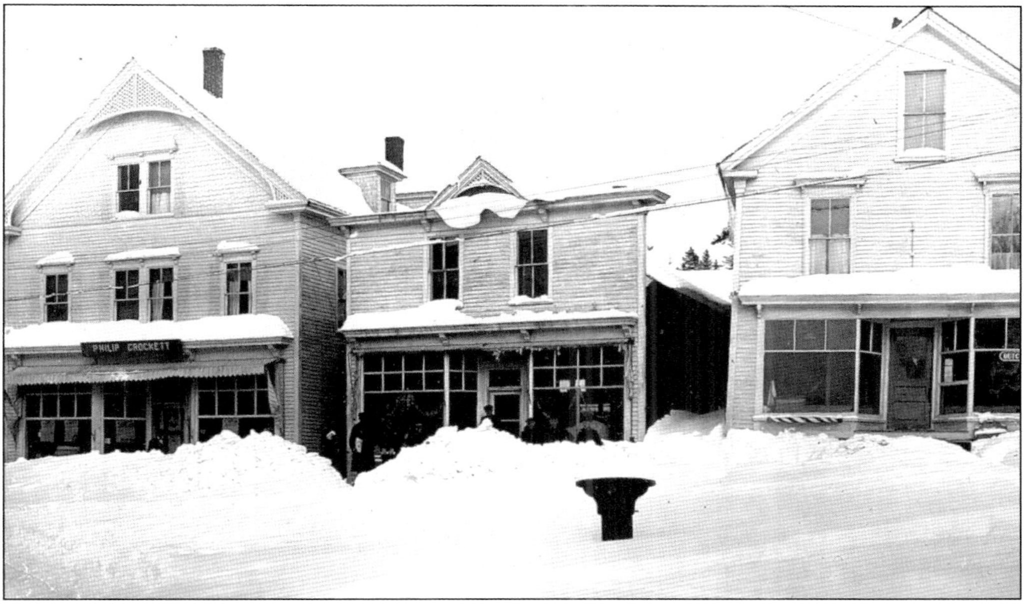

This c. 1920 photograph shows, from left to right, Phillip Crockett's Store, Small's Drug Store, and a building that housed the telephone office, all on Main Street in Stonington. The object in the foreground, a horse watering trough, is now located on the lawn of the town hall.

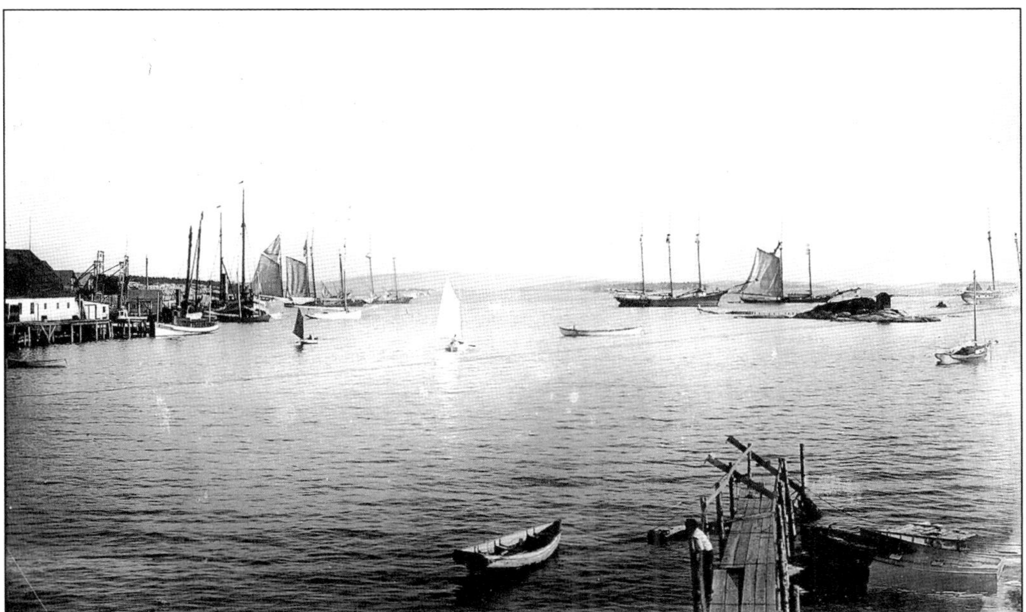

The little steamer *Minnehaha* is just visible at the far left of this c. 1910 view of Stonington Harbor. The building at the left, used for coal and wood, occupies the site later used by Atlantic Hardware.

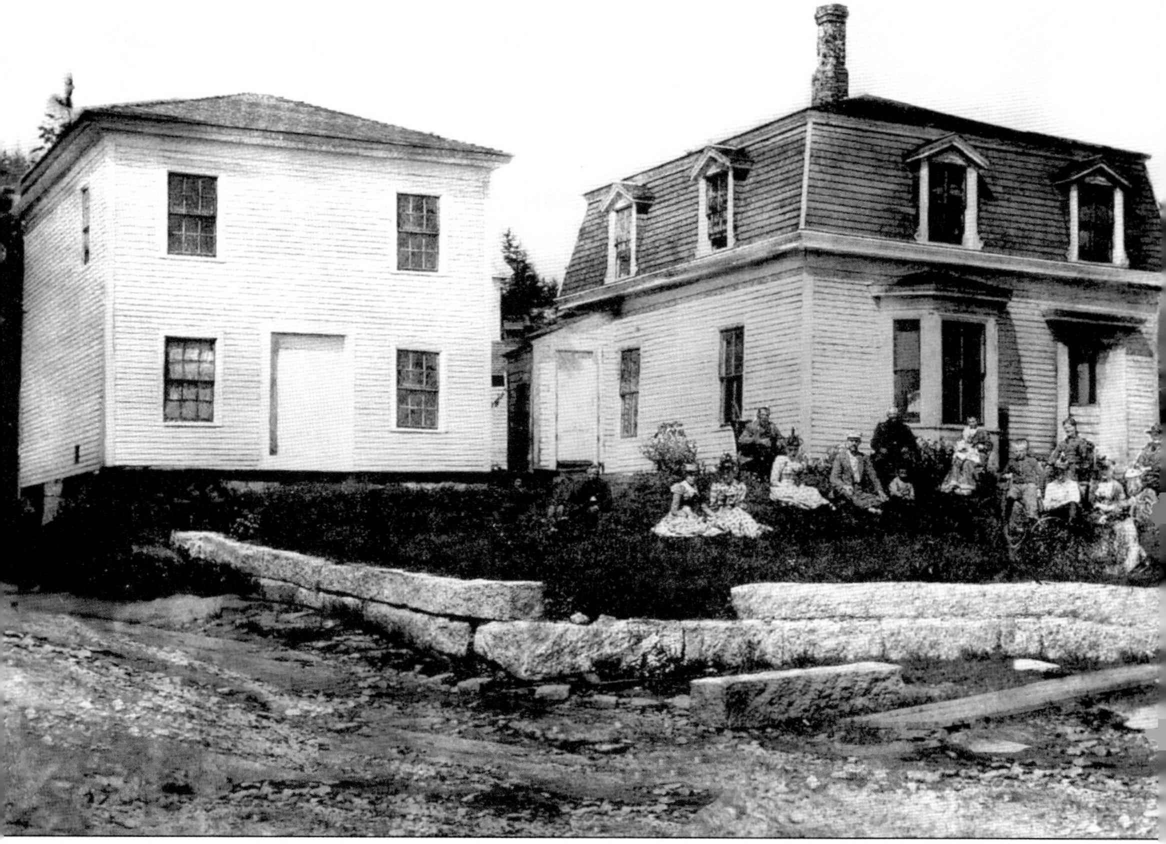

Winfield Scott Thurlow (1847–1917) was a fisherman and dairyman who also conducted an ice business and lobster trade. On a fishing trip to the Bay of Fundy, he was anchored at Grand Manaan, where he had a view of the home and medical office of Dr. George B. Noyes (father of B. Lake Noyes of Stonington). Thurlow admired the house so much that he decided to build one like it when he returned to Stonington. He did so, and it later became the home of Rev. Horace Haskell and his wife, Bessie (Thurlow) Haskell.

Three

Day to Day

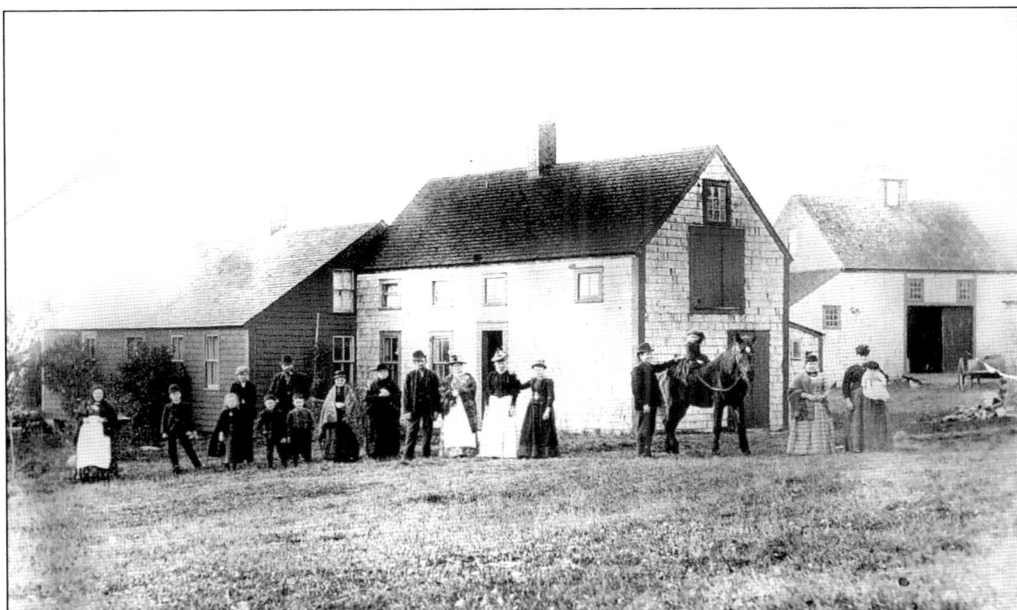

The large house on the left was built by Nathaniel Bray c. 1804. He left it to his son, who "became crazy"; Mark Sawyer and his wife, Susan Bray, cared for him for 20 years and took the house in exchange. Later owners built the house that appears in the middle of the photograph and added the barn. The larger house was eventually torn down. To see what became of the barn, turn to page 114.

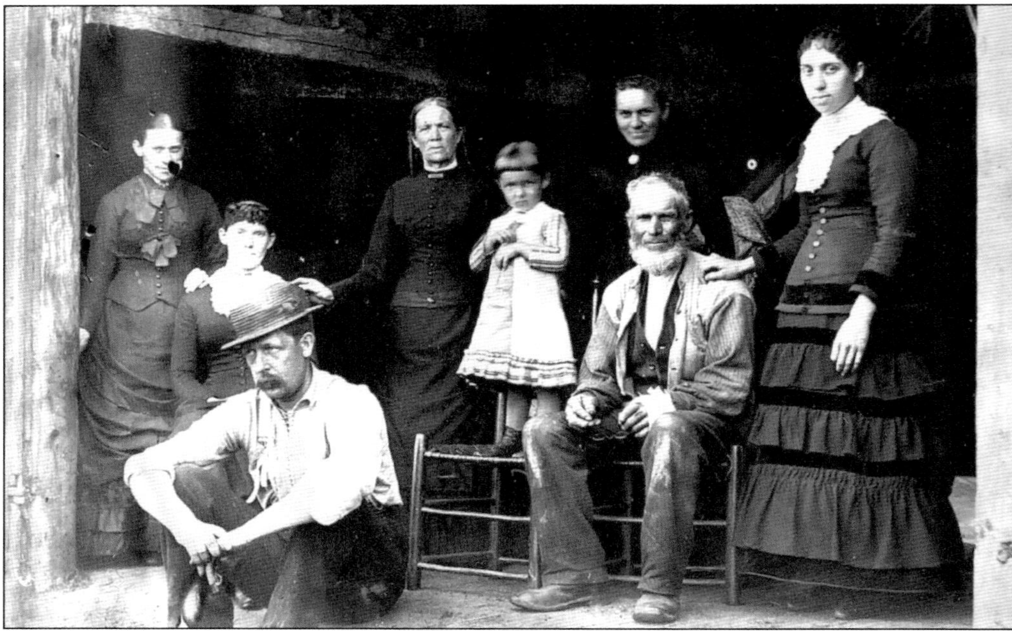

This 1890s photograph depicts the family of Capt. Amos Torrey. The man in the foreground is unidentified. From left to right, the others are his daughter Comfort (Torrey) Greenlaw; his granddaughter Lottie Greenlaw; his wife, Sarah; two unidentified people, Captain Torrey, and an unidentified woman.

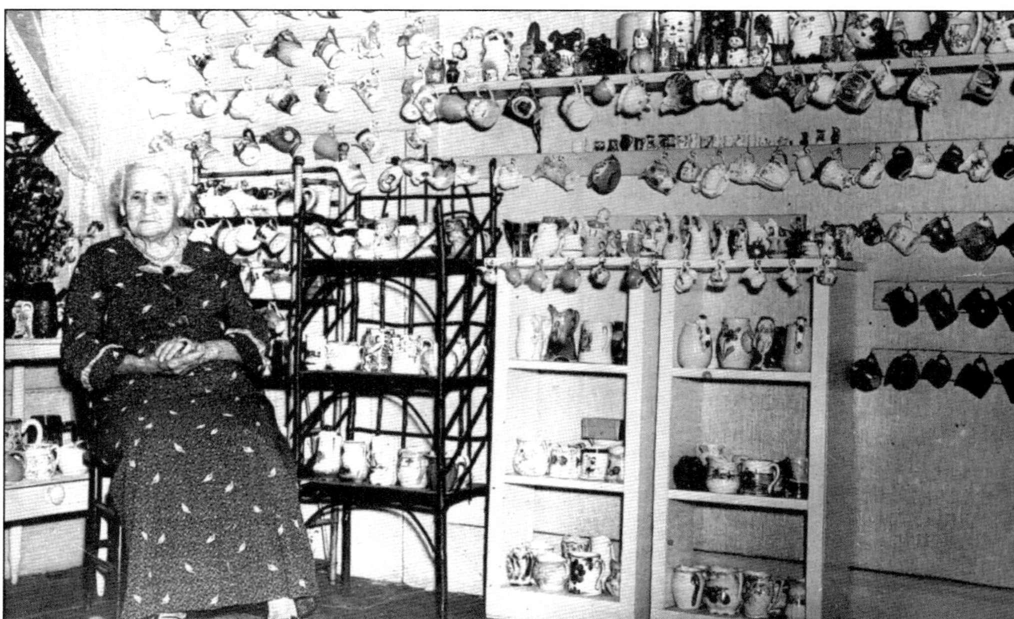

Arvilla "Granny Bill" (Saunders) Lufkin was born in 1852 and died in 1951. She and her husband, George William Lufkin, lived in Sunset. He was lost at sea while their six children were still very young. Her collection of 400–500 pitchers was widely admired. Granny Bill remembered the assassination of President Lincoln and the high prices caused by the Civil War.

Nathaniel Robbins of South Deer Isle lived to be almost 103 years old. Known to all as "Uncle Tan," he had nine children by his first wife, Betsy Babbidge; after her death, he married Mary Sylvester. He followed the America's Cup race of the *Columbia* with great interest and was a sympathizer with the Boer cause in South Africa. Robbins attributed his long life to "wasting no time in worrying over things he could not prevent."

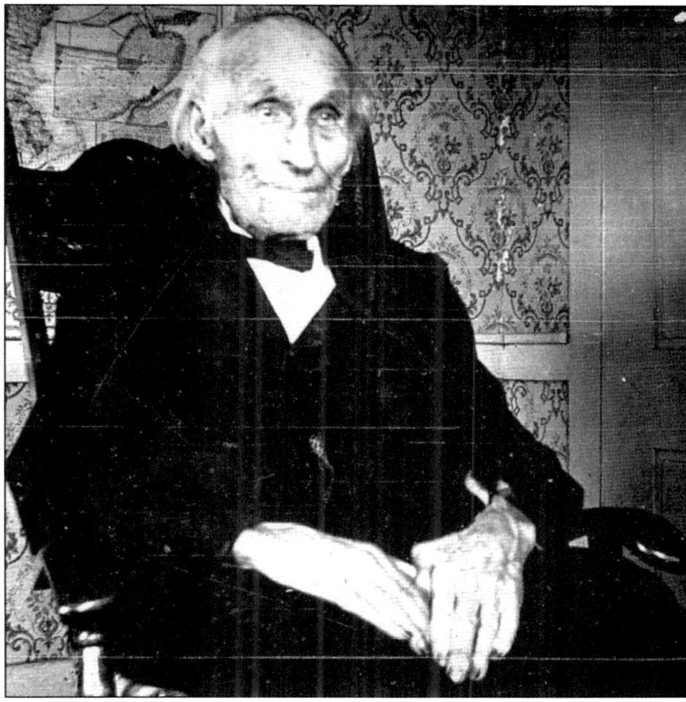

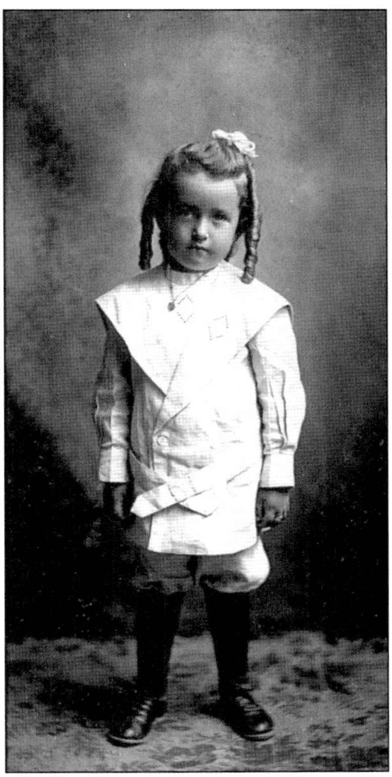

Walker Pickering was born in 1909 to Emery and Caro Pickering of Deer Isle. He graduated from the University of Maine in 1931 and became principal of McKinley High School that same year. He served in that position until the death of his father in 1939, when he took over the store S. Pickering & Son, which had been in the family since 1840. It was destroyed by fire in 1971. Walker was very active in town affairs, serving as selectman, master of the Marine Lodge, and trustee of the Congregational church. He had a special talent for storytelling. As a boy, he would join the men who sat around the stove telling stories every evening. He remembered the tales the men told and related them to others in great detail. He died in 1988.

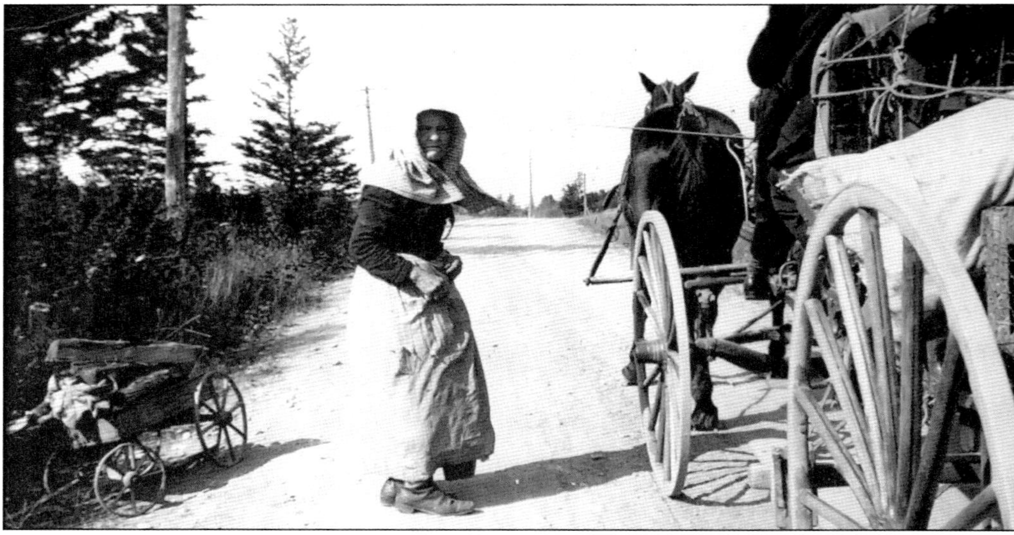

Nancy Conary appears beside a wagonload of summer boarders and their trunks on the way to the ferry landing in North Deer Isle. Nancy was born in Deer Isle the daughter of John and Mary (Sellers) Conary. She was a well-known character in town, always seen pulling a wagon (at left) containing her chickens and other belongings. She and her chickens would go visit acquaintances, stay two or three days, and then visit someone else. Long ago, to a child carrying too many things at once, a mother would say, "You're worse than Nancy Conary." Nancy died in 1914 at the age of 77.

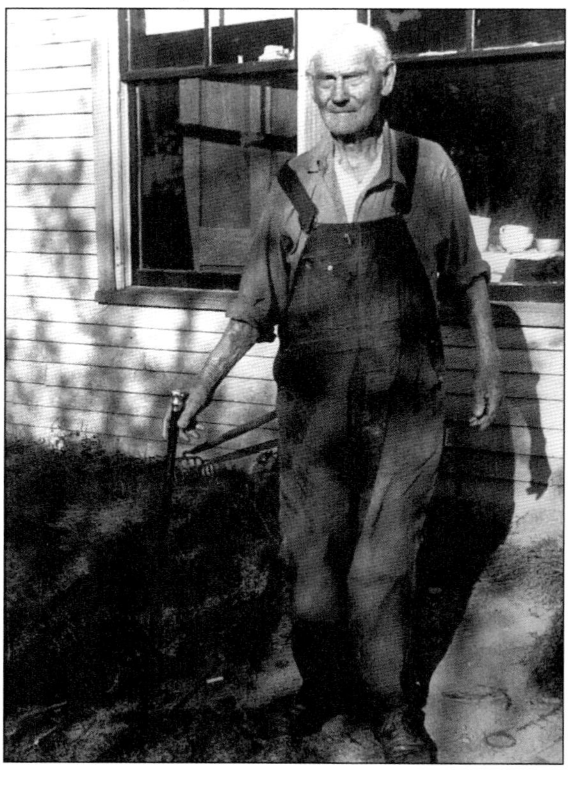

In 1909, the *Boston Post* distributed gold-headed ebony canes to the oldest residents of 700 New England towns. Walter Small of Sunset, pictured here, received the cane in 1950. Well over 90 years of age, Walter never needed to use the cane; he worked in his garden, cut wood in his wood lot, and was digging a well the day of this photograph. The cane is passed on from one individual to the next, with the presentation made by the selectmen. The present holder of the cane is Willie Haskell of Little Deer Isle.

This photograph of Billy Jarvis was taken in 1892. He worked for many years for "Dode" Spofford, who owned land on the Center District Road. Jarvis drove the cows from Spofford Hill to the Center District every day. At the time, the Center District included the first church, town hall, and schoolhouse of the town of Deer Isle.

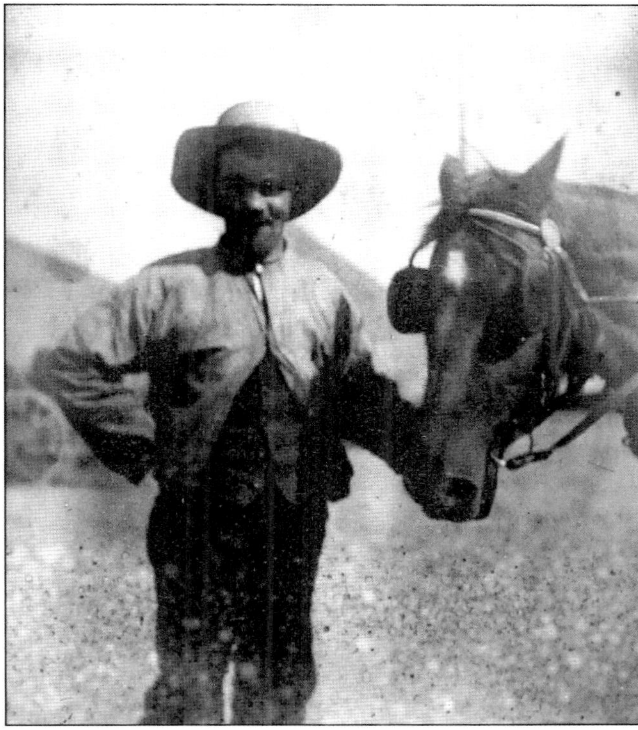

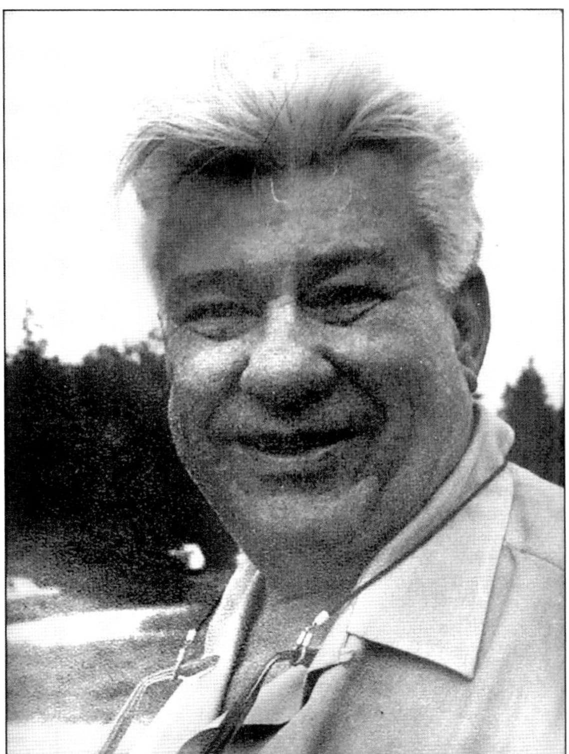

Dr. Harry Kopfmann was born in 1909 in Union City, New Jersey. He received his degree in medicine from the University of Marburg, in Germany. He and his wife, Patricia, moved to Deer Isle in 1940, where he set up his office and home in the former Edwin and Carrie Haskell house, near Deer Isle Village. He was a well-loved country doctor who had office hours morning and night, made house calls, and was always available for emergencies. For years, he was the only doctor on the island. Office calls were $2, house calls $3, and no charge was placed on patients who were financially unstable. Dr. Kopfmann died in 1984.

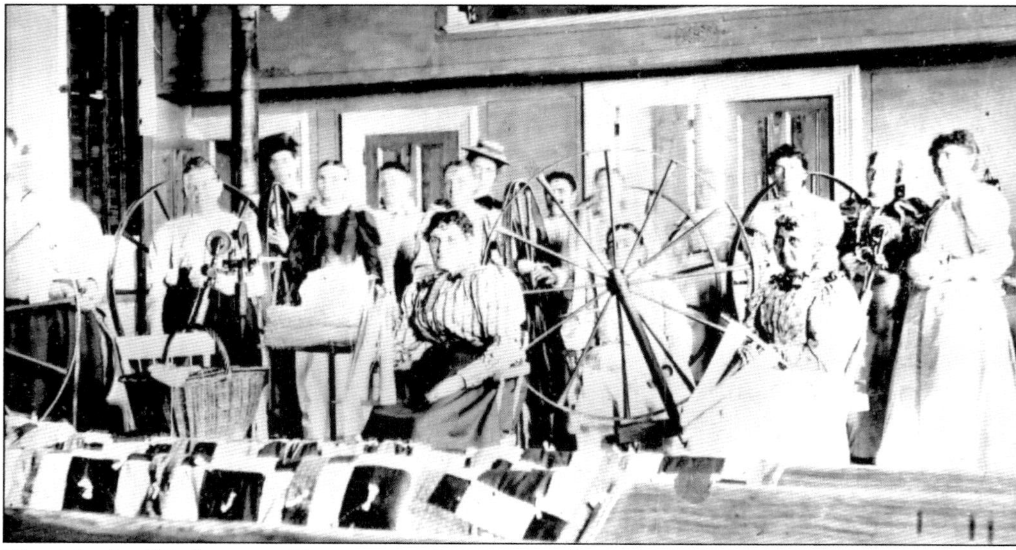

The Martha Washington Temperance Society was formed in 1835, when a group of strong-willed women joined together to keep Deer Isle free of "evil liquor intemperately consumed." Years later, the group changed its name to the Martha Washington Benevolent Society and turned its attention to the needs of less fortunate island neighbors. The society's motto, "Whatever Thy Hand Finds To Do, Do It With Thy Might," can still be seen in the balcony of the Sunset Congregational Church.

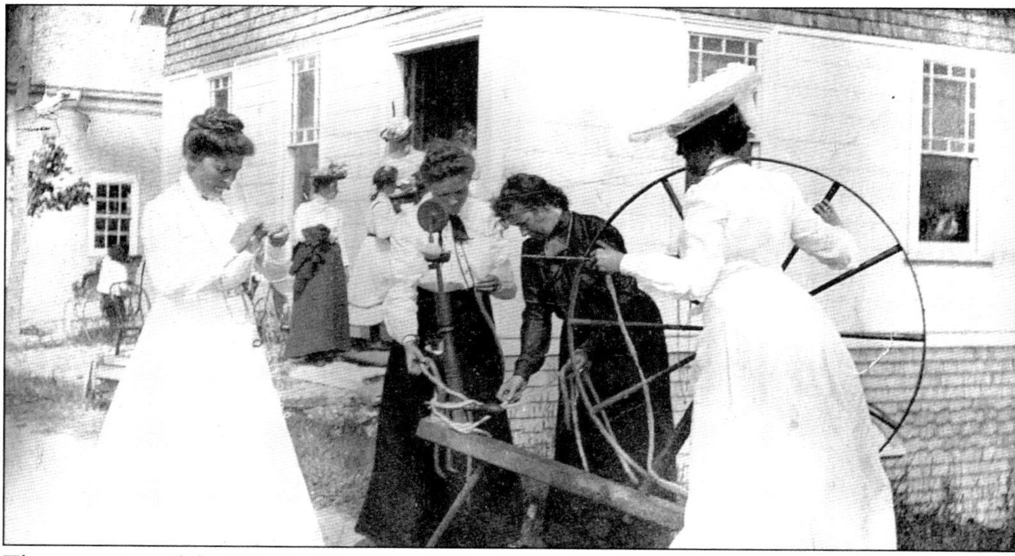

These women of the Martha Washington Benevolent Society work in front of what is now the parish house of the Sunset Congregational Church. The society, which had been meeting in the homes of its members, offered to help the South West Chapel Society build a church on the condition that the society could hold its meetings there. The church was completed *c.* 1884, and the society used its balcony as a meeting place. By April 1902, the Martha Washington Benevolent Society had accumulated $800 for its own building, which was completed that year. The society continued to meet there until 1943, when the members disbanded and deeded the building to the Sunset Congregational Church.

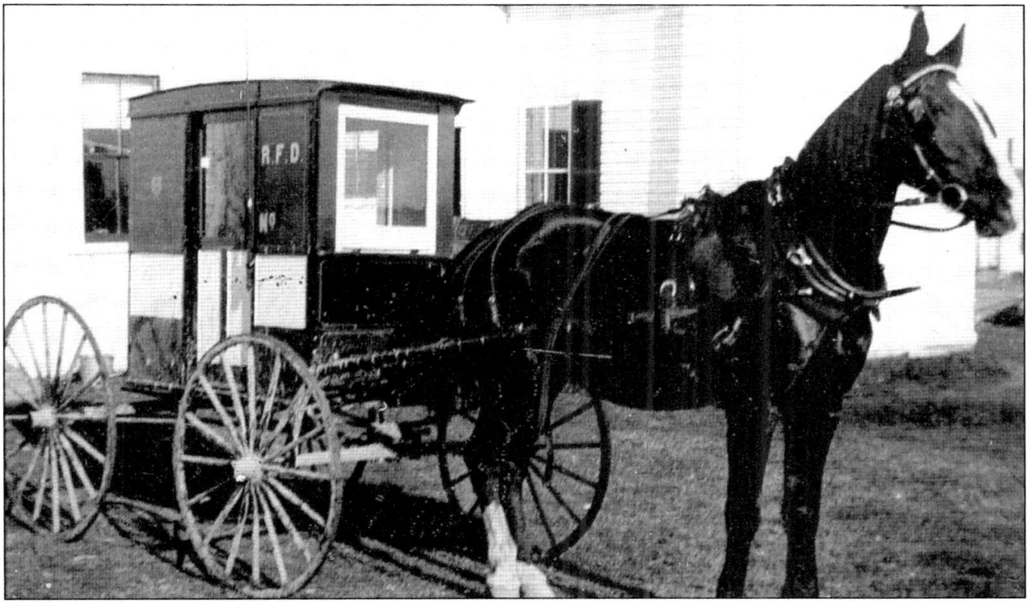

Rural free delivery (RFD) began in 1904, and M. D. Joyce served as the first RFD carrier in Deer Isle. His route included Deer Isle, the Reach, and Sunset and was later expanded to include Sunshine. This photograph was taken in front of Joyce's house at Hallet's Corner (where Bridge Street meets the Pressey Village Road). The delivery cart was painted red, white, and blue. In 1907, Joyce resigned in order to found the M. D. Joyce Company in partnership with George L. Beck. Fred Eaton took over the mail route. In those days, mail was delivered to the island twice a day by steamer—one landing in Stonington and the other in North Deer Isle. Contracted carriers took the mail from one post office to the other, where the RFD carriers took over. Parcel post began in 1907.

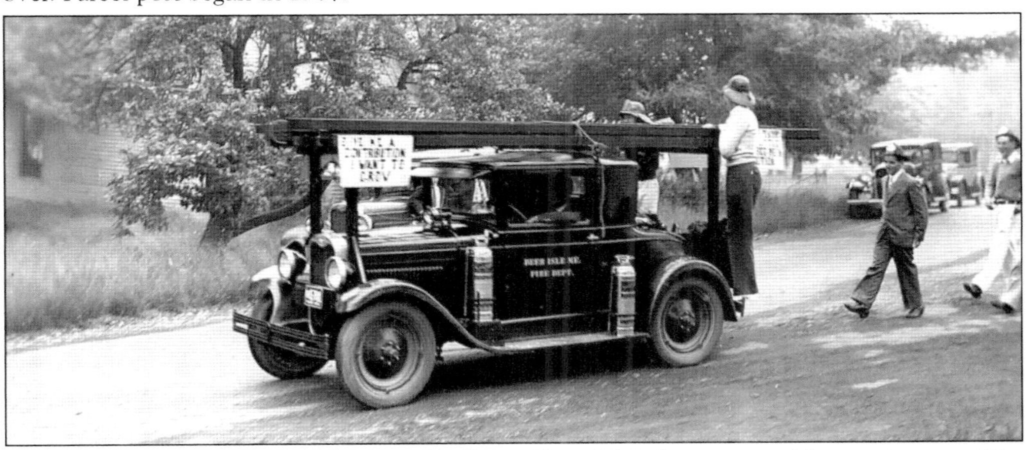

This photograph, taken on July 4, 1937, shows Deer Isle's first piece of fire equipment. The truck, a 1928 Chevrolet coupe, was converted into a fire truck by a group that included George Cole, Sylvanus Haskell, George J. Haskell, and Lawrence Pickering. It was equipped with a siren, a bell, eight brooms, 12 pails, two pyrene guns, four fire extinguishers, two fire axes, two smoke masks, a shovel, two electric lanterns, a rope, and two ladders. George Cole and Maurice Greenlaw were chief and assistant chief, respectively. All firemen were volunteers, as they are today. The sign on the truck reads, "Give me a contribution—I want to grow."

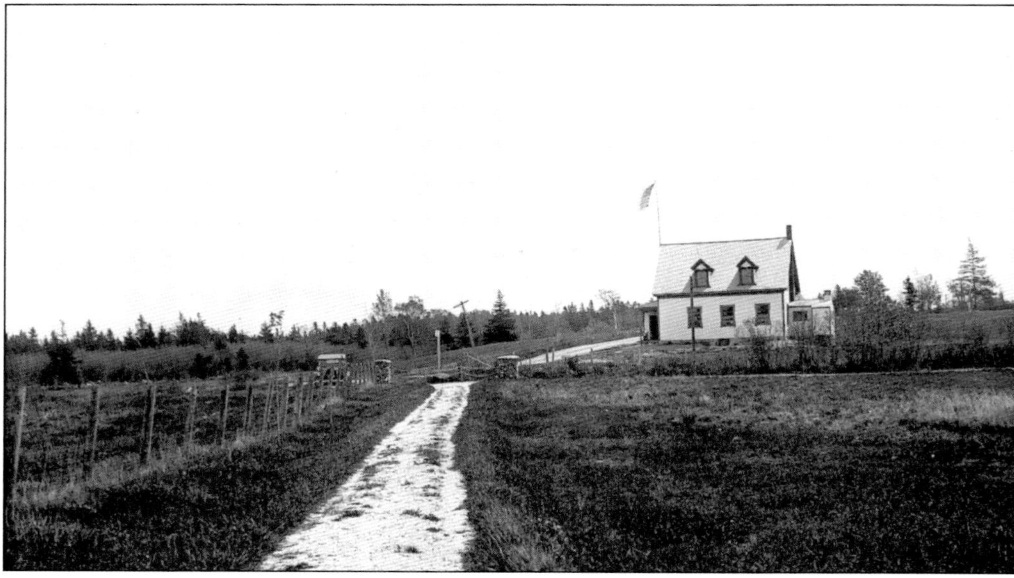

The Burnt Cove School was moved from its original location at Fifield Point to here, its present location (now opposite the Burnt Cove Market). The building is now the Stonington Pharmacy. Burnt Cove and Burntland Pond were named in remembrance of a fire in the mid-18th century that swept across the island. The fire was started by Joseph Colby, an early settler, who was trying to clear his land.

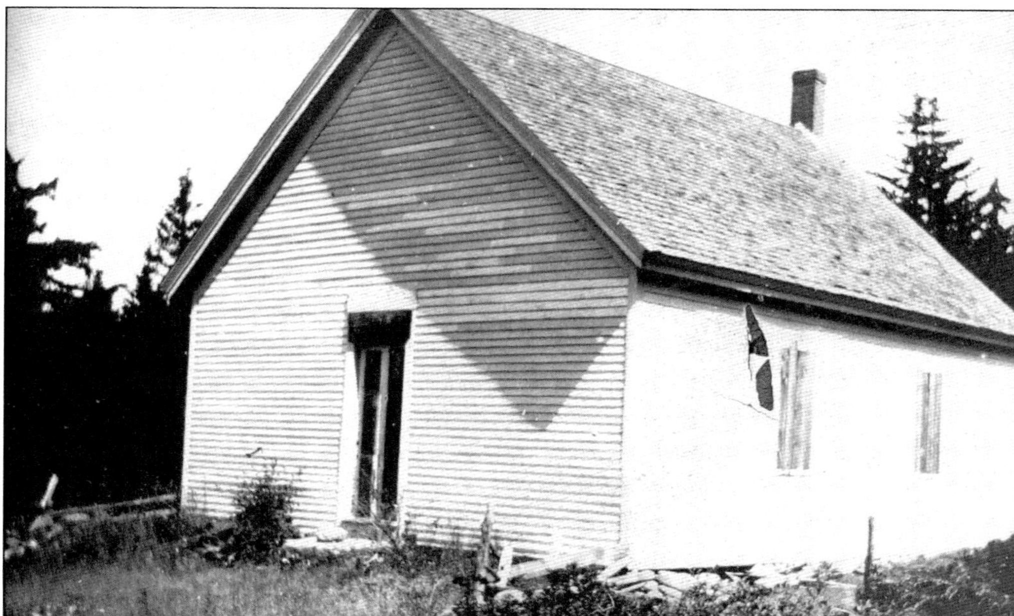

The Pressey Village Schoolhouse, seen here, is typical of the schools built in the first half of the 19th century. In 1847, there were 28 schools in the area—19 on Deer Isle and 9 on the smaller islands. In the early 20th century, there were 15 or 16 on Deer Isle. Some burned or were torn down, but most are in use today in one form or another. This schoolhouse was moved and became part of a summer cottage.

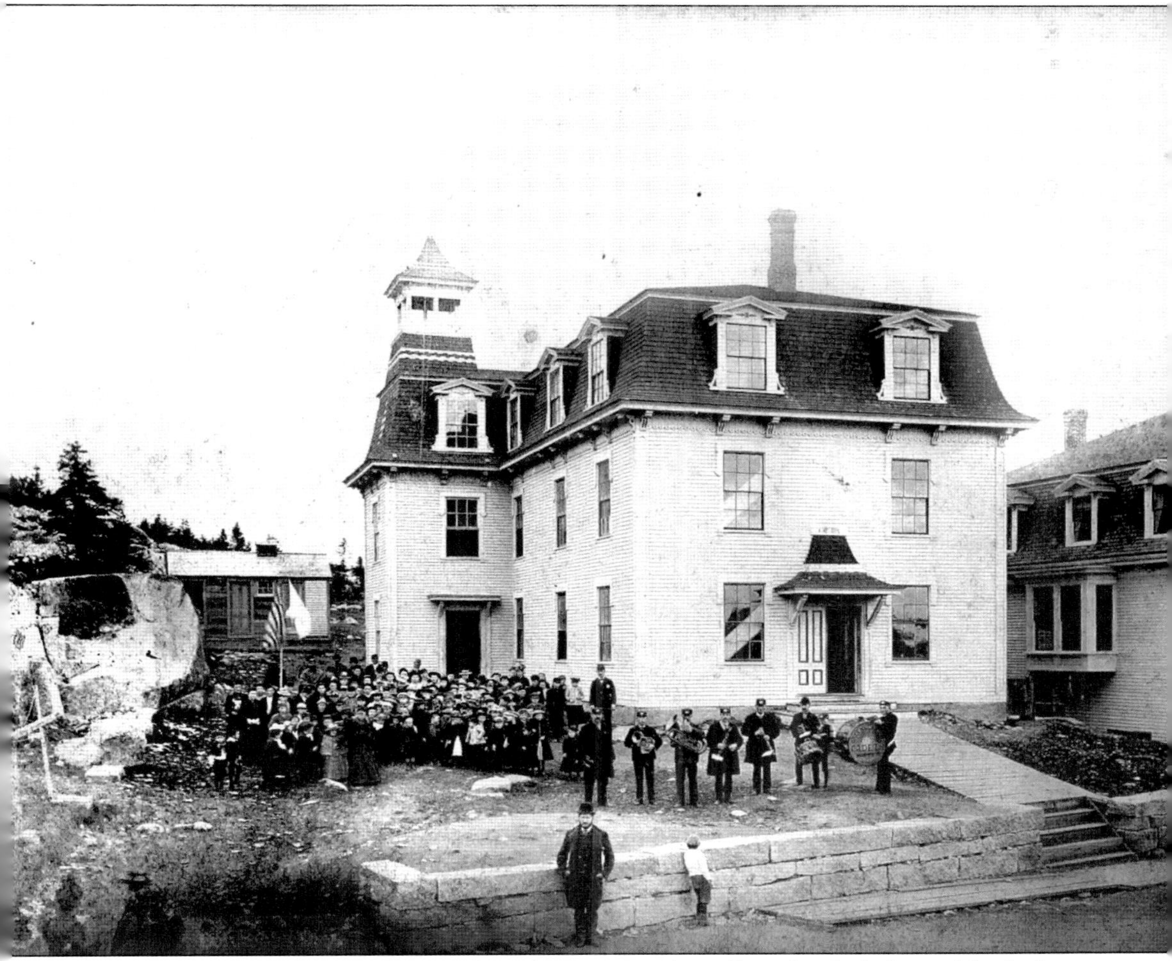

The Rockbound School opened in 1895, replacing several smaller schools. It housed both the high school and some elementary grades, with the smallest children taught in another building. In 1905, Rockbound was replaced by a new school, which served grades 1 to 12. This old school, without the bell tower, now serves as the Stonington Town Hall. This photograph was taken on Columbus Day 1892, the 400th anniversary of the discovery of America. Note the Green's Landing Cadets, a local band.

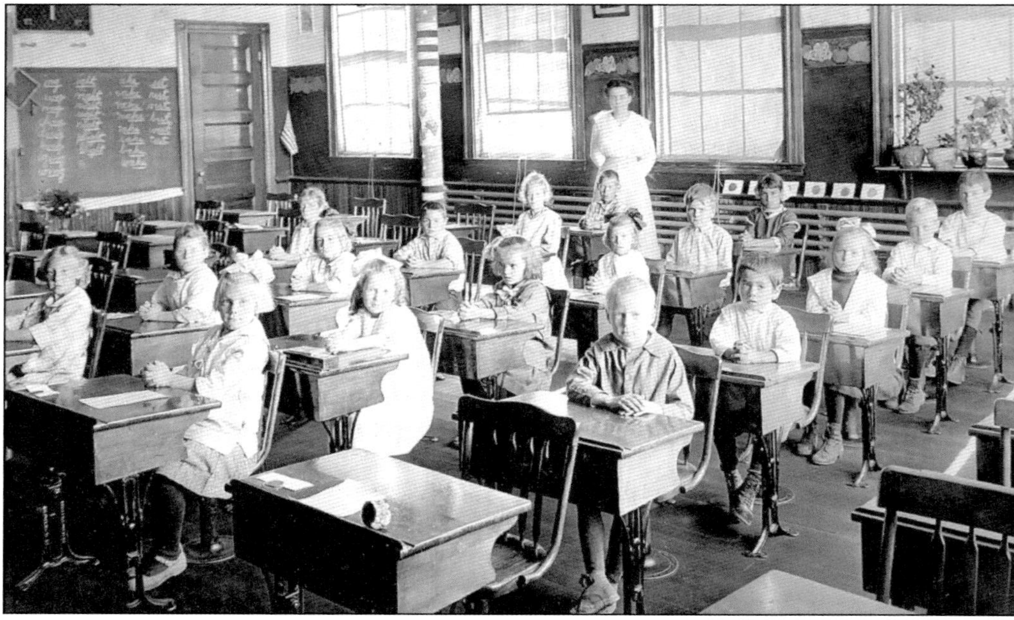

This photograph was taken *c.* 1915 at the Stonington School. Teacher Annie Thurlow (1873–1938) taught for 32 years, starting when she was 15 years old.

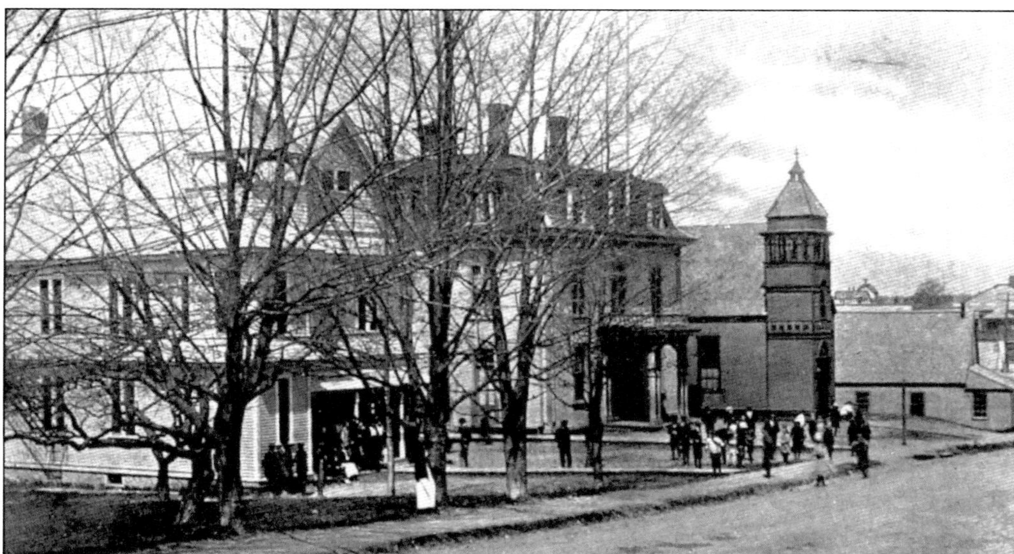

This *c.* 1915 postcard photograph of Deer Isle shows, from left to right, McKinley High School, the Masonic hall, the parish house, and a skating rink built on the site of a former tannery. The high school was built in 1897, the first year of William McKinley's term as president, and was in use until 1976, when the Deer Isle-Stonington High School opened. A room in the back of the building and two rooms in the Masonic hall housed the elementary school. They were replaced when the Deer Isle Elementary School opened in 1953. The parish house, built for the use of the Congregational church, was the site of the school lunch program; it is now an antiques shop. The skating rink is now gone.

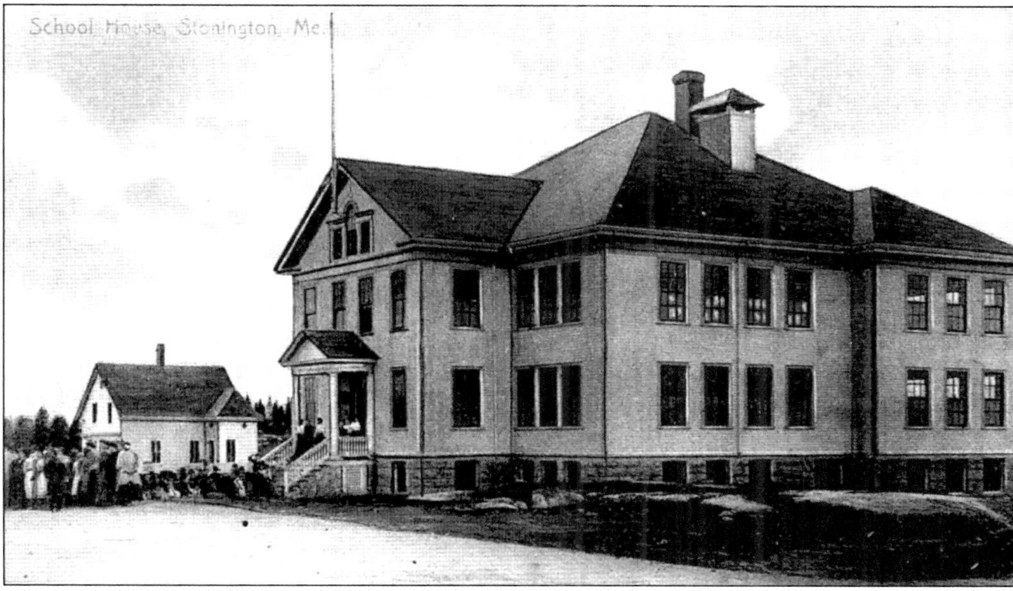

The Stonington School opened in 1905, with the high school upstairs and the elementary school downstairs. It was designed by Dr. B. Lake Noyes. An annex, built in 1951, housed a gym, a stage, and classrooms. With the consolidation of high and elementary schools into island-wide facilities, both the Stonington schools and the old Deer Isle Elementary School await new futures as community centers of one type or another.

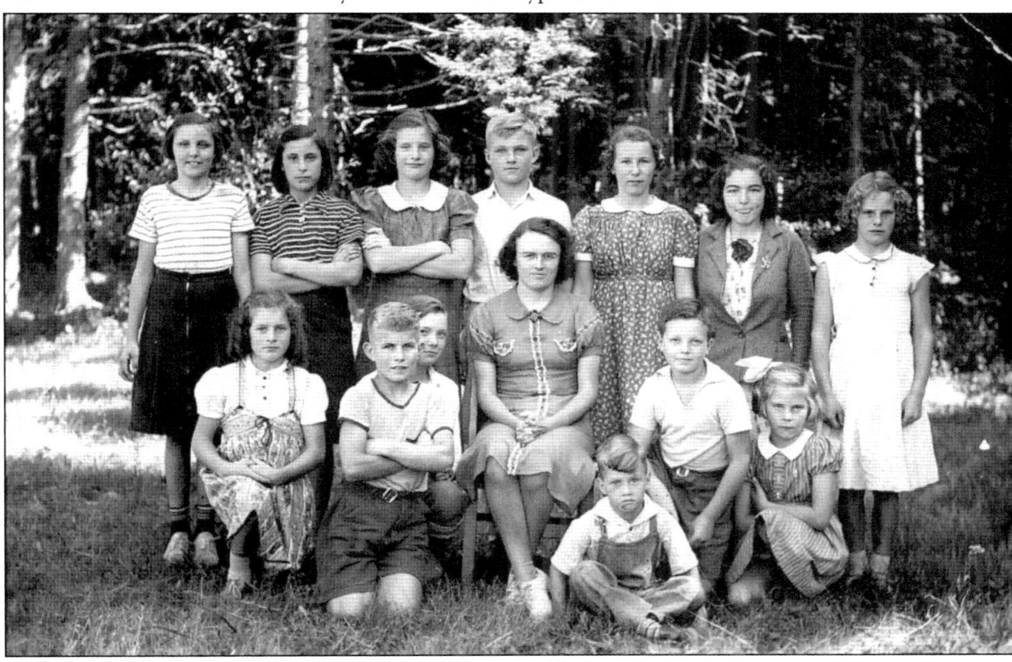

Students at the Eggemoggin Grammar School in 1939, from left to right, are as follows: (first row) Norma Billings, Sheldon Eaton, Gilbert Powers, teacher Alice Barbour Eaton, Jerould Hutchinson, Duane Gray, and Denise Snowman; (second row) Sadie Eaton, Barbara Eaton, Miriam Billings, Elwell Hutchinson, Betty Powers, Mary Douglass, and Myrtle Billings.

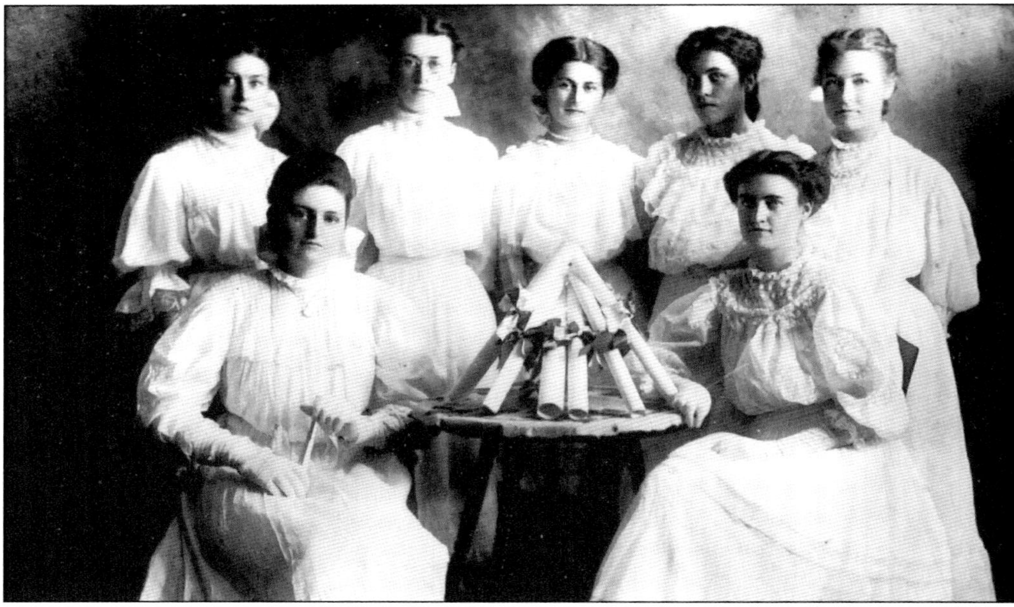

Graduating in 1906 from McKinley High School in Deer Isle were the following, from left to right: (first row) Amy (Sylvester) McVeigh and Breta (Haskell) Harris; (second row) Irene (Haskell) Ferris, Linwood Pickering, Mabel (Gray) Green, Grace (Haskell) Mitchell, and Hazel (Beck) Carman. There were also two boys in the class—Harry Pickering and Jasper Phillip Haskell.

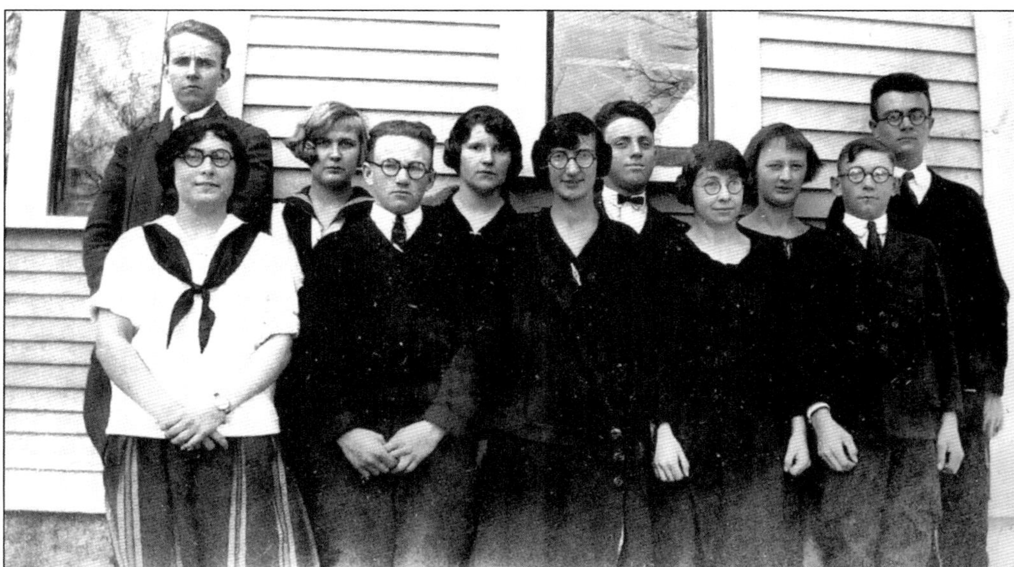

The Deer Isle High School class of 1925 poses for a photograph. Seen here, from left to right, are the following: (first row) Kay (Black) Milan, Lloyd Conary, Josephine (Cole) Pickering, Muriel (Hardy) Sellers, and Sheldon Conary; (second row) Kenneth Greenlaw, Fannie (Conary) Reynolds, Christine (Lufkin) Pickering, Elwyn Sylvester, Ethelyn (Eaton) Matthews, and James Robbins. Frank Milan was principal of the high school, and John Dunton was superintendent.

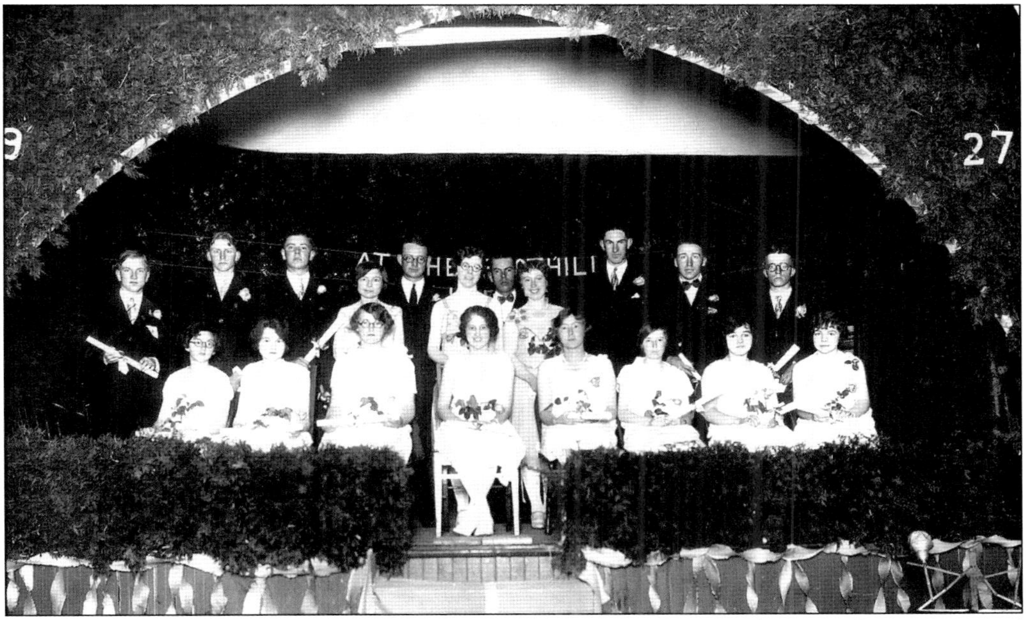

The Stonington class of 1927 and the faculty gather on the stage of the opera house. Pictured here, from left to right, are the following: (first row) Ruth Ott, Eleanor Sellers, Lyndell Stinson, Kathleen Billings, Gertrude Snowden, Doris Gross, Madeline Gross, and Margaret Hardy; (second row) Robert McGuire, Benjamin Carter, Dwight Thurlow, teacher Marjorie Smiley, superintendent John Dunton, teacher Doris Gray Gross, principal Harold Blackwood, teacher Esther Wood, Harry Annis, Harold Collins, and George Webb.

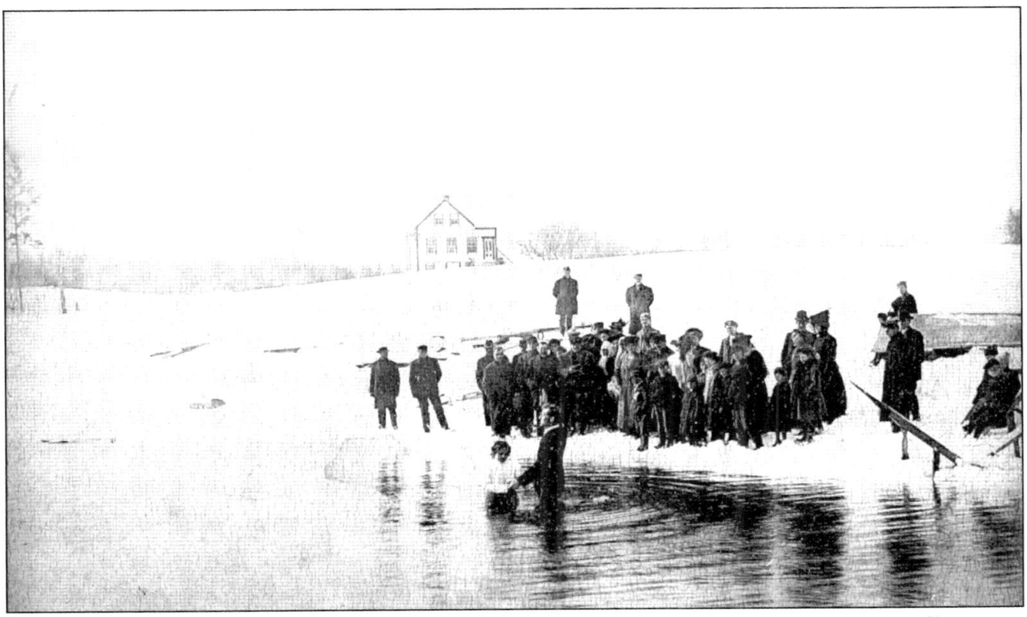

A baptism takes place in Little Deer Isle in February 1909 with Elder Dan McGregor officiating. The elder was likely one of several itinerant evangelists who worked with the Reformed Latter Day Saints Church in Little Deer Isle.

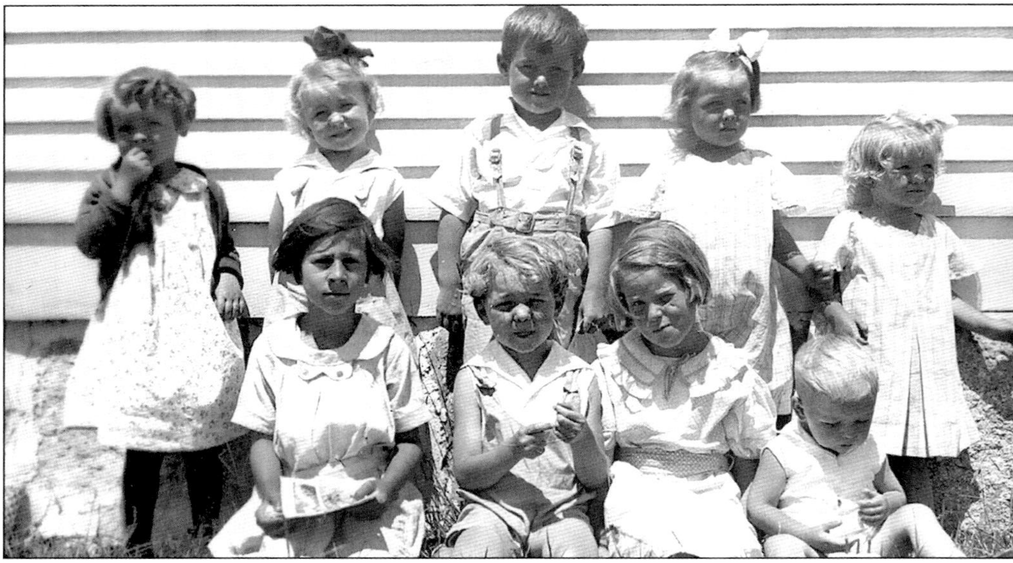

This 1936 photograph is of a Sunday school class at the Methodist church in South Deer Isle. From left to right are the following: (first row) unidentified, Neville Eaton, Augustine Barter, and Elmer Spofford; (second row) Rosamond Eaton, unidentified, Gilbert Taylor, E. Goldie Spofford, and Wilma Spofford.

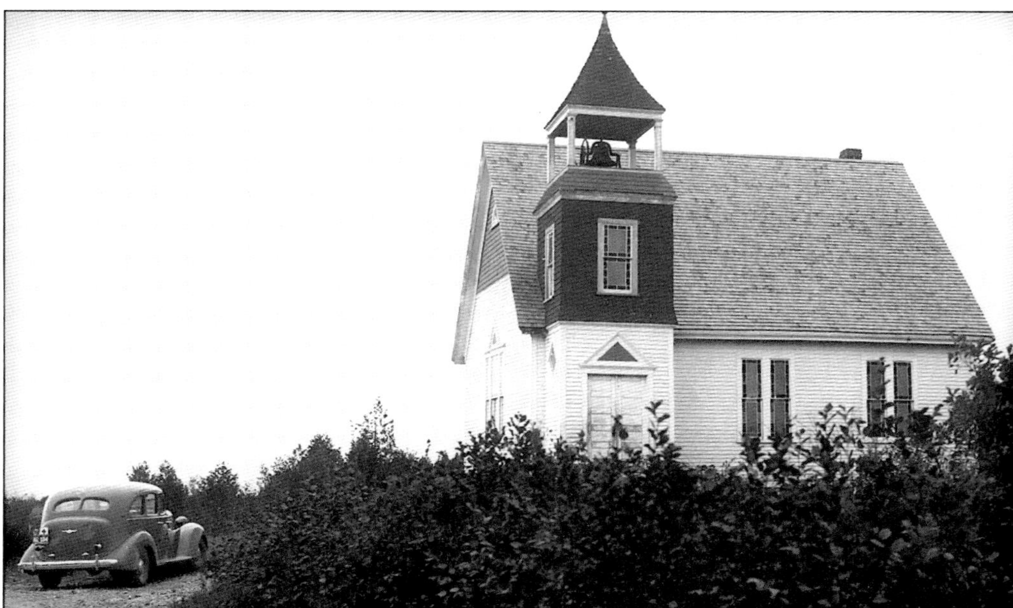

The Reformed Latter Day Saints Church in Little Deer Isle was torn down c. 1958. Some of the lumber was used to build Milton and Priscilla (Capen) Haskell's house in North Deer Isle.

In 1857, Larzous Gott came to Stonington from Ellsworth to organize a Baptist society. Soon after, a sewing circle was established to raise money for the building of a church. Each woman in the group contributed one egg and one skein of yarn. Some of the eggs were hatched; the yarn was made into mittens and sold. The group worked for 13 years before construction began on the Burnt Cove Church in Stonington. The first preacher was Lafayette Collins. In 1887, 10 people—including Gov. J. R. Bodwell, Sens. James G. Blaine and Eugene Hale, and Congressman Seth Milliken—contributed funds to purchase the first bell. Extensive repairs were made in 1958, and a new steeple and restoration of the building took place in 2004.

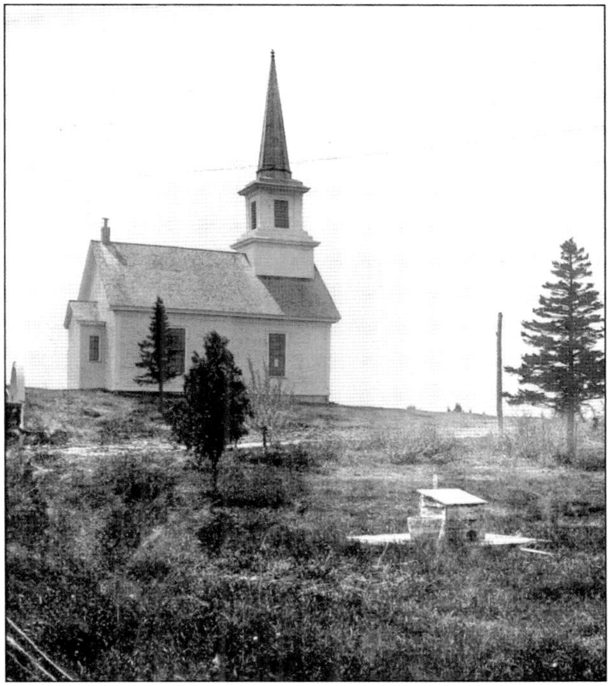

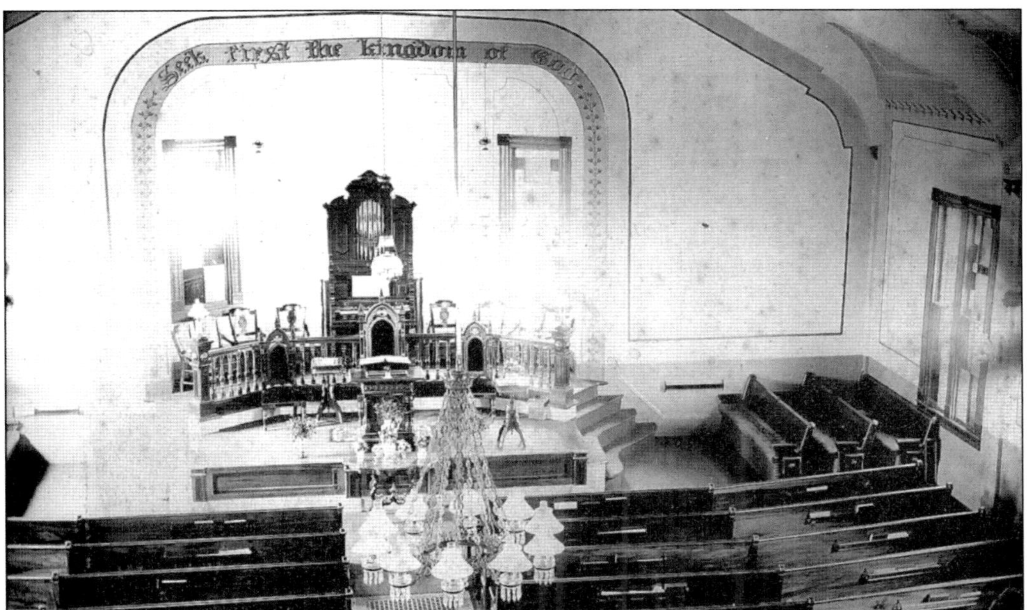

This photograph, taken from the choir loft, shows the interior of the Congregational Church of Deer Isle, known as "the Church on the Hill." It has held continuous services since 1773, when its first minister was Rev. Peter Powers. The first church was located at another site. Two have been built at the present site; the first, built in 1800, burned. The present church was dedicated in 1886.

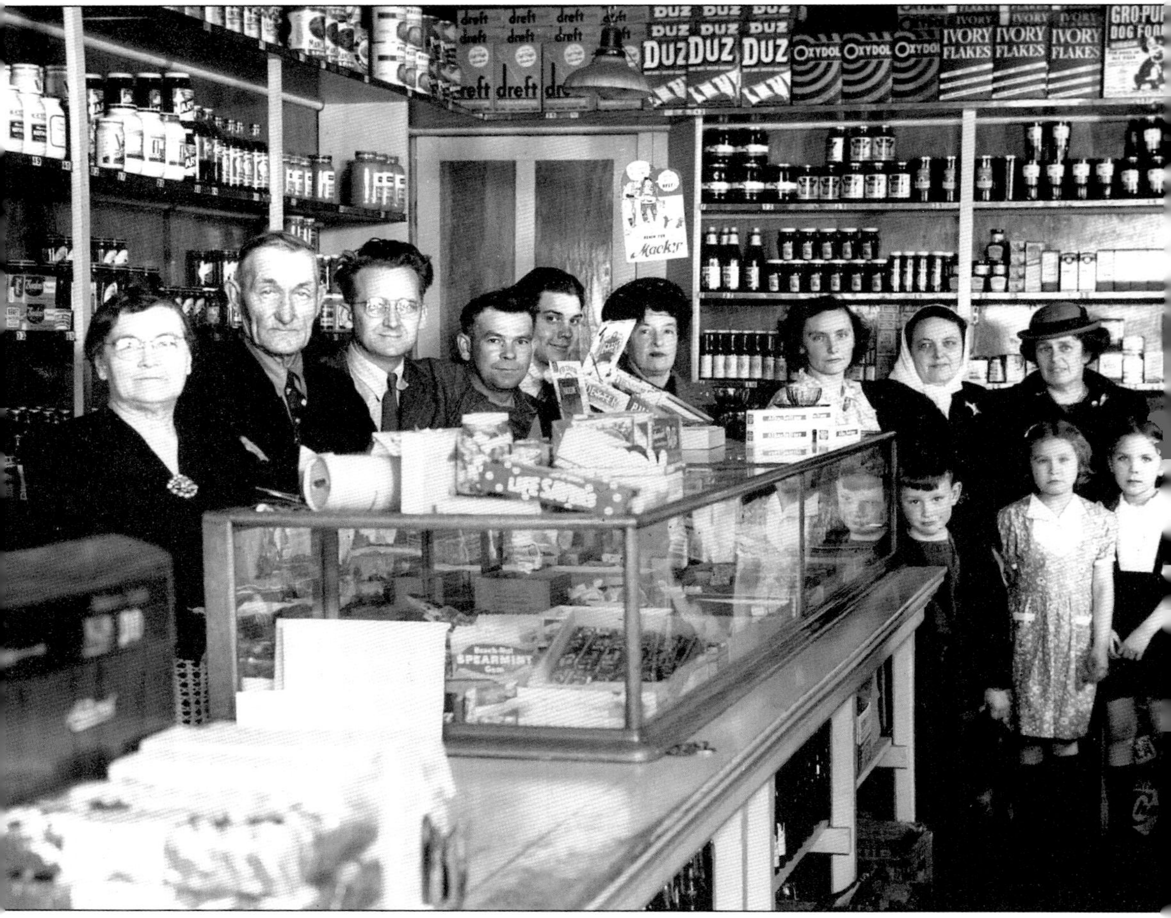

The 50th anniversary of Prescott Eaton's General Store is celebrated in 1948 in Sunset. Pictured, from left to right, are Ethel Eaton, Prescott Eaton, Rev. Robert Snelling, Arthur Jenkins, Charles Snelling, Essie V. Torrey, Gwendolyn Eaton, Gertrude Snelling, Bea Marshall, Sandra Eaton, Audrey Eaton, and Tommy Cole. The store was a popular spot where men gathered to talk. One of the store's benches is on display at the historical society.

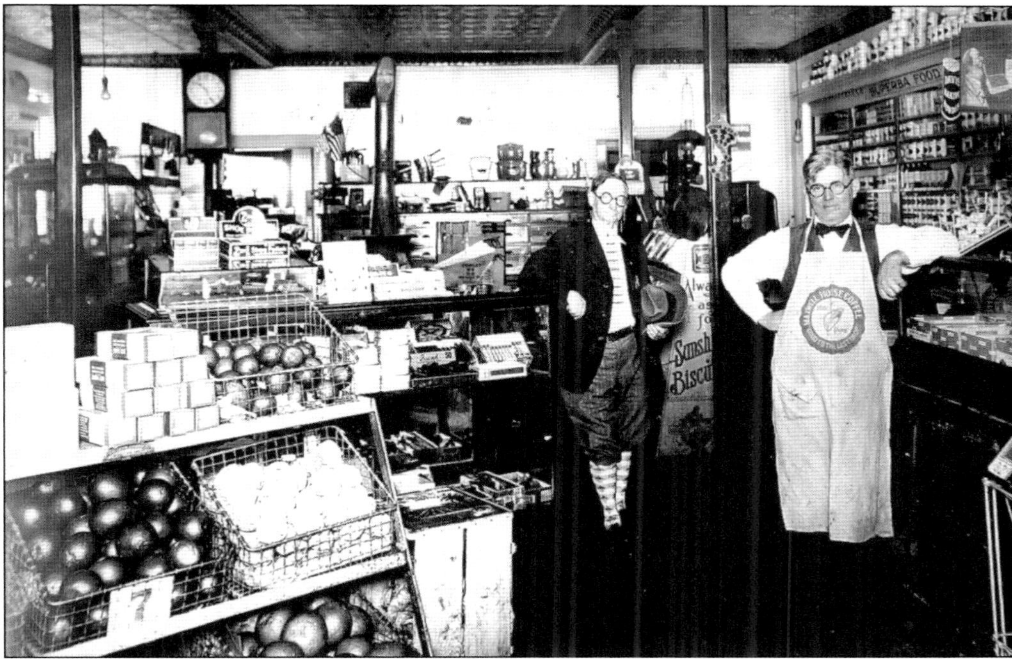

Frank Webb (in the apron) appears in his grocery and hardware store on Main Street in Stonington probably in the 1940s. The man in the golf outfit is clearly a "summer person." Later, the building became Peterson's Pharmacy and is now the Deer Isle Granite Museum.

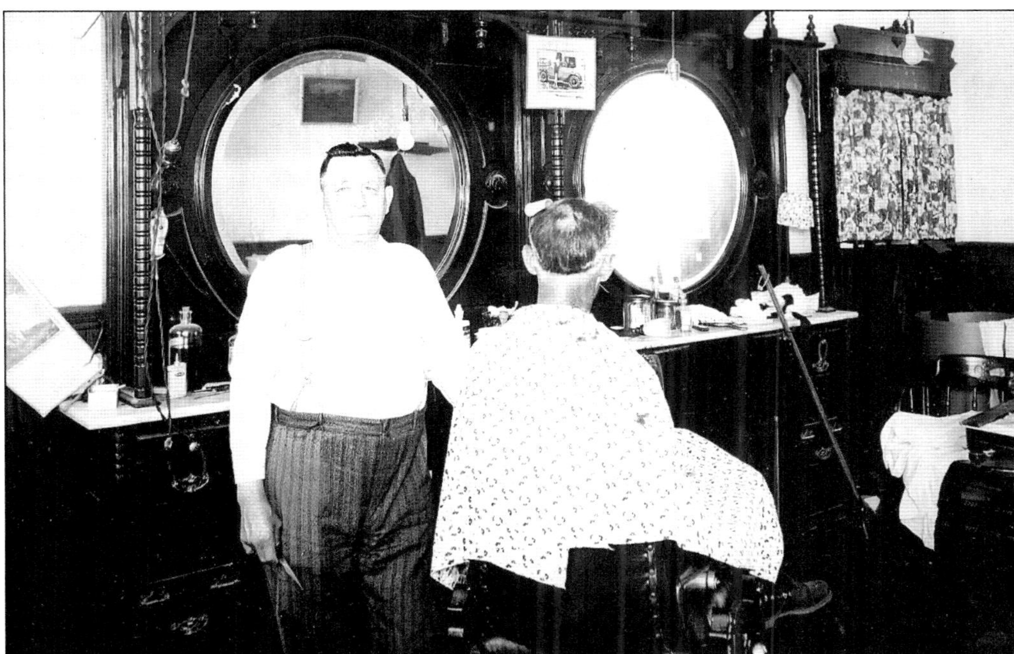

Charles William Brimigion, known as "Bill the Barber," is at work in his shop on Main Street, Stonington, *c.* 1925.

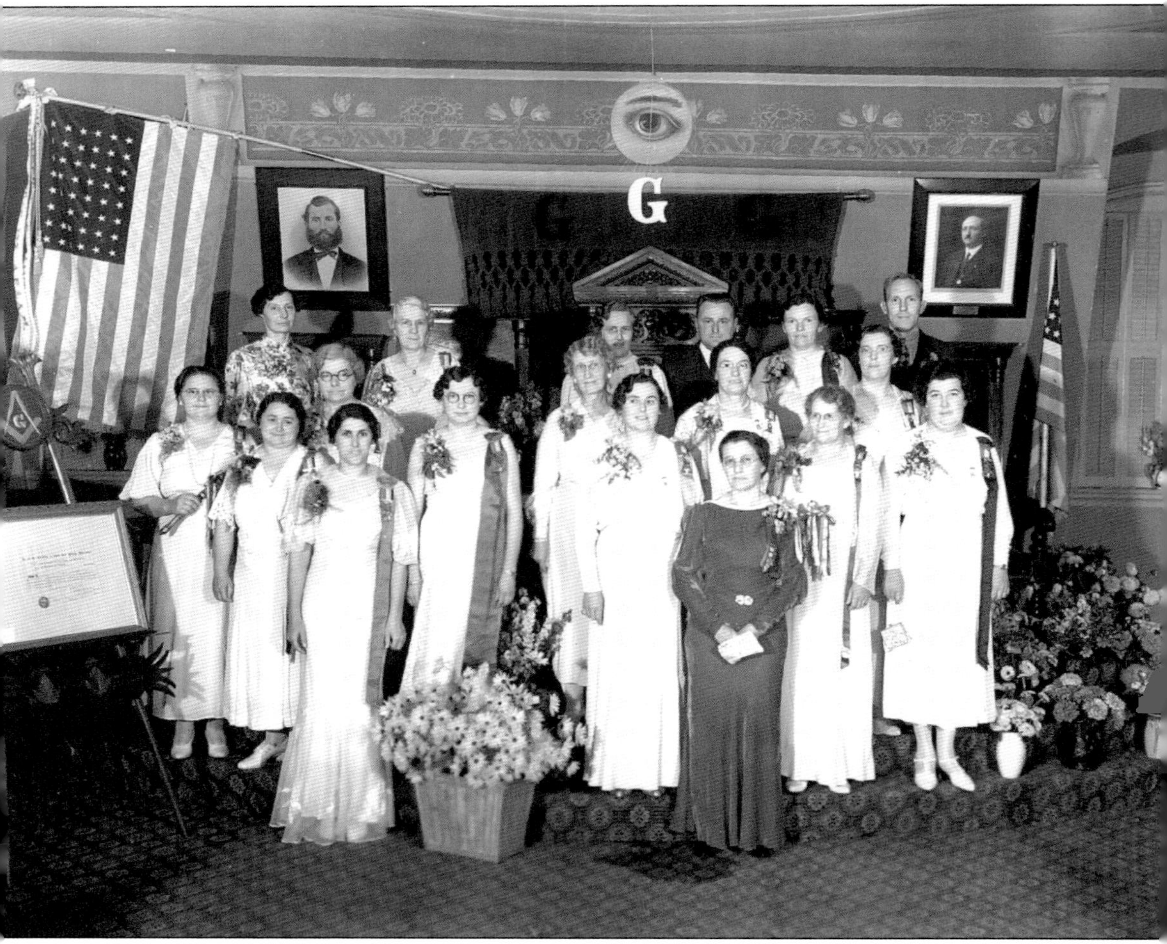

The officers of Harbor View Chapter No. 136 of the Order of the Eastern Star pose for a photograph in 1936. Seen here, from left to right, are the following: (first row) Vesta Pickering and Effie Hinkley; (second row) Myrtle Conary, Leah Lowe, Rose Beck, Grace Haskell, and Annabelle Weed; (third row) Elleeta Johnson, Electa Weed, Harriet Haskell, Essie Torrey, and Minnie Greenlaw; (fourth row) Beatrice Knowlton, Adelaide Joyce, Helen Haskell, Lawrence Pickering, Sadie Powers, and Leon C. Weed.

Four

INDUSTRY

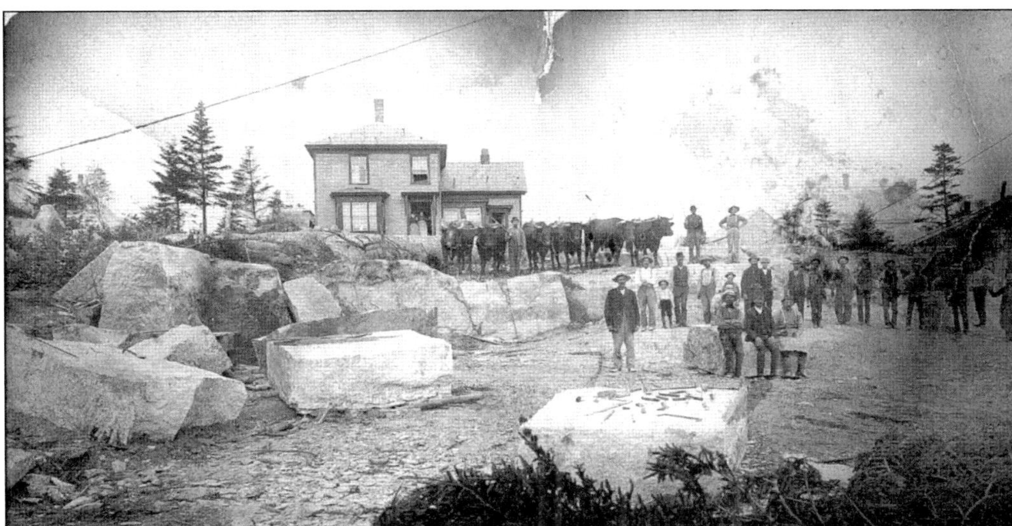

A number of small quarries existed on the site of what is now downtown Stonington. The house in this undated photograph is presently located on Church Street. Note the oxen. These small quarries produced mostly foundation stone and paving blocks.

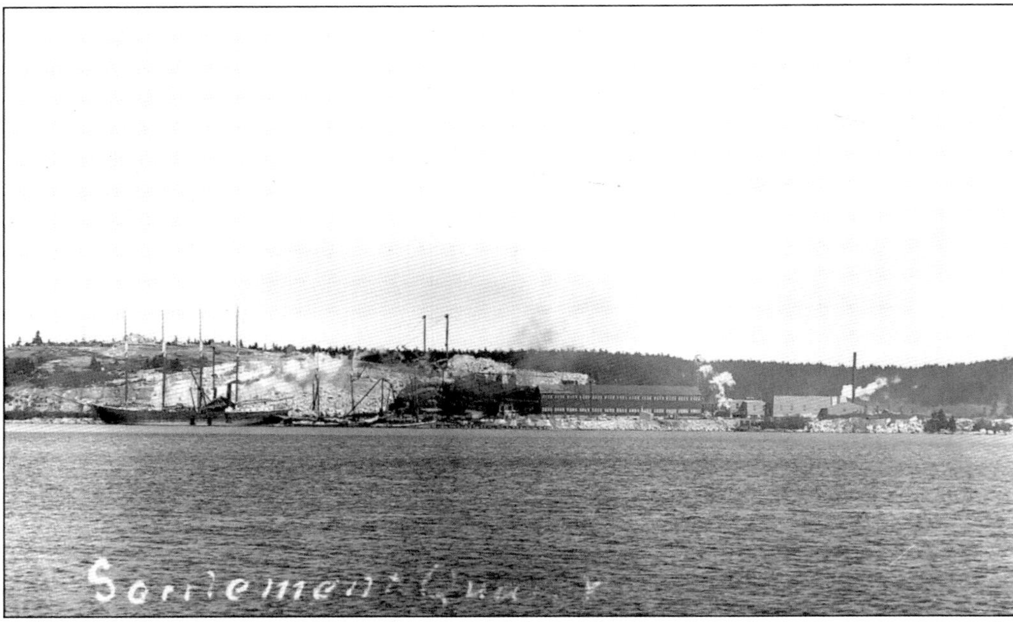

The Settlement Quarry was located in Oceanville and was open only for a short time in the early 1920s. Its major project was the Fuller job, which supplied granite for the construction of a courthouse in New York. In this photograph, the four-masted schooner *Nancy Hanks* takes on a load of granite.

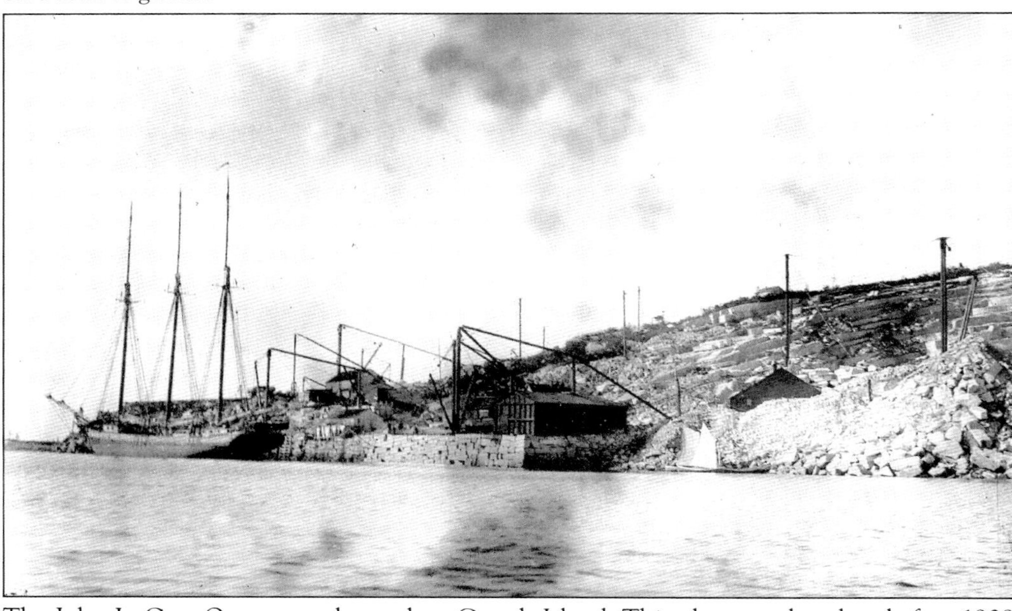

The John L. Goss Quarry was located on Crotch Island. This photograph, taken before 1908, shows the schooner *Donna Briggs* ready to pick up a load of granite. Quarrying on Crotch Island began c. 1870 and continued until the end of World War II. The John L. Goss Quarry reopened in 1965 to take out stone for the John F. Kennedy Memorial at Arlington Cemetery. It is now operated on a limited basis by the New England Stone Company, largely for the manufacture of decorative items.

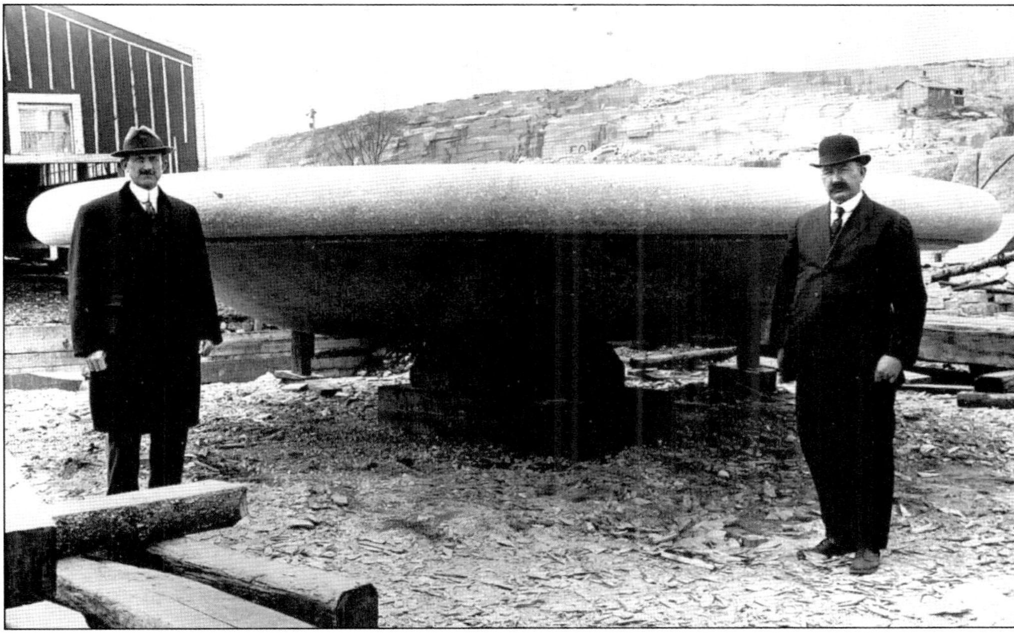

In 1913, John D. Rockefeller hired the John L. Goss Corporation to make a fountain bowl for his estate in Tarrytown-on-Hudson. It was to be an exact replica of one he had seen and admired in Venice. Above, Fred A. Torrey (left) and William McKenzie (right) pose with the completed bowl. Made from a single block of granite, the bowl is almost 21 feet across and weighs 55 tons.

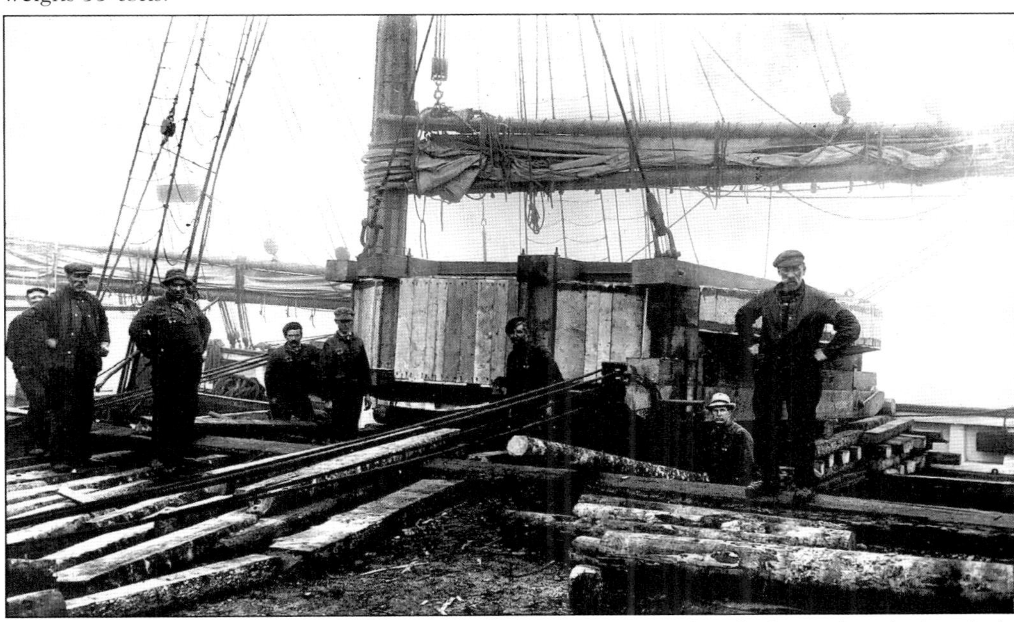

The Rockefeller bowl was crated with heavy lumber and rolled to the deck of the *Susan N. Pickering*, whose captain, Frank Haskell, delivered it to Tarrytown in May 1914. Seen here, from left to right, are an unidentified worker, John Reid, Marion Allen, unidentified, Merrill Knowlton, unidentified, Max Button, and John Merchant.

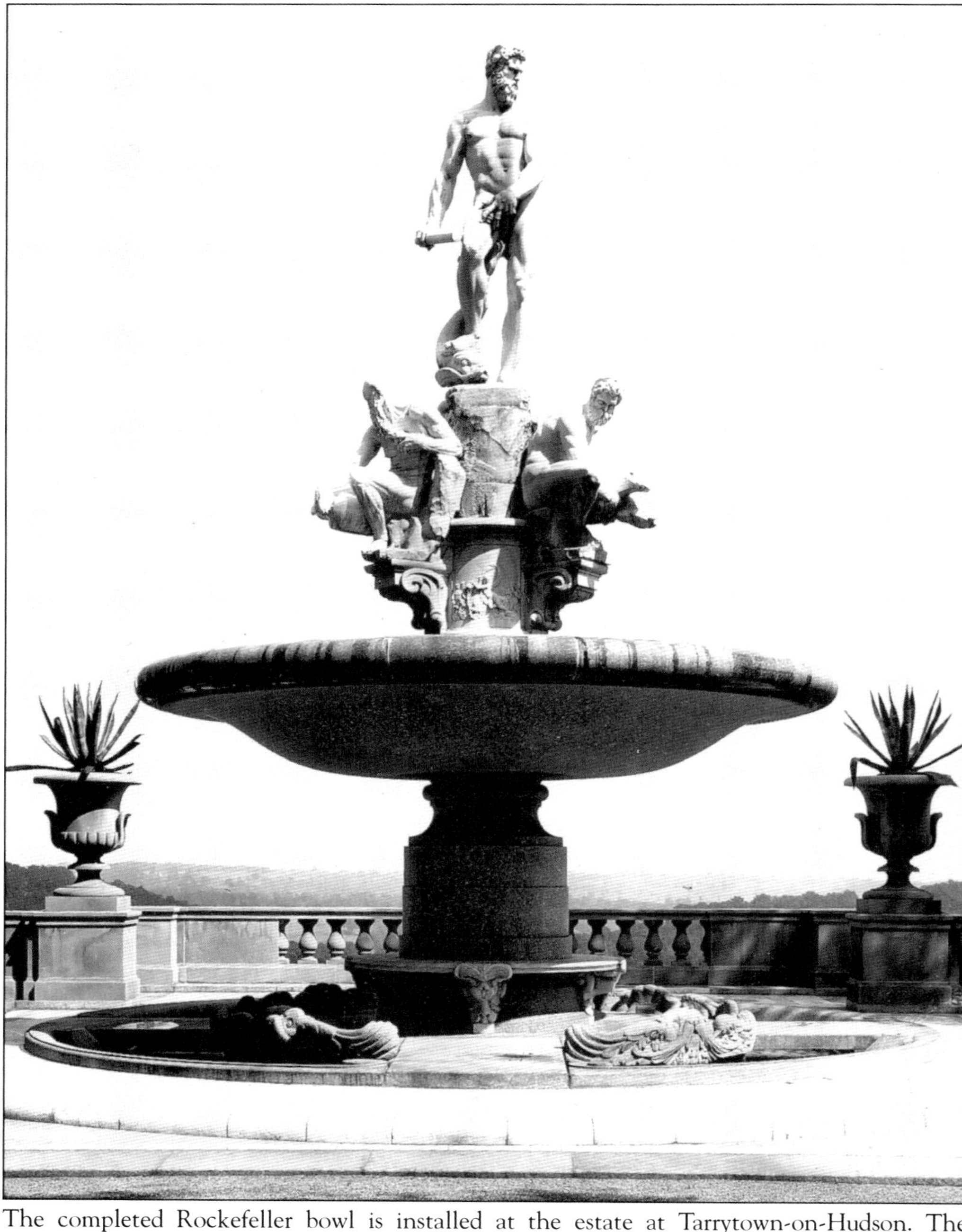

The completed Rockefeller bowl is installed at the estate at Tarrytown-on-Hudson. The journey from Stonington was an eventful one. Rockefeller had agreed to have the *Susan N. Pickering* towed up the Hudson River from the Battery. The bowl was unloaded at the shore and carried by a team of both horses and oxen. En route to the estate, the bowl arrived at a railroad bridge that was not constructed to carry its massive weight. Rockefeller, who was a director of the New York Central Railroad, ordered the railroad closed while the bridge was shored up and the pedestrian guard rails removed to accommodate the bowl's width. This caused some unhappiness among commuters, some of whom traveled in their privately owned railroad cars.

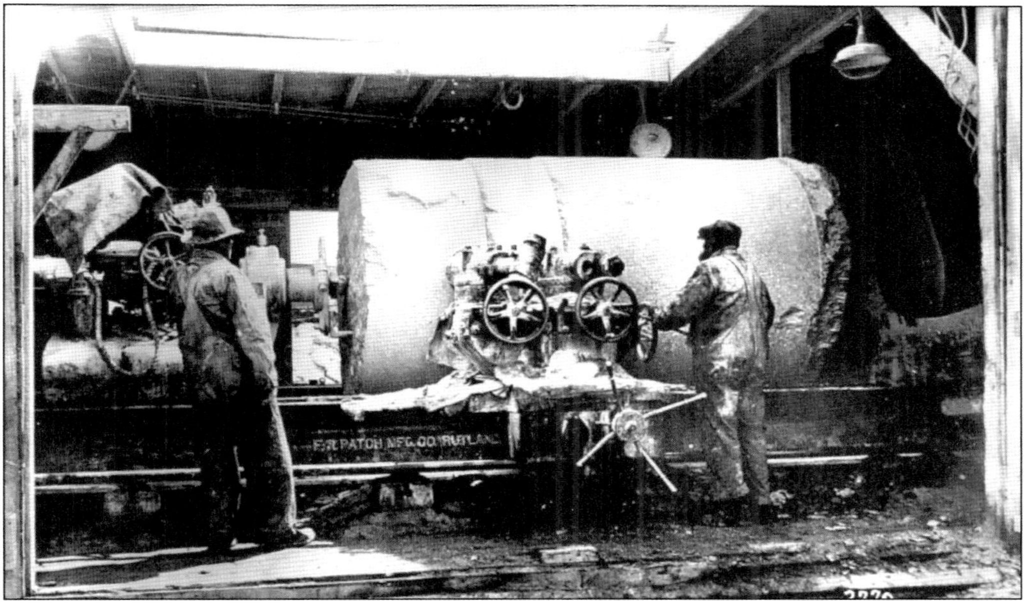

This 1923 photograph, taken at the Settlement Quarry, shows a lathe for turning large granite columns for the Fuller Construction Company. Part of the Settlement Quarry is now owned by the Island Heritage Trust and is open to the public for use of several walking trails.

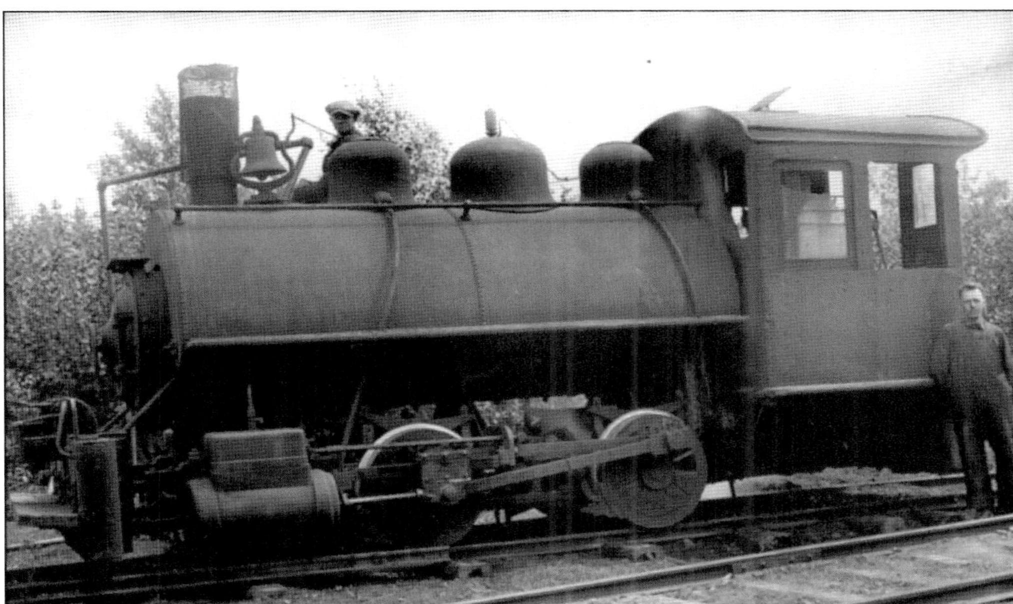

This Vulcan locomotive was brought over to the Deer Island Granite Corporation from the Settlement Quarry when the Fuller job was done. The engineer, standing by the cab, is Charles Brimigion. The brakeman, sitting by the stack, is Harry Bye.

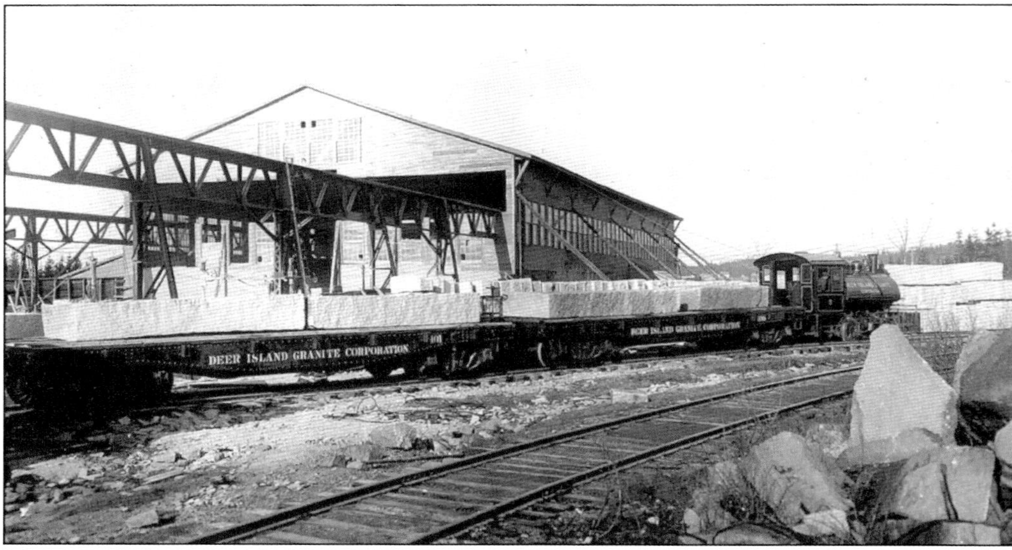

This 1931 photograph of the Deer Island Granite Corporation shows a newly purchased locomotive with cars carrying cut granite, which will be taken to the shore and loaded onto a schooner. It also shows the cutting shed and the overhead crane, which delivered stone to the shed. Lloyd Brimigion is in the cab as engineer. The locomotive was purchased from the Baldwin Locomotive Factory.

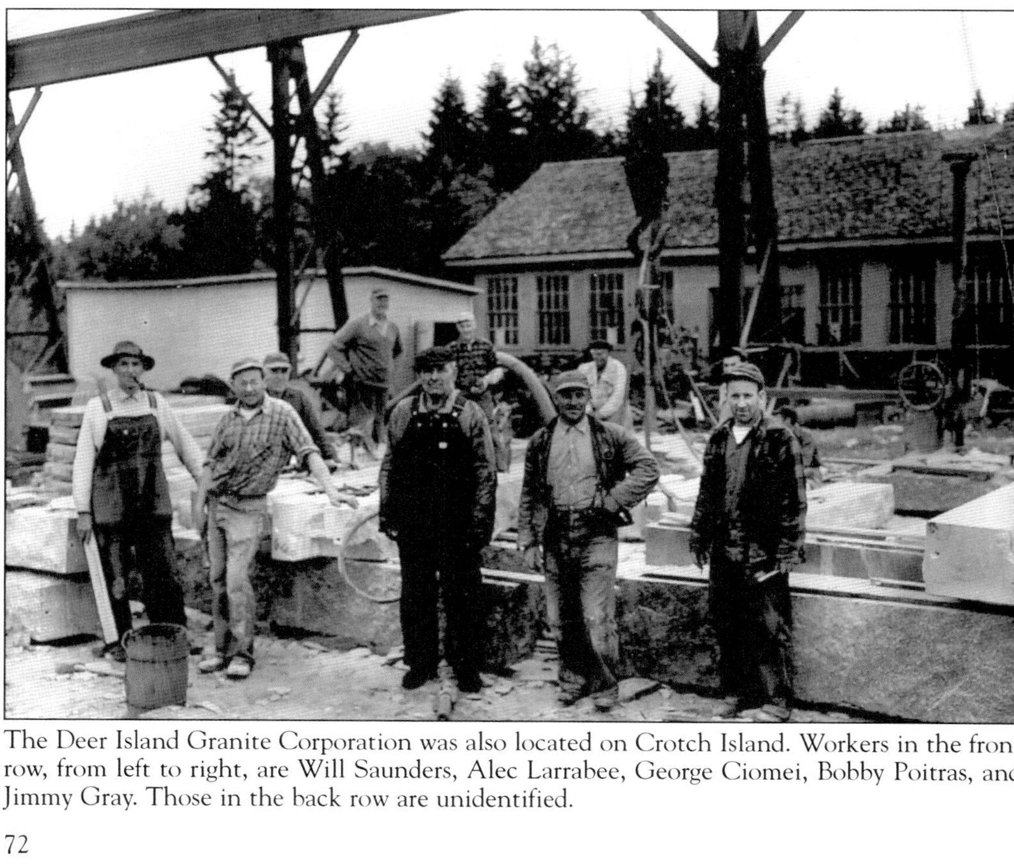

The Deer Island Granite Corporation was also located on Crotch Island. Workers in the front row, from left to right, are Will Saunders, Alec Larrabee, George Ciomei, Bobby Poitras, and Jimmy Gray. Those in the back row are unidentified.

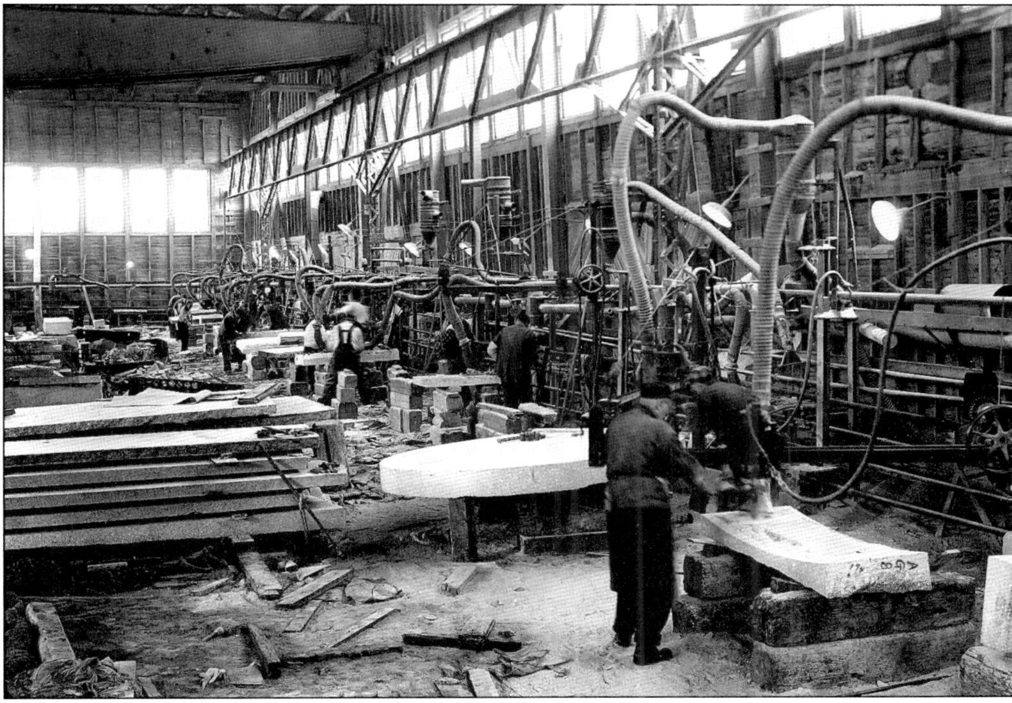

In this photograph of the cutting shed at the Deer Island Granite Corporation, note the variety of sizes and shapes being cut. Each workplace has a vacuum device, which attempts to clear stone dust from the air.

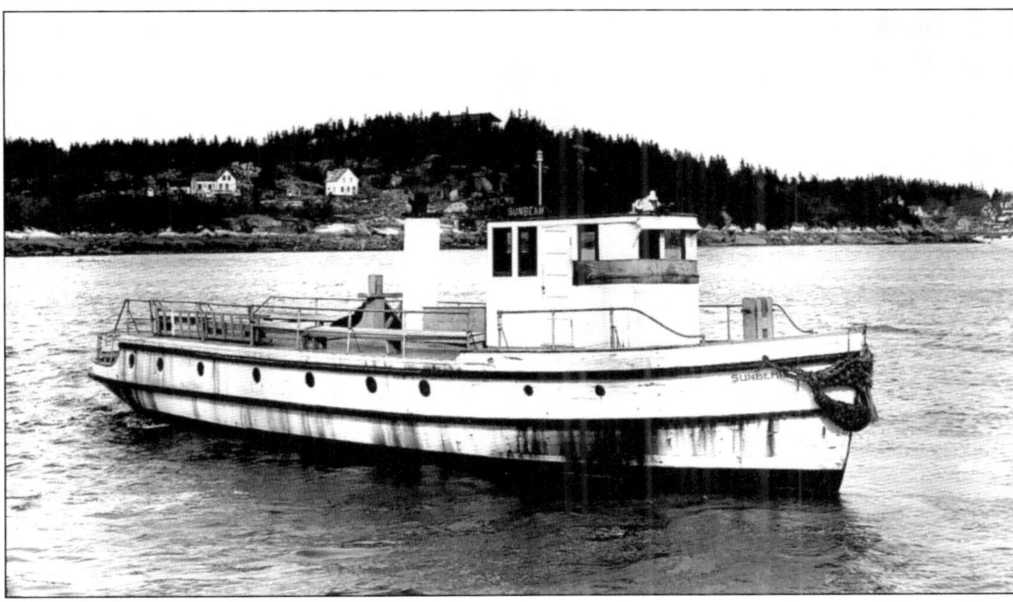

The *Sunbeam*, which belonged to the Maine Seacoast Mission, carried its staff from island to island to conduct church services until it was purchased in the 1930s by the Deer Island Granite Corporation. It was then used to carry quarry workers back and forth from Stonington to Crotch Island.

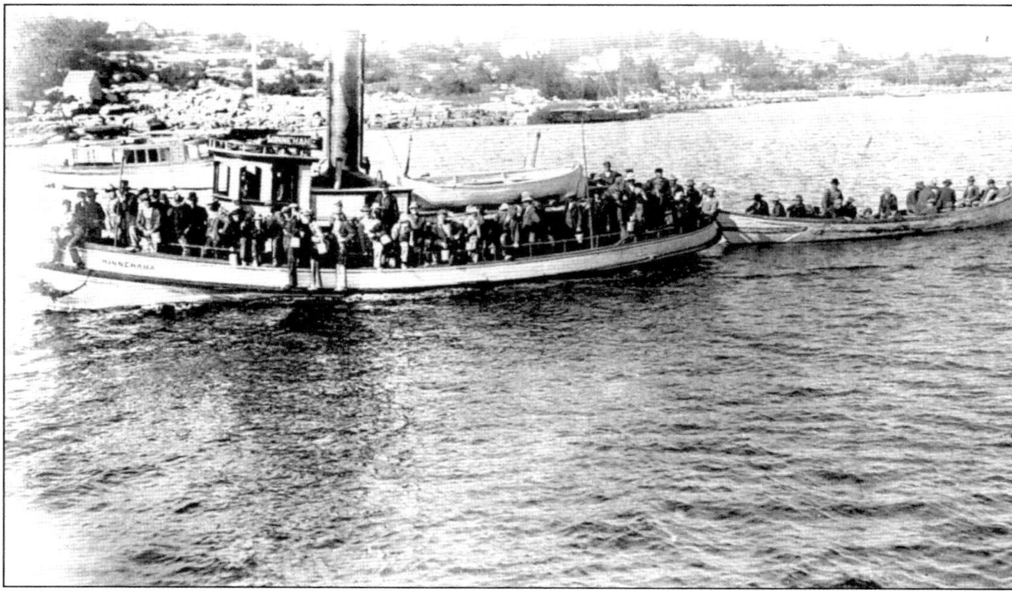

The *Minnehaha* tows a seine boat, bringing quarry workers home to Stonington from quarries on some of the small islands at the end of a day. In the background, the stone sloop *A. L. Hamilton* sets the granite on which the Clam City road lies. Most of the small quarries were closed by the end of the 19th century.

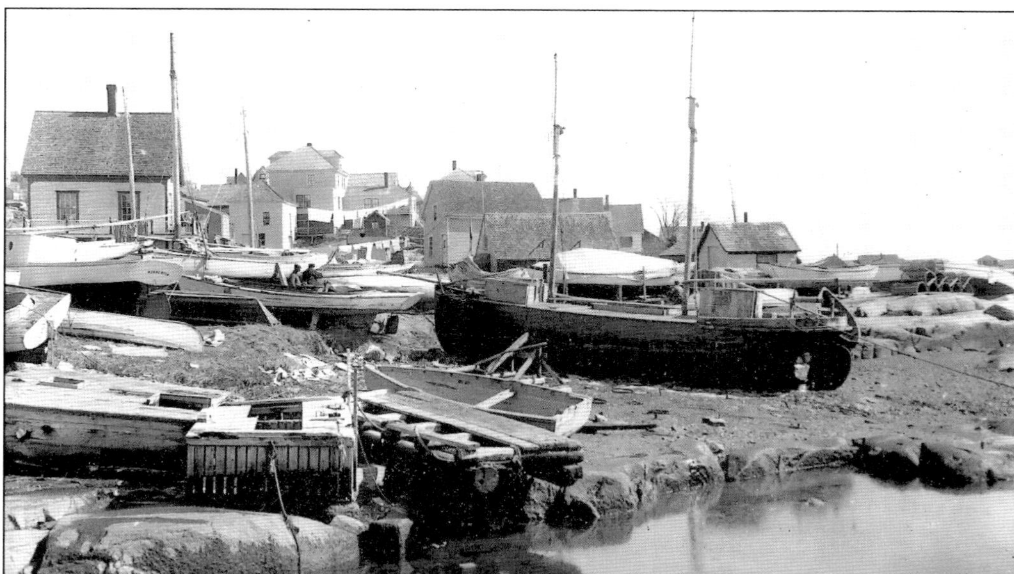

The *Aqua Pura* is drawn up at Green Head in Stonington. Originally a catboat rig, she was built in Gloucester, Massachusetts. There and in New London, Connecticut, she was used to provide fresh water to coasters, freighters, and yachts. When this picture was taken *c.* 1912, she had been re-rigged as a schooner. The *Aqua Pura* was in use in Stonington to provide water to quarries on small islands, such as St. Helena and McGlathery, which used steam for power but had no water.

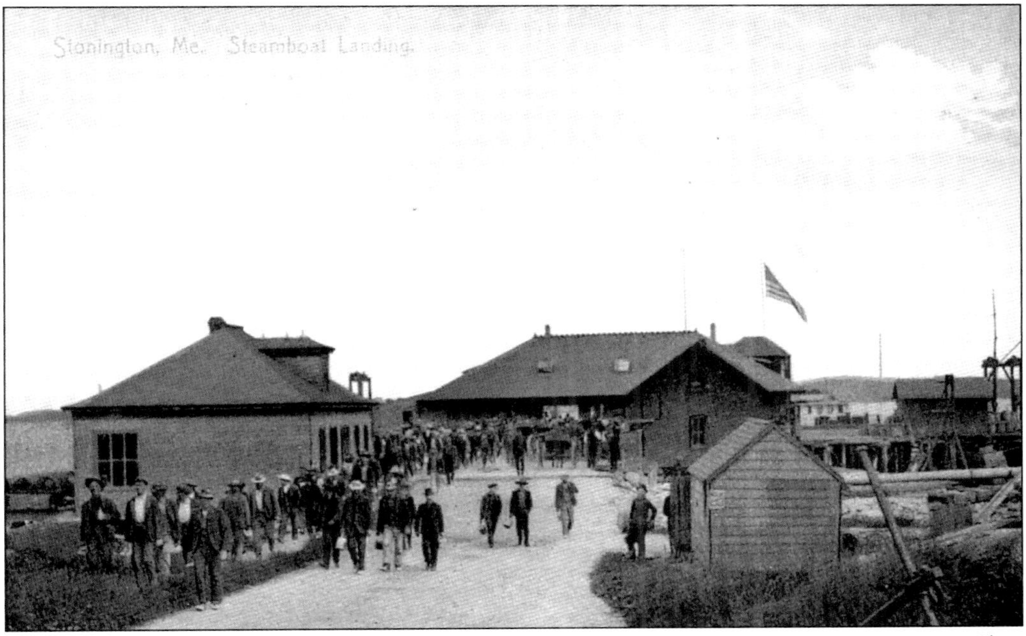

This postcard photograph shows quarry workers who have just landed at the Eastern Steam Ship wharf in Stonington at the end of a work day. Many of the men lived near the landing—some in the boardinghouses on Main Street, others in homes as near as possible. Someone who grew up in Stonington at this time recalls the drumming sound of the men's boots as they tramped by on the wooden boardwalks. Notice their lunch boxes.

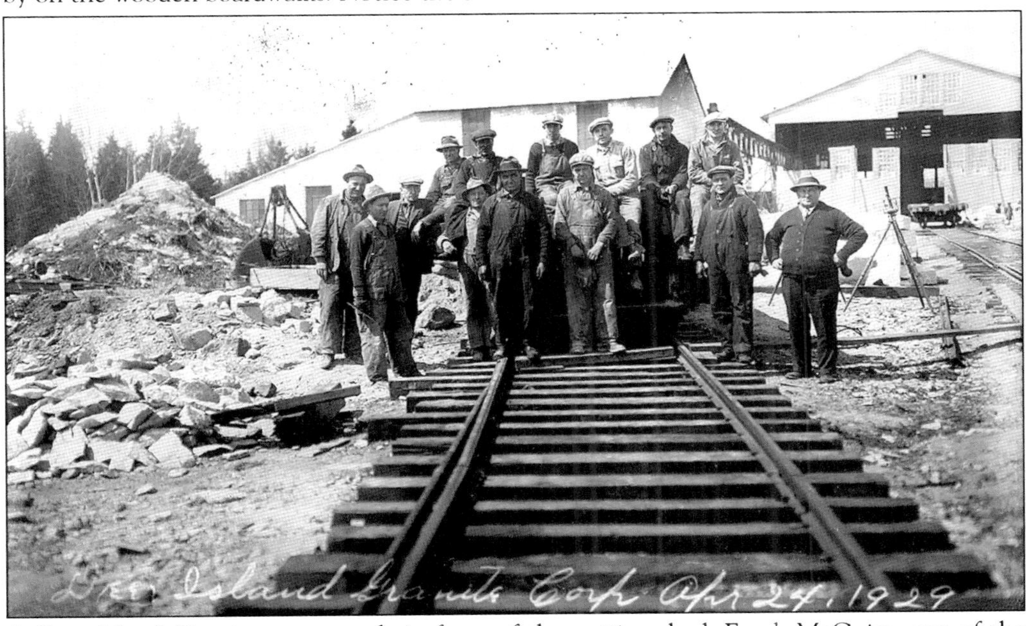

A Deer Island Granite crew stands in front of the cutting shed. Frank McGuire, one of the brothers who owned the quarry, appears at the extreme right. Derricks at the quarry loaded cut stone onto railroad cars. The locomotive then took them to the cutting shed and from there to the dock, where cranes put the stone aboard the barges.

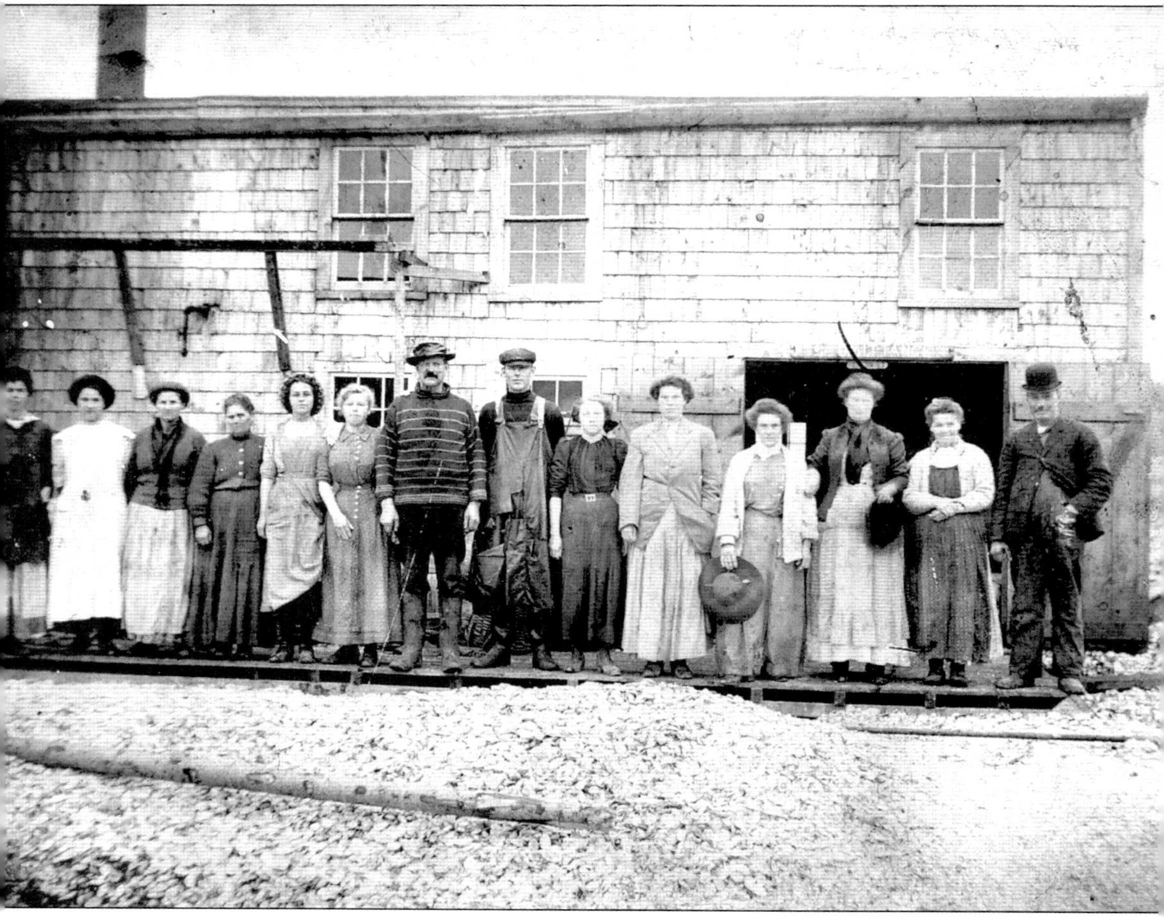

Sylvanus "Venee" Eaton's clam factory was located at Blastow's Cove in Little Deer Isle. A notation on the photograph states that it was taken in 1888. Sylvanus stands seventh from the left. In addition to clams, Eaton canned blueberries, brown bread, and string beans, which he raised. His wife made the brown bread. A tinsmith constructed a continuous strip of metal that ran above the length of the picking bench, which held oil lamps so that workers could see to pick out clams at night. Neighbors recall seeing Venee soldering the cans by hand. He sold the factory c. 1919; after several changes of ownership, the land was purchased by Eugene B. Eaton sometime in the 1950s. It is now the site of the Lobster Pool, a popular restaurant.

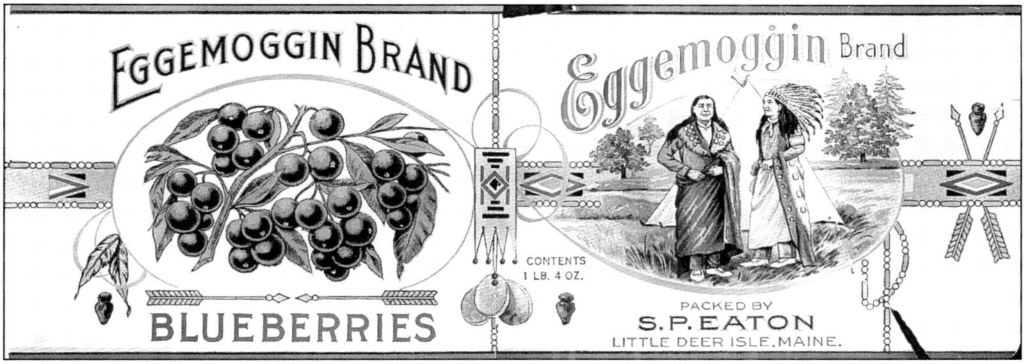

Shown here are Eggemoggin brand labels.

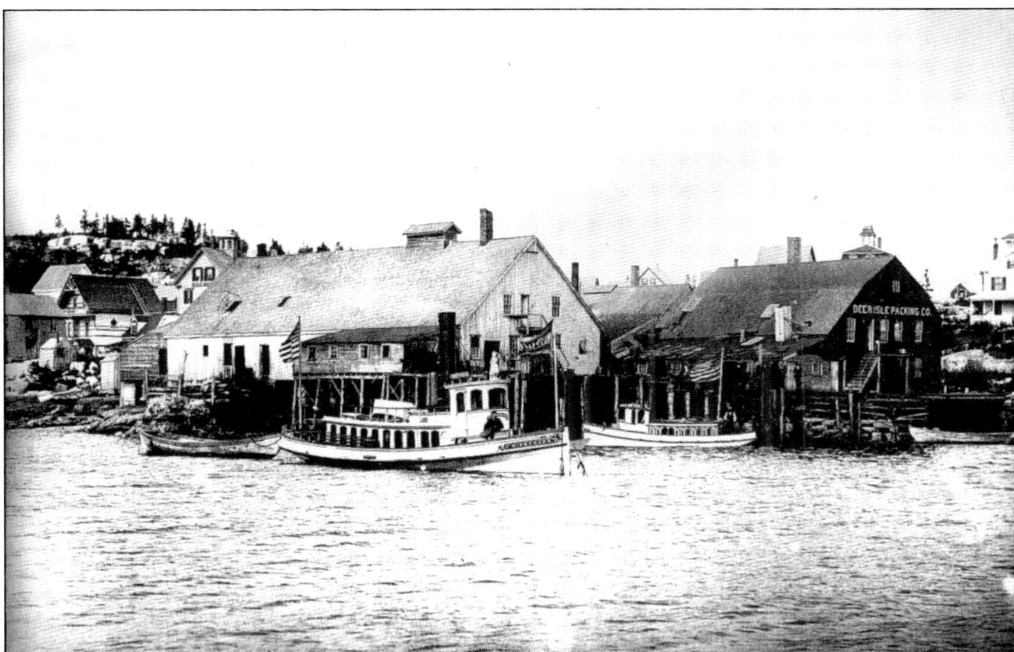

This waterfront scene shows the Flye Brothers factory and the Deer Isle Packing Company. Oscar Flye and his brother Charles came to Stonington c. 1890 and bought the cannery that was formerly operated by W. K. Lewis. Here, the steamers *Minnehaha* and *Jane McCray* are pulled up at the sardine cannery. The *Minnehaha* was also used in general towing and ferrying business. Note the statue of *Minnehaha* on the pilothouse.

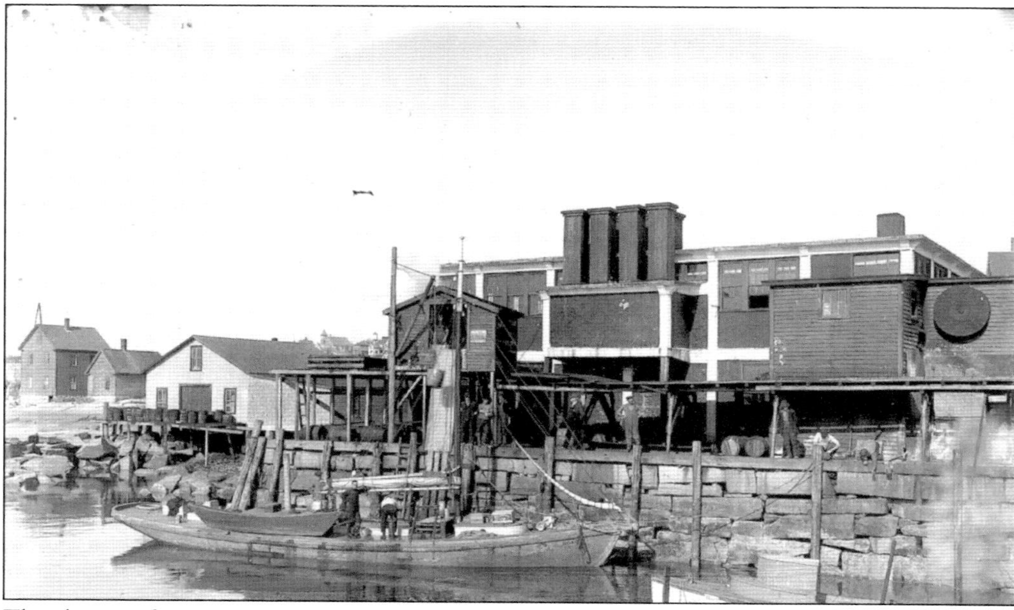

The sloop *Nokomis* was built in 1914 at the Adam Yard in East Boothbay for the North Lubec Canning Company in Eastport. In this photograph, she is at the factory in Stonington, where sardines are unloaded by buckets to go to the canning floor. The sardines were caught in weirs, or by stop-seining (closing off the mouth of a cove).

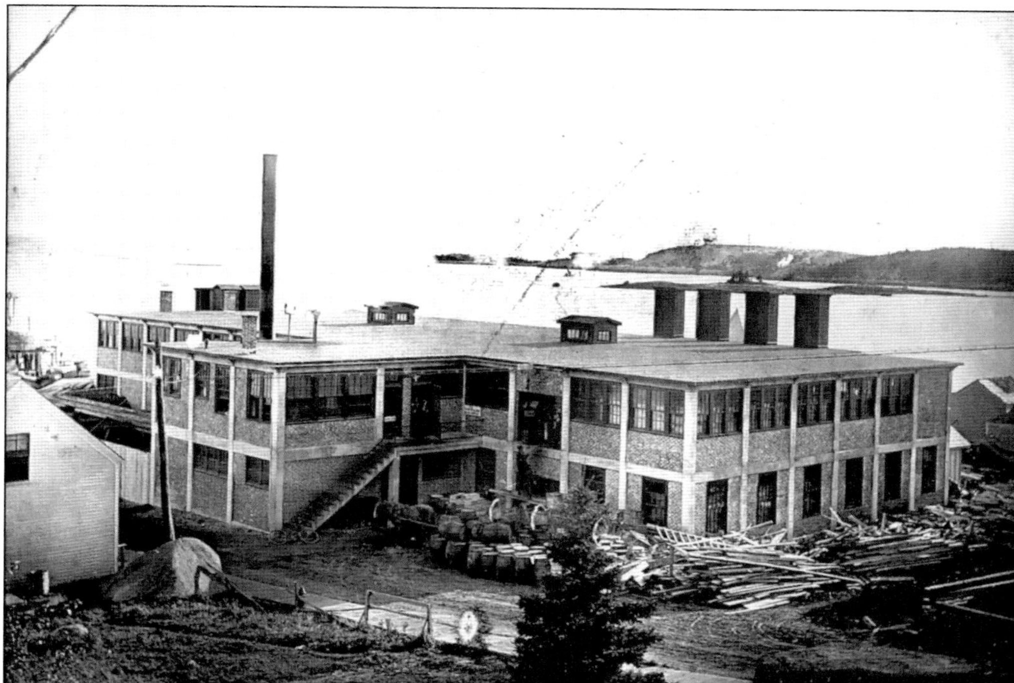

The North Lubec Canning Company built this factory in Stonington *c.* 1910. It had several owners over the years before it closed in 1992. With its wharf, the site is now the headquarters for the Isle au Haut Stonington Dock Company.

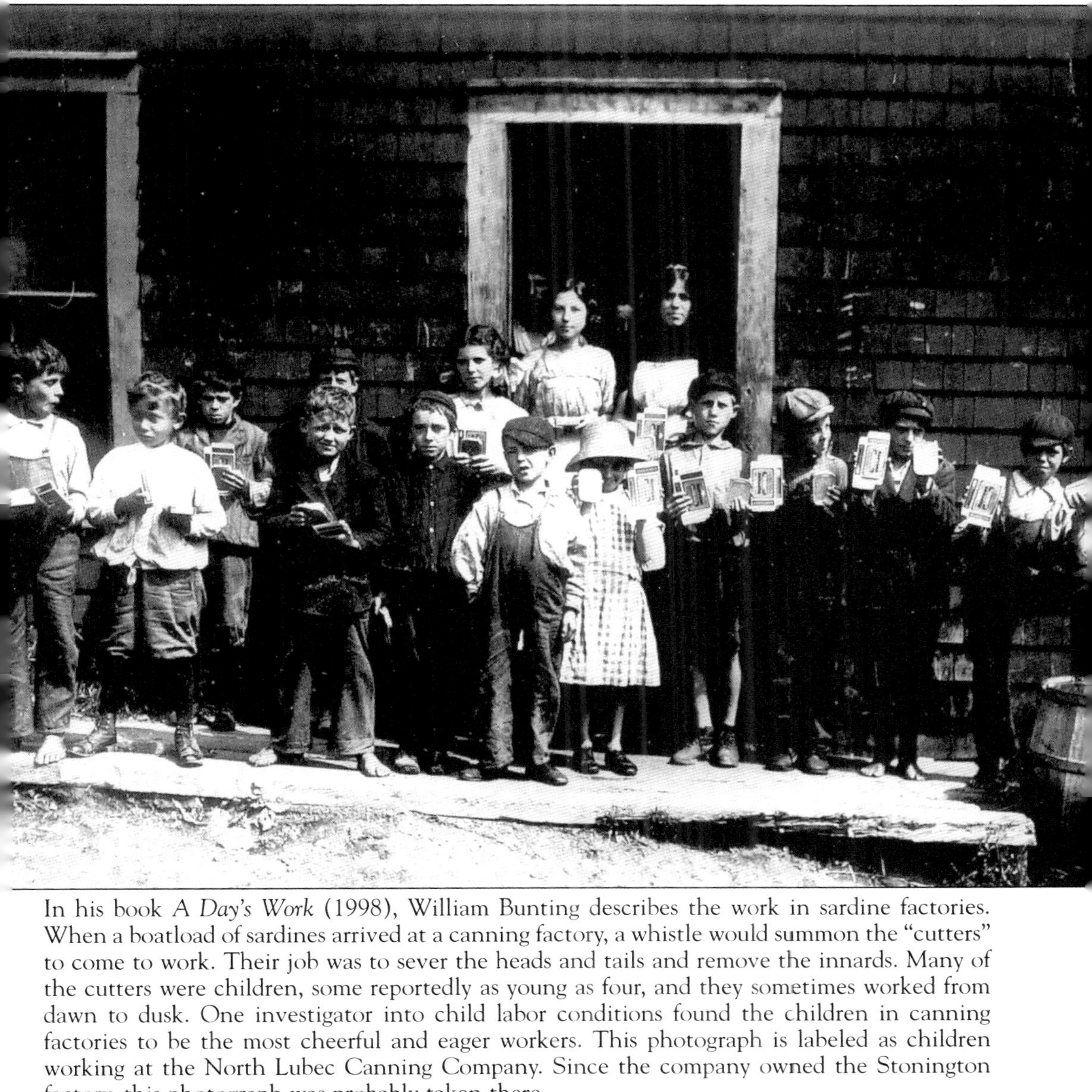

In his book *A Day's Work* (1998), William Bunting describes the work in sardine factories. When a boatload of sardines arrived at a canning factory, a whistle would summon the "cutters" to come to work. Their job was to sever the heads and tails and remove the innards. Many of the cutters were children, some reportedly as young as four, and they sometimes worked from dawn to dusk. One investigator into child labor conditions found the children in canning factories to be the most cheerful and eager workers. This photograph is labeled as children working at the North Lubec Canning Company. Since the company owned the Stonington factory, this photograph was probably taken there.

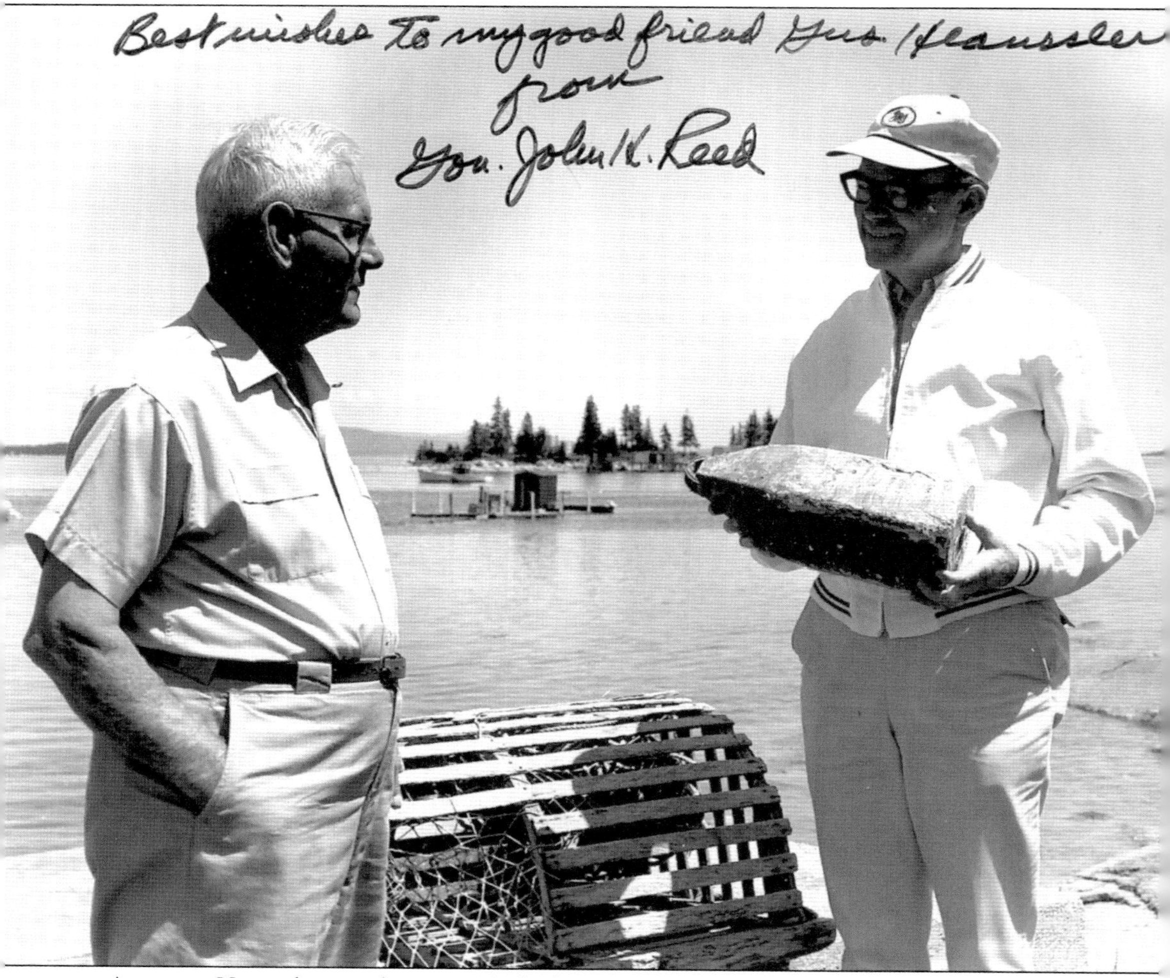

Augustus Heanssler was born in 1895, the son of Julius and Frances (Conary) Heanssler of Deer Isle. He married Frances Taylor. Starting in 1929, he developed a well-known lobster business in Sunshine; he built his first lobster pound in 1935. Gus had a dockside store where he sold marine hardware, fishing supplies, and boat rigging of every kind. He also had a fish weir in Greenlaw Cove. He served two terms in the Maine legislature and was on the Marine Resources Advisory Committee for 26 years. Gus liked to say, "Every penny I've got came out of the Atlantic Ocean." He died in 1976.

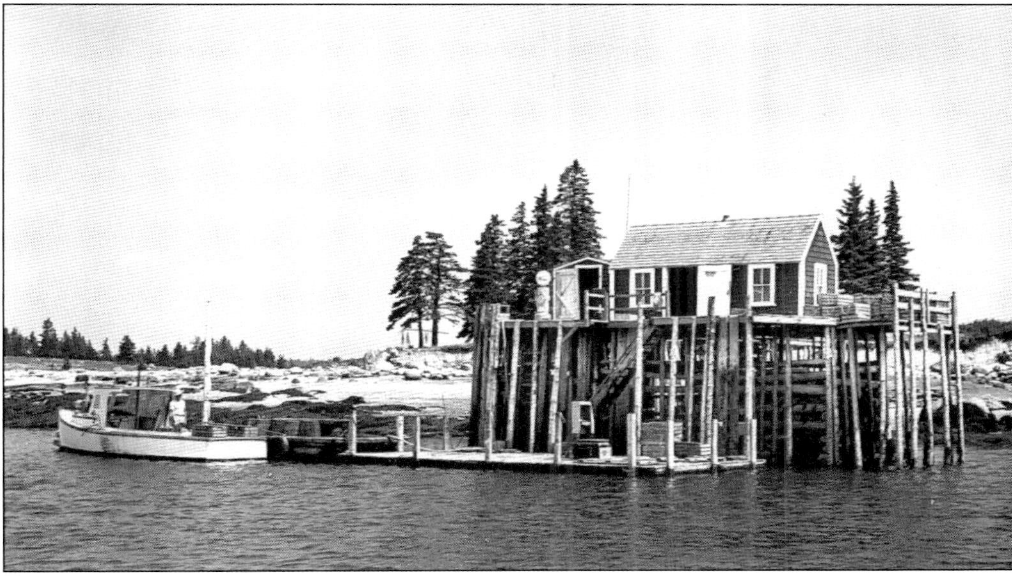

Hen Island lies just off Sunshine, near the Heanssler lobster pounds. Gus Heanssler owned it; he bought lobsters there and sold gas and snacks. Lobster boats could come right in to the dock where his marine supply store was. He opened it in the early 1930s, and it was in use until 1983, when the harbor was dredged.

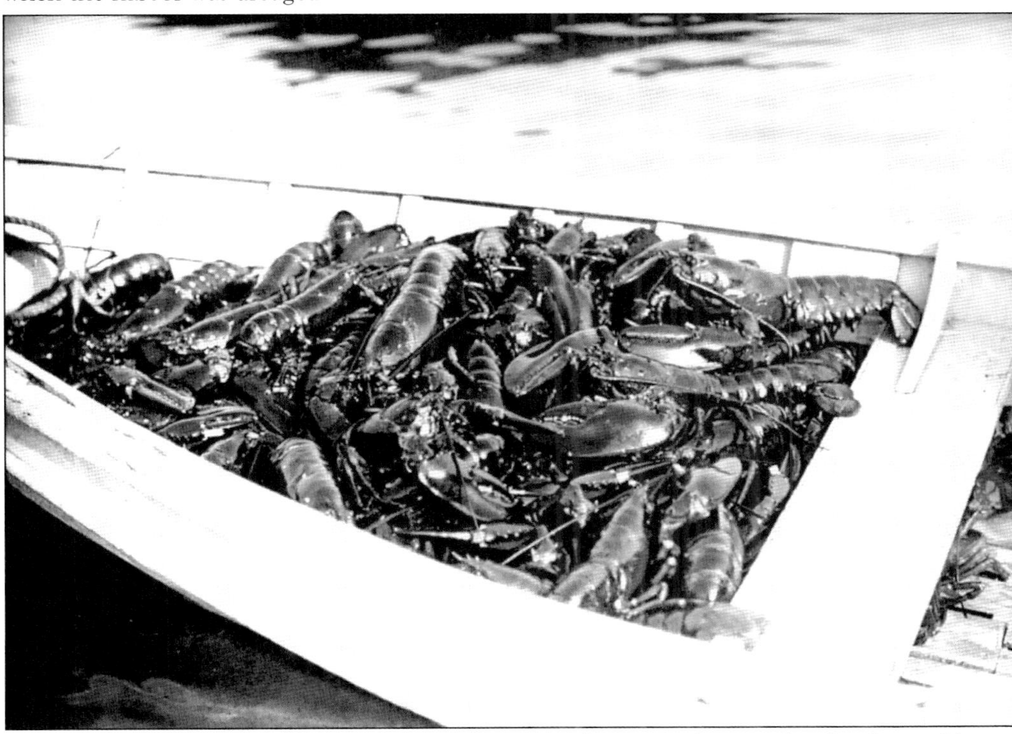

In 1947, 700 pounds of lobster were sent from Heanssler's pound to London for the wedding of Princess Elizabeth and Phillip Mountbatten. The lobsters pictured here are in a skiff belonging to Nelson Coombs of Stonington.

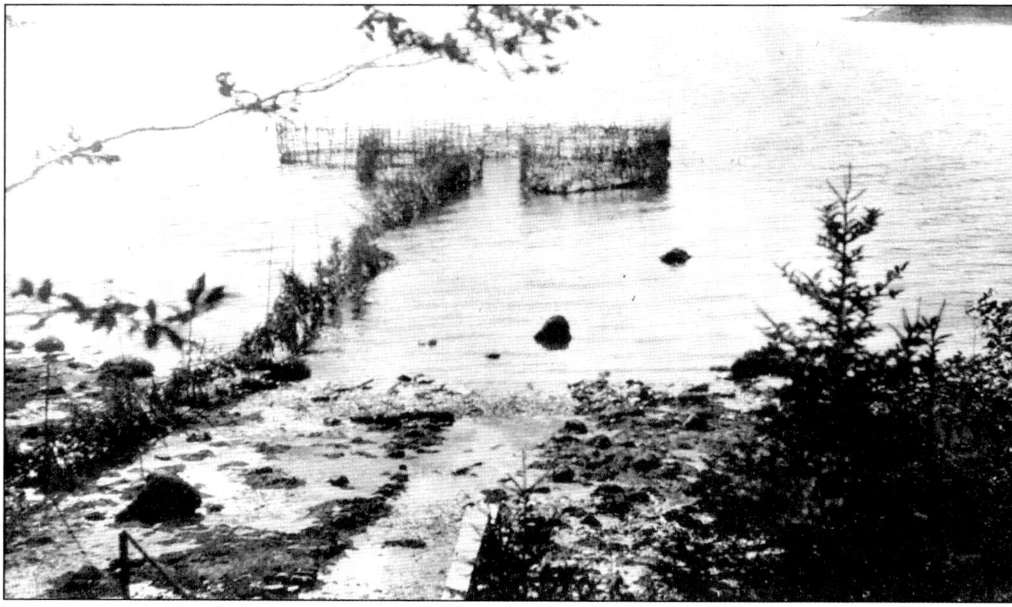

This weir, seen here *c.* 1916, belonged to Elmer Hardy. It was located off Haviland's Beach, near the southwest corner of the original Hardy farm. During the 1930s, there were several stop-seines and seven weirs on the shores of Deer Isle. Though there are none in Deer Isle now, weirs are still used in the Maritime Provinces of Canada.

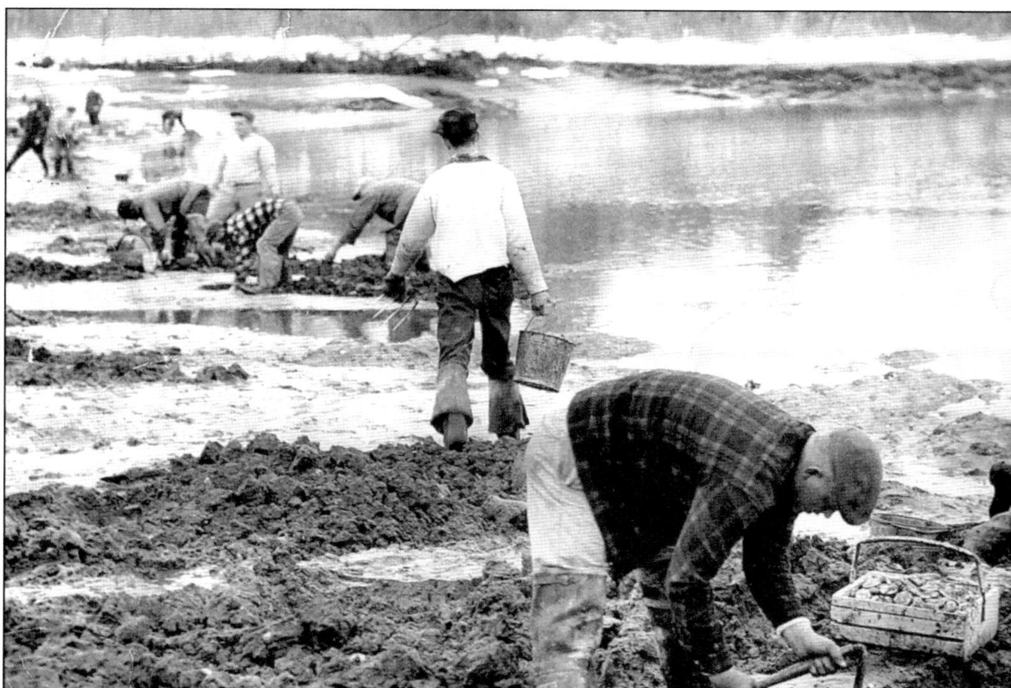

The location and date of this photograph are unknown. A lot more clams existed then than now! Note the snow still blanketing the shoreline.

Capt. Stephen Babbidge Haskell was born in 1828 and went to sea in 1850. He was the master of a number of ships, including the *Norwest* and the *Financier*. A few years after his marriage to Elizabeth Austin, he left the sea and started to make sails in his barn. Two years later, he acquired land on the shore of Northwest Harbor and built the Haskell Sail Loft. He died in 1893.

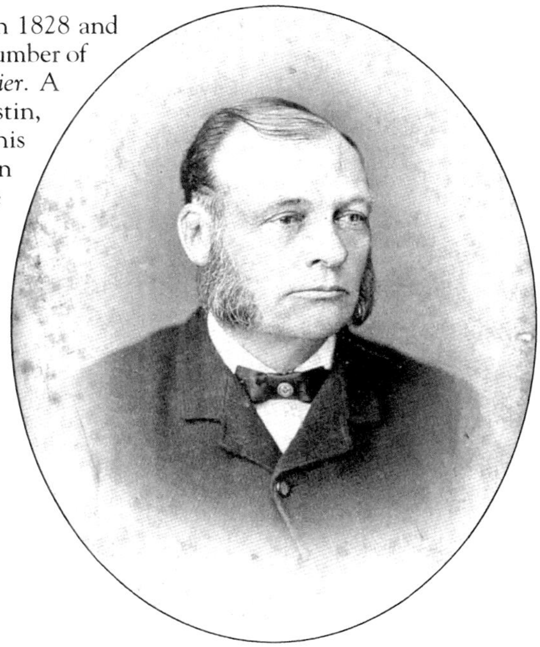

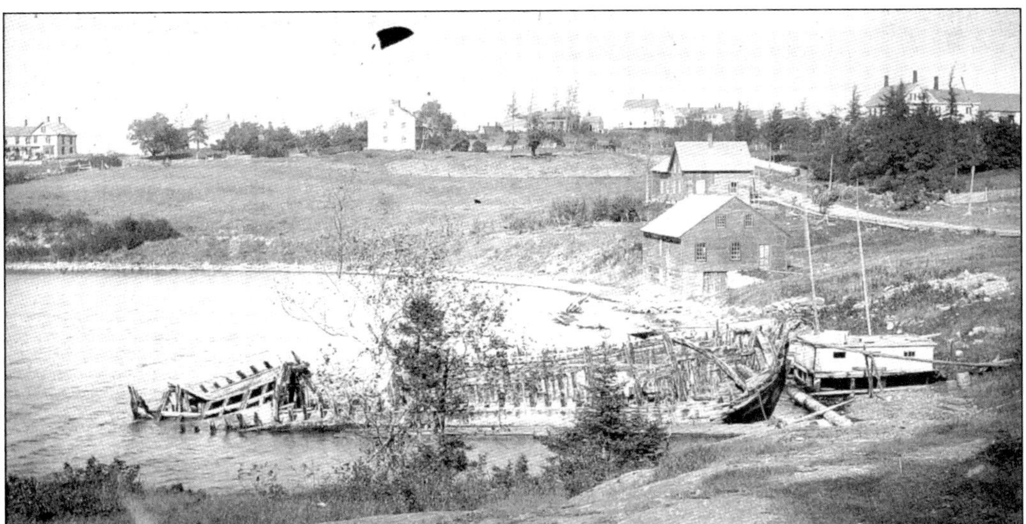

At the Sail Loft at Northwest Harbor, Capt. Stephen Haskell and his son Austin made sails for the Deer Isle fleet—almost 100 schooners in all. Anchored schooners lay in Northwest Harbor for the winter, while their sails were repaired and re-roped at the Sail Loft. According to Captain Haskell's great-grandson Winthrop, "With the passing of the fleet have gone scores of Deer Isle captains who, when at home, made Mr. Haskell's loft a rendezvous, and it is said that some most interesting and miraculous yarns were spun there."

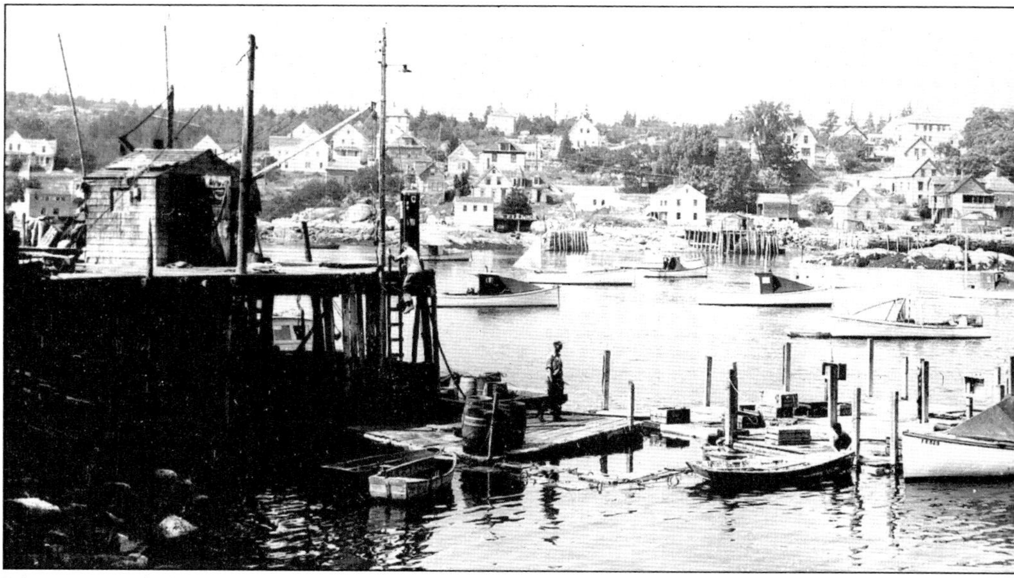

This postcard photograph, taken in the late 1940s, shows Clyde Conary's wharf at Green Head Cove in Stonington. Here, he bought lobsters and sold gas.

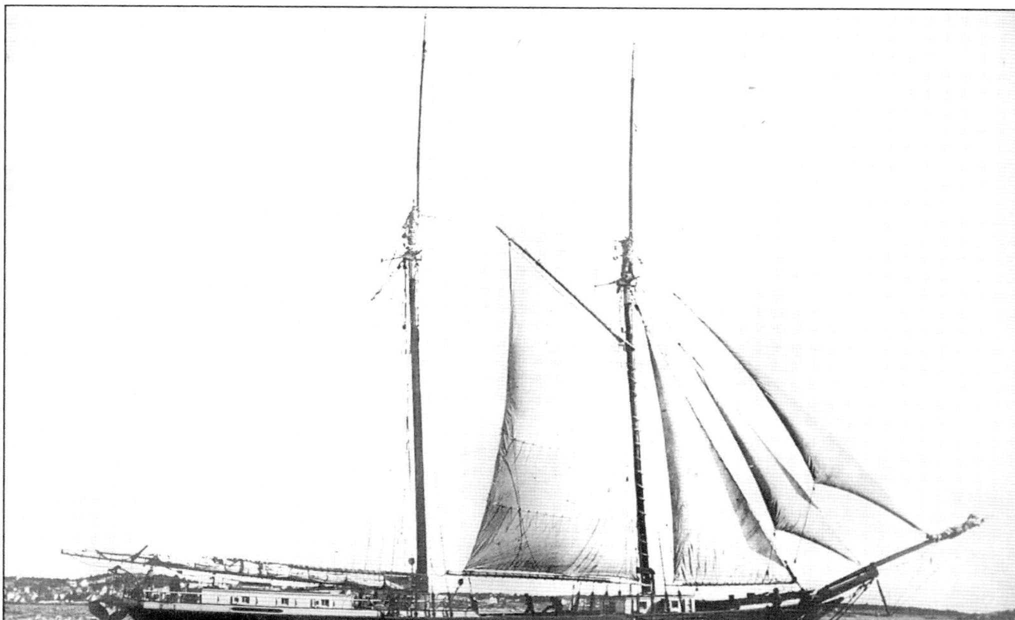

The *Carrie E. Pickering* was a 277-ton schooner owned by the Deer Isle Pickerings. She was used to carry granite to New York and to return with coal from Philadelphia. On her last trip, on Thanksgiving Day 1903, she ran into a gale off Cape May. Trying to get to the Delaware breakwater, the ship ran aground on Cape Henlopen and broke up. The crew of six men from Deer Isle was taken off by breeches buoy by the Coast Guard.

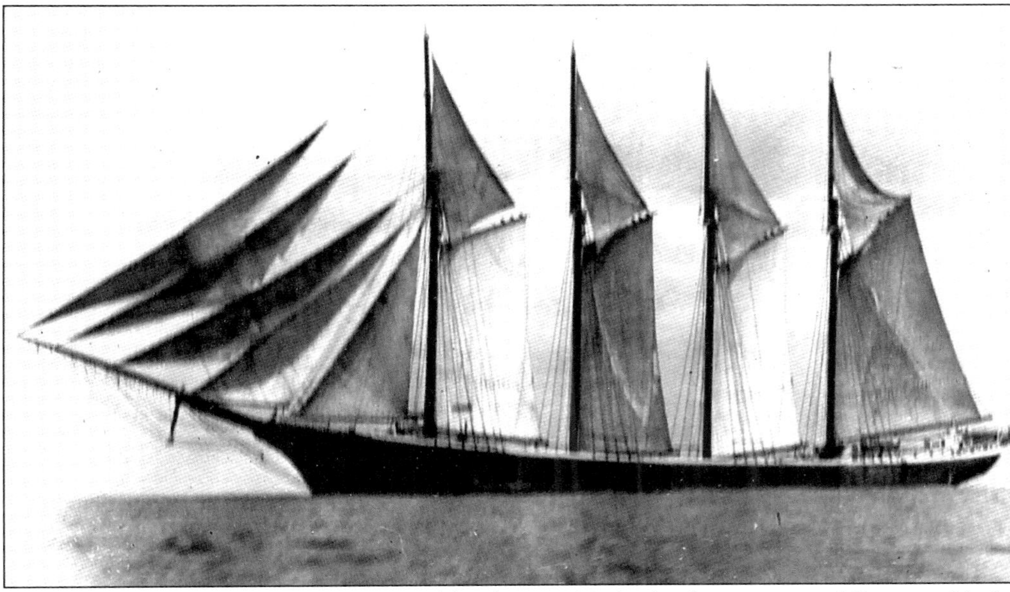

The *Ella Pierce Thurlow,* built in Rockland in 1939, had a home port of Boston. Under Capt. George Washington Torrey of Deer Isle, she was a cargo ship carrying such things as coal, pine, and molasses. In 1920, she sailed from Lisbon to Norfolk in 45 days. The ship was often moored in Northwest Harbor while Captain Torrey awaited orders.

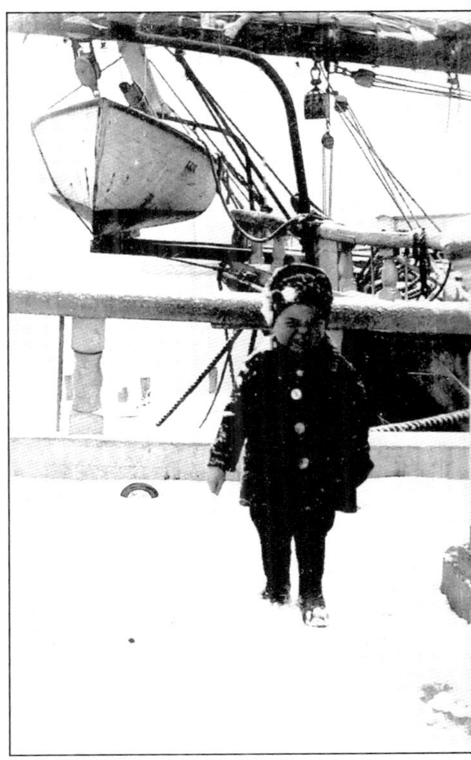

Capt. George Washington Torrey often took his family with him. In this 1923 photograph, his son George Washington Jr. is three years old. Captain Torrey's wife, Essie, was a teacher and home-schooled her son on board, year round. When George Jr. discovered that children in Deer Isle did not have to go to school in the summer, he chose to stay with his grandparents so that he, too, could enjoy vacations.

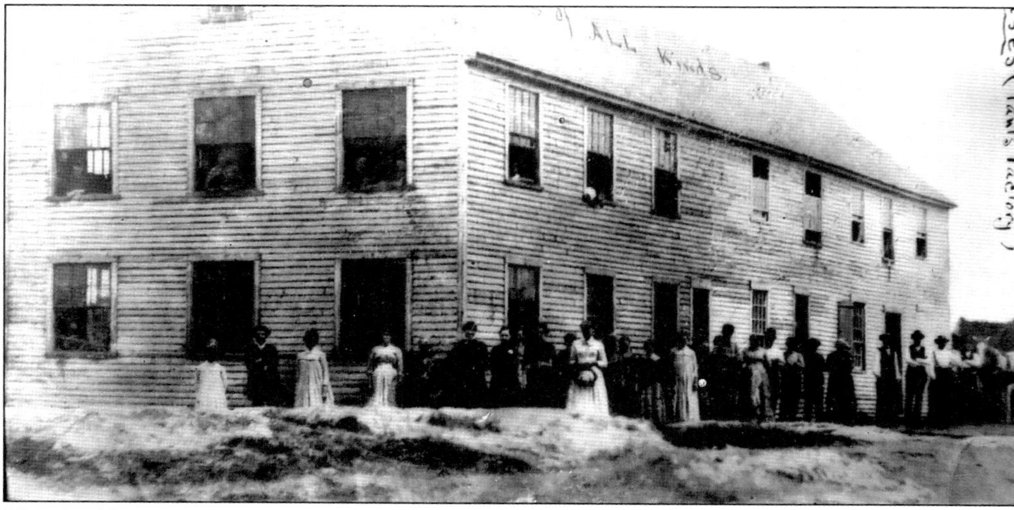

This building was constructed c. 1845 by Farnum Haskell, who used it as a sail loft. After his death during the Civil War, the building was acquired by Sylvanus Haskell. He rented it to a Boston company, which ran a pants factory there for 10 years. The pants were cut out in Boston and shipped to Deer Isle for finishing. Some of the cloth was distributed to the homes of women who were unable to work at the factory; they received 50¢ a dozen. After the factory closed, the building remained empty for a while. Ralph Barter then bought it and used it for his coal and lumber business. In the 1930s, Arthur Barter purchased it, and in 1974, the building was extensively renovated. Located at the Mill Dam in Deer Isle Village, it now contains two apartments.

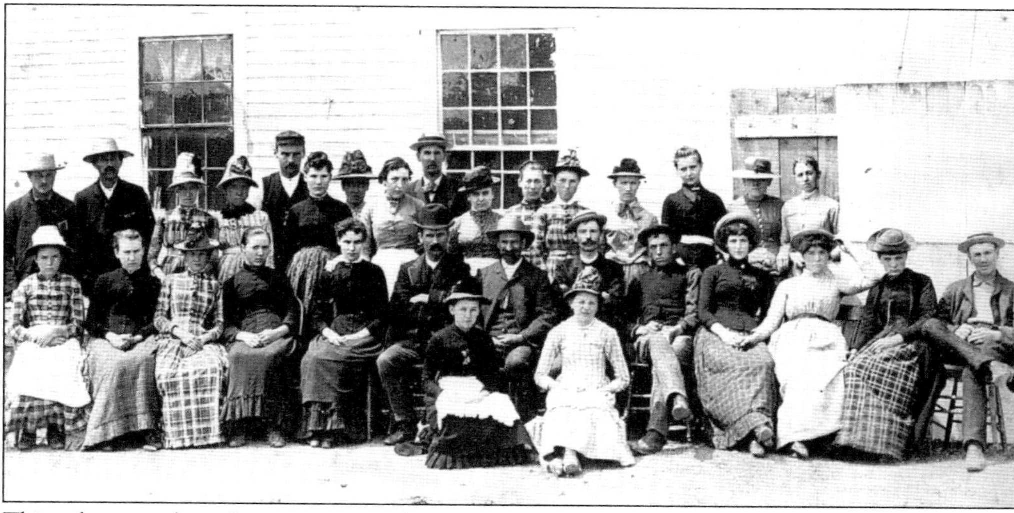

This photograph, taken c. 1882, shows the employees of the pants factory operated by Moses S. Joyce at the Mill Dam in Deer Isle. Pictured here, from left to right, are the following: (first row) Gertrude Greene and Julia Greene; (second row) Annie Thompson, Rose Eaton, Asenath Staples, Jennie Eaton, Alberta Pickering, John H. McGorrill, Moses S. Joyce, unidentified, Ernest "Smug" Haskell, Mabel Small, Kate Small, unidentified, and Edward "Dickie" Greenlaw; (third row) Moses "Dell" Joyce, Henry Bray, Minnie Haskell, Carrie Jordan, Bentley Raynes, Lottie Marshall, Alice Hatch, Vinnie Pressey, Rollins Stinson, Olive Pickering, Sarah Pickering, Eliza Eaton, unidentified, Maud Burgess, Etta Greenlaw, and Sarah Morey.

Before World War I, Ralph Barter was a lobsterman with a string of 200 traps. He lost one arm at the battle of the Argonne. When he returned to the island, his father told him, "A seagull can't soar with one wing, and a man can't handle a pitching small boat with one hand. Better forget it." After a fall overboard from a dory when he tried to balance himself, Ralph decided that his father was right. In the process of finding a way to make a living, Ralph eventually founded the Barter Coal Company, the Deer Isle Canning Company, and, with his brother Arthur, the Barter Lumber Company.

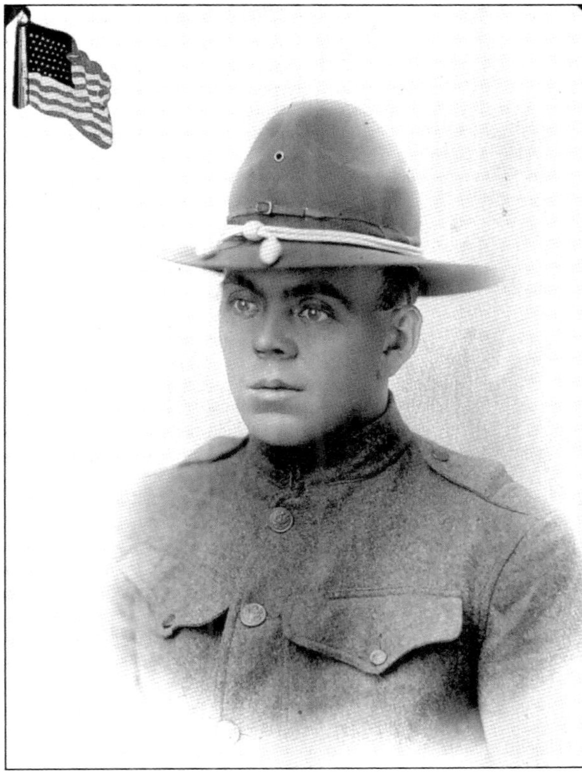

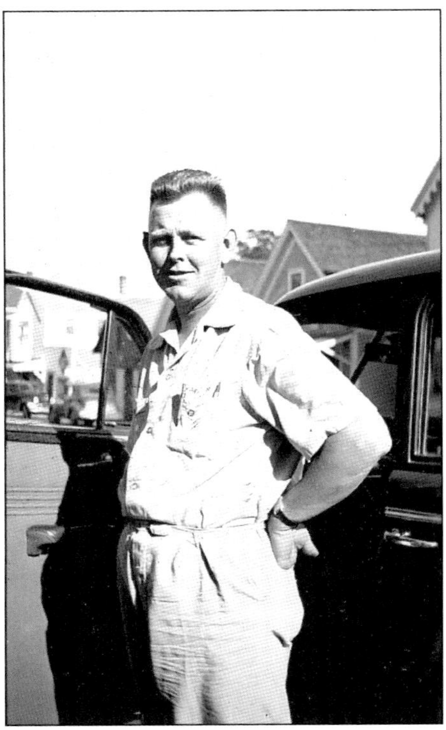

In addition to founding the Barter Lumber Company, Arthur Barter purchased the M. D. Joyce Hardware Company from George Beck in 1932; both are still run by the family. During the war years, Arthur also operated a bus service (in what would now be called a stretch limousine) that traveled from Stonington to Bangor making stops at all the towns along the way.

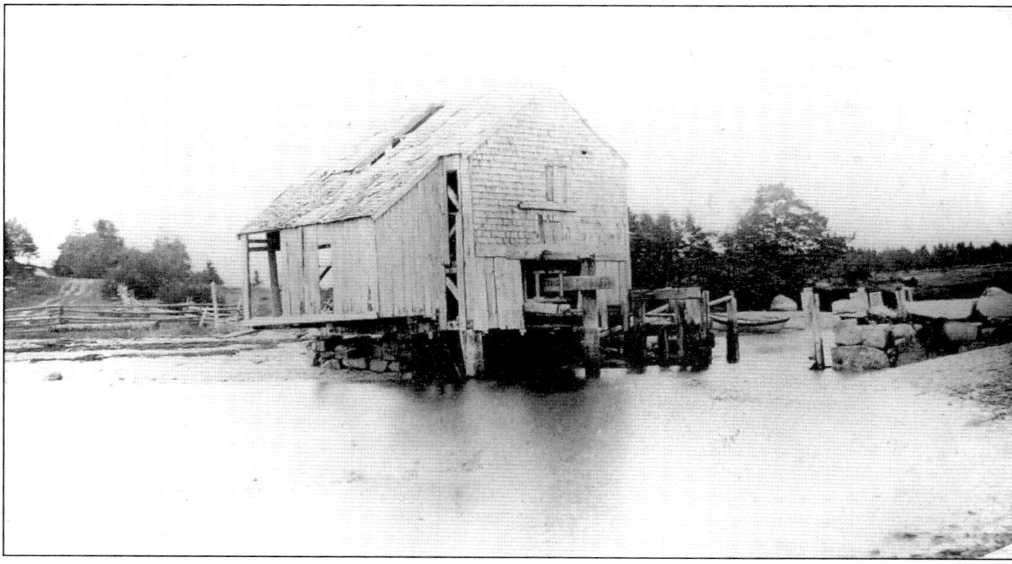

This gristmill was located at the Mill Pond on the Reach Road. Constructed in 1837 by Capt. John Torrey, who built a dam across the mouth of the cove, it used tidal power to turn the mill wheel. A bushel of corn could be ground in five to seven minutes, and the charge was one quart of grain for each bushel ground. The mill was torn down in 1883; one of the grindstones is on display at the Deer Isle-Stonington Historical Society.

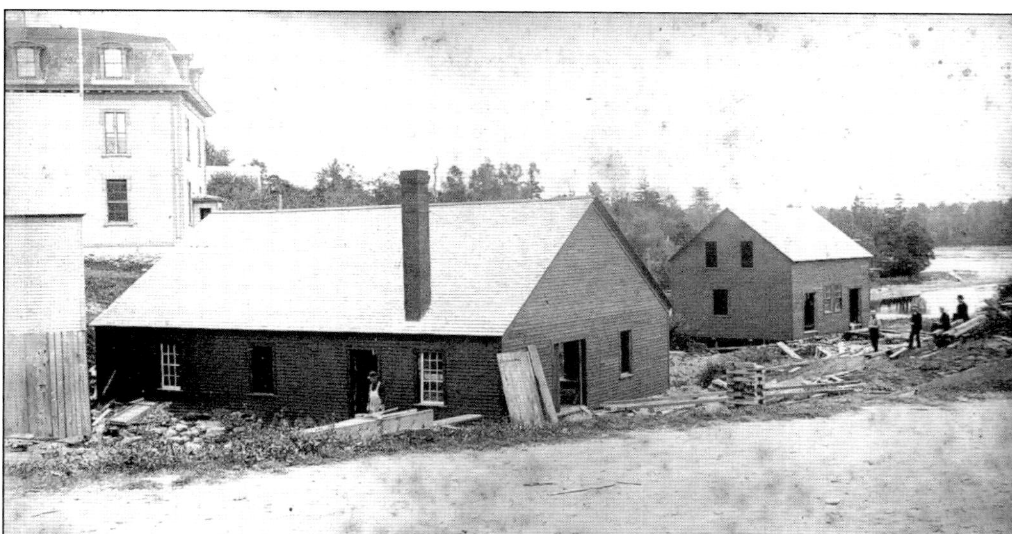

This 1880s photograph shows a tannery and gristmill located at the mouth of the brook that runs from the Lily Pond to the Mill Pond, behind what is now the Terrell Lester Gallery in Deer Isle Village. The tannery was built c. 1797 by Ignatius Haskell and was operated by his son Aaron. It included a mill that was used to grind hemlock bark. The bark aided in creating tannic acid for the tanning of hides later sold to local shoemakers. The Haskells also owned the gristmill (at right in the photograph); it was eventually moved to Main Street and is now the Deer Isle Photo Studio.

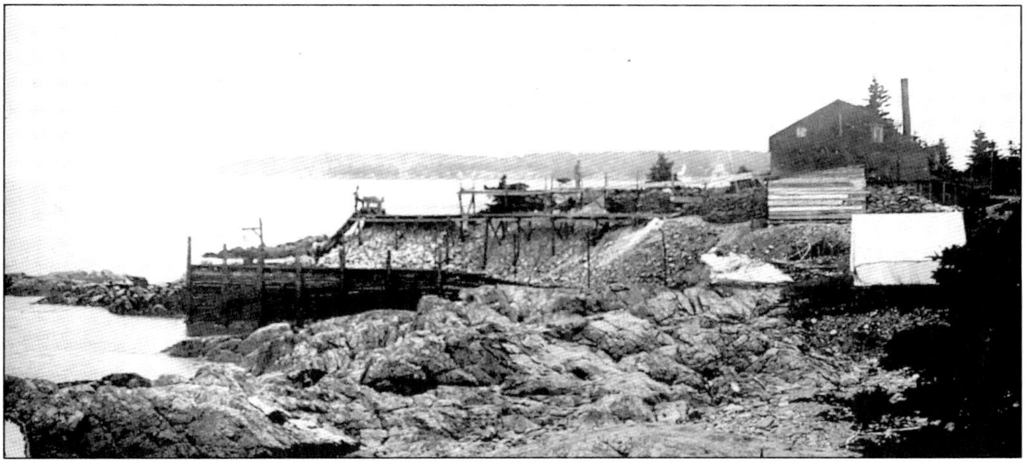

This postcard photograph shows the silver mine at Dunham's Point, which operated briefly from 1882 until its final closure in 1908. Although the mine was called the Deer Isle Silver Mine, most of the metal found was lead and zinc, with a little gold, silver, and copper. "Silver" was probably used in the mine's name to help sell shares. A crew of 20 men worked the mine. Deer Isle men made up the day crew, whereas the night shift consisted of experienced miners from the Blue Hill copper mine. The schooner that delivered ore from the mine to Elizabethport, New Jersey, would return with coal to operate the mine. However, between 1905 and 1908, only three shipments were made. The mine's bankruptcy was caused by the great expenses and long distances involved (and by the lack of silver ore).

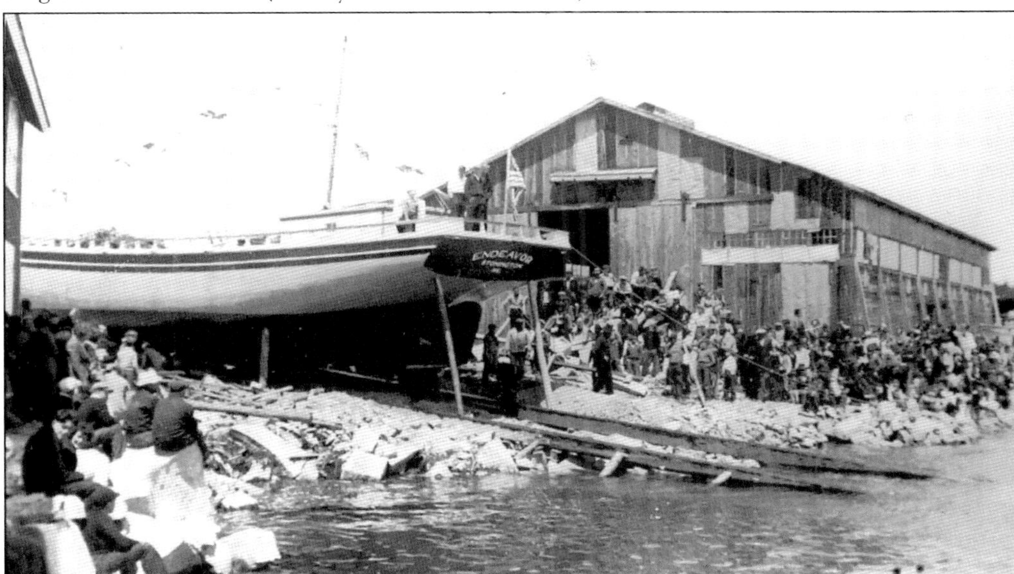

Harlan Billings and his four sons had a shipyard on Little Deer Isle, where a schooner was built for each of the brothers for commercial use. In 1929, the Billings family purchased the site of an abandoned quarry on Moose Island and started the Stonington and Deer Isle Yacht Basin. Here, the *Endeavor* is being constructed in 1938. It is believed to be the last schooner built on the East Coast during the cargo-carrying era. In 1967, Dick Billings, the son of one of the founders, bought the yard from the bank. His son, Harlan, now operates it as Billings Diesel and Marine, one of the largest employers on the island.

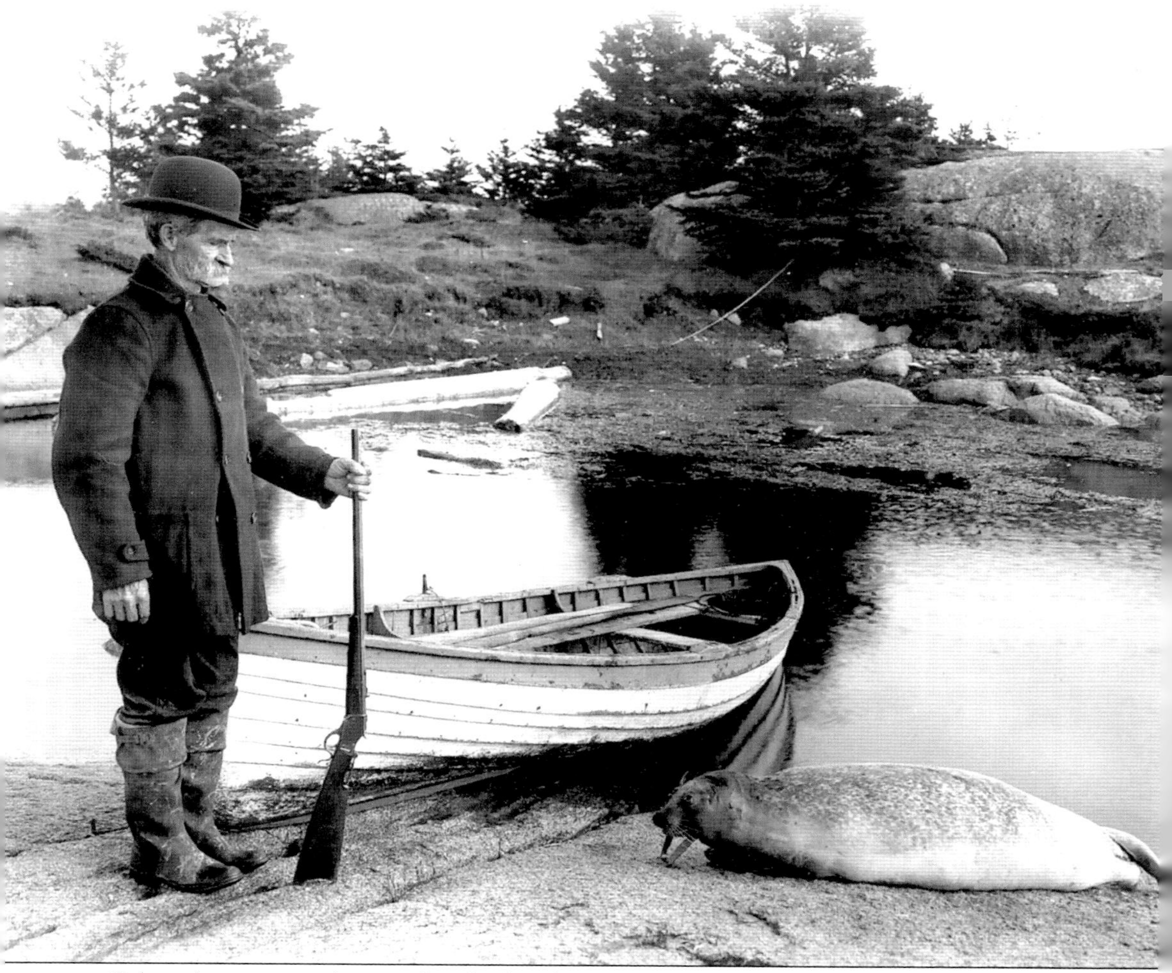

Calvin Ames is seen here with a dead seal. A note on the back of the photograph reads, "It has been said that when his barn needed painting he would kill a seal for oil and mix it with red ochre for stain." The term "barn red" for paint originated in the Penobscot Bay area, where there were numerous porpoises and seals during the late 1700s and early 1800s. Their oil provided a base for paint that served as an excellent preservative and retained its color for years.

Five

RECREATION

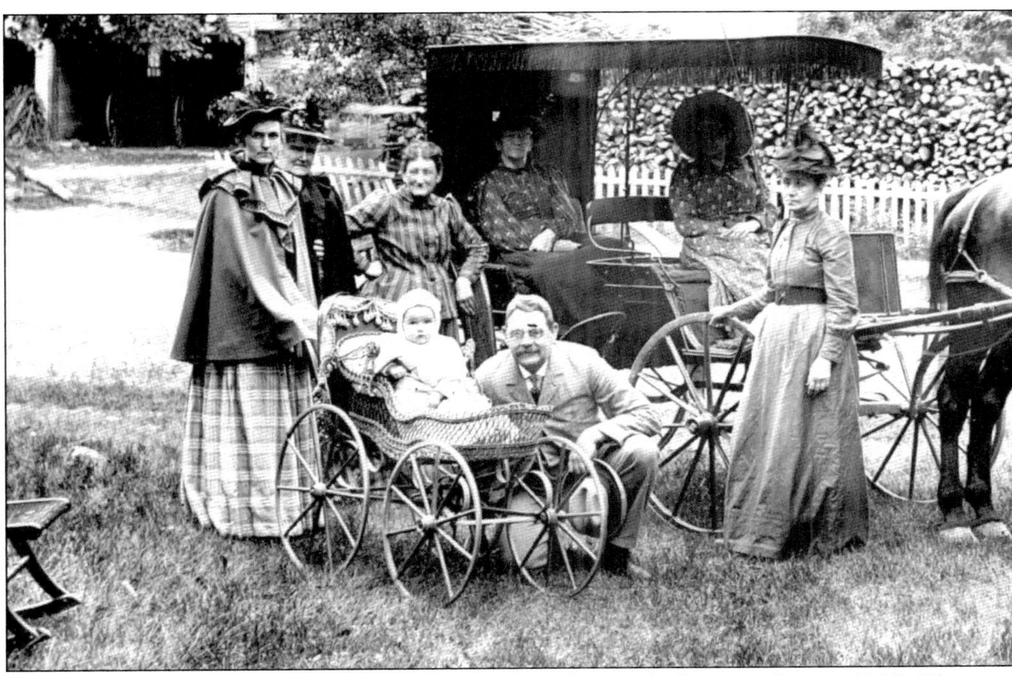

This photograph was taken by Walter Fowler, a professional photographer, *c*. 1895. These are probably members of his family, residing in the Reach area of Deer Isle. Note the wicker baby carriage, "the surrey with the fringe on top," and the impressive woodpile.

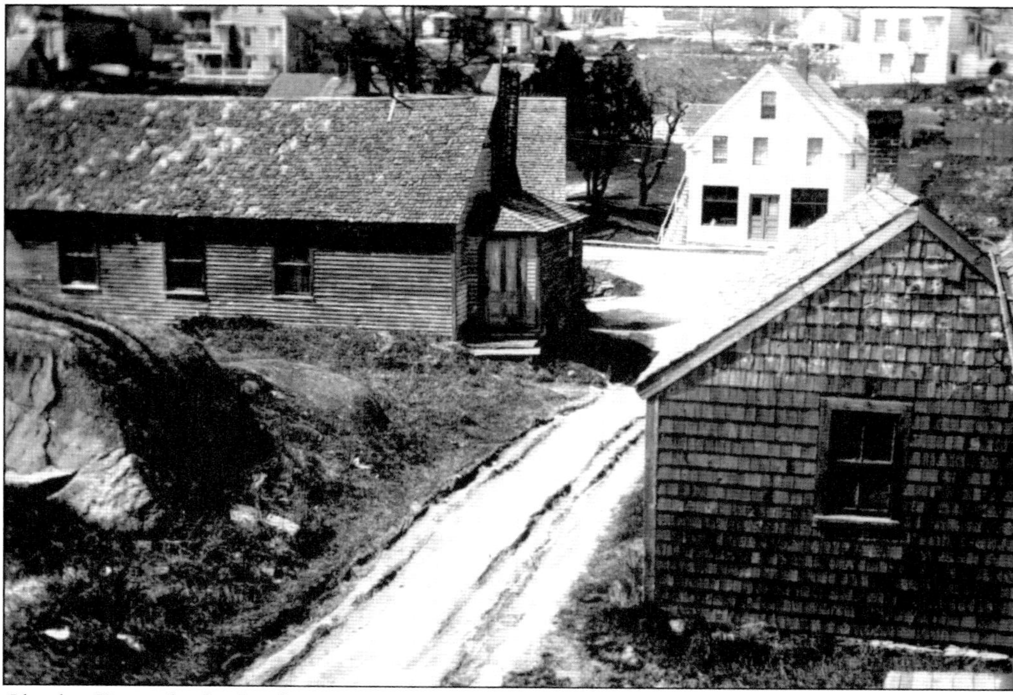

Charles Eaton built the first recreational structure (the building on the left) in Stonington c. 1870 and called it Olympic Hall. Soon after, Solomon Green built Eureka Hall nearby. Eventually, the building in the photograph became residential and was called Seaside Hall by the people who lived there.

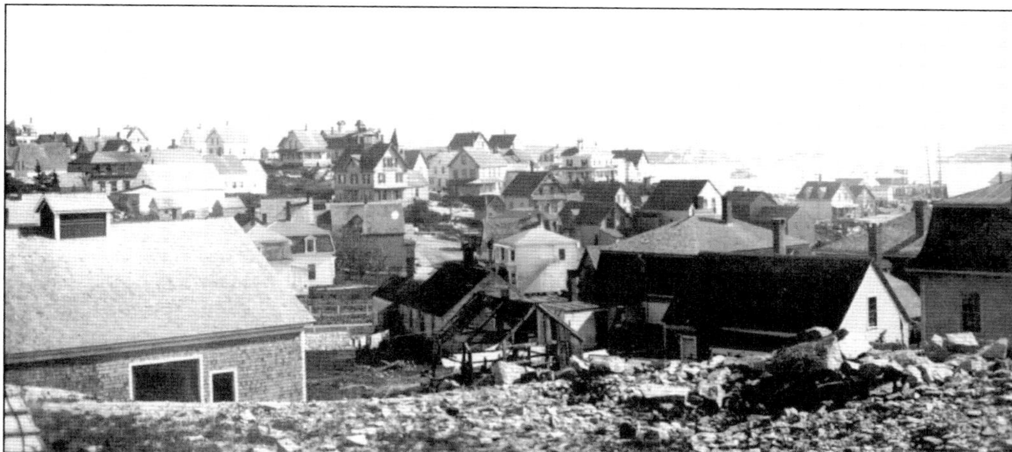

The building on the left in this photograph served many uses. In the 1840s, it was built as the Deer Isle Town Hall. The building was sold c. 1890 and was moved to Pink Street in Stonington, where it served as a barn, slaughterhouse, and butcher shop. Sometime in the 1920s or 1930s, it began to house a church group and to serve as a movie theater. In 1946, the Community Building Association formed to purchase and renovate the building, which became known as the Red Barn, the social center of Stonington. At the Red Barn, the Stonington High School basketball team played its games, and activities such as dances, band practices, wrestling, and fund-raising events were held.

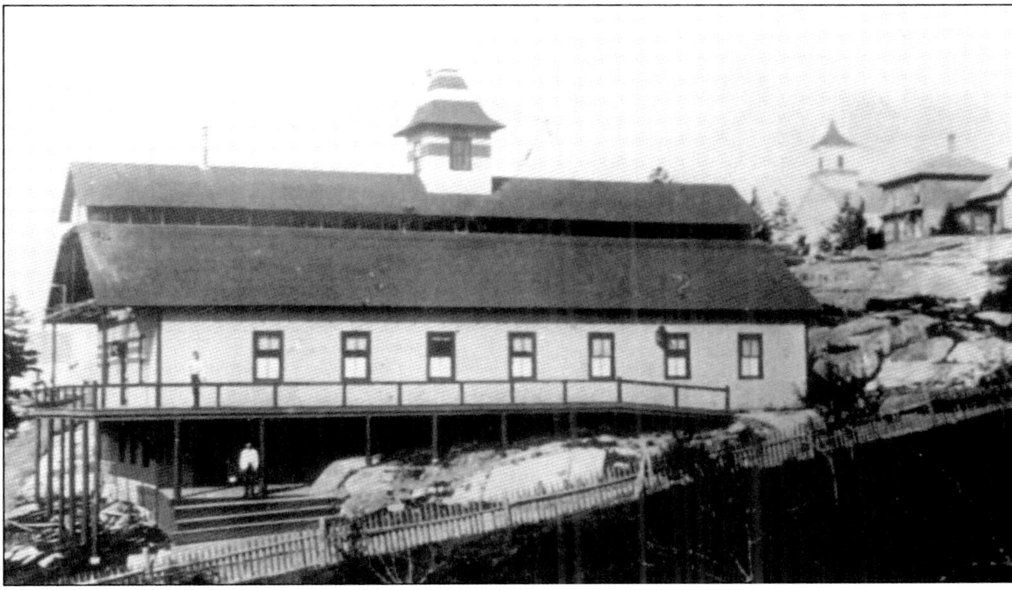

The first amusement hall on this site on Russ's Hill was named the Music Hall by its owner, Charles U. Russ. A store was located on the lowest level. After a tower was erected on the south end for opera company scenery, the name was changed to the Stonington Opera House. The building burned down on the night of March 6, 1910. Ironically, that was the first day that water had been turned on to the hydrant at the foot of the hill.

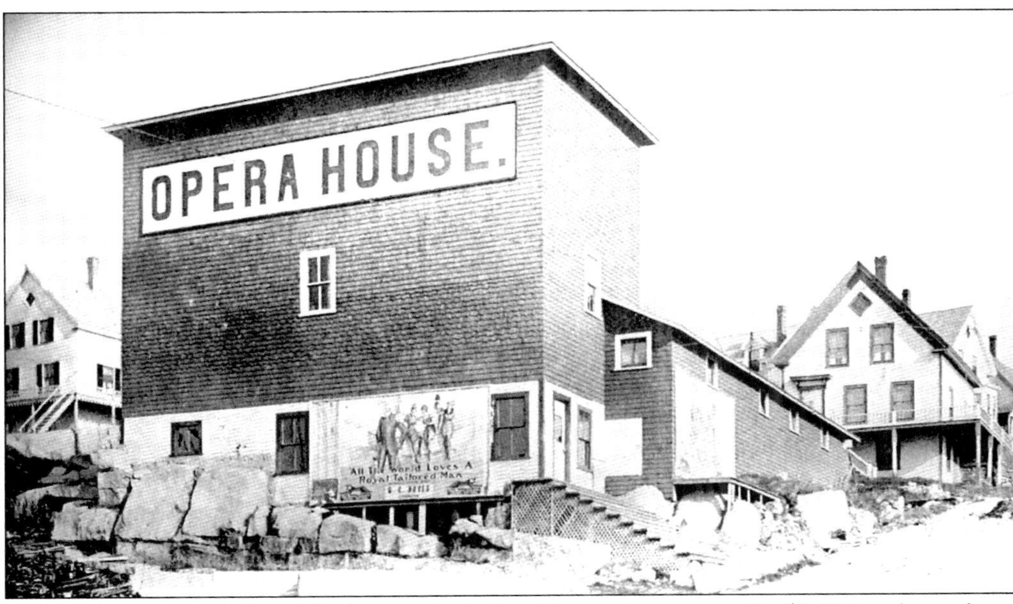

Dr. B. Lake Noyes purchased the lot on which the old opera house stood for $1,500 and transferred it to the newly organized Stonington Opera Company. The opera house stood empty, off and on, for many years. It now houses a group called Opera House Arts, which enjoys tremendous community support. In the summer, it has a busy schedule of performances and classes.

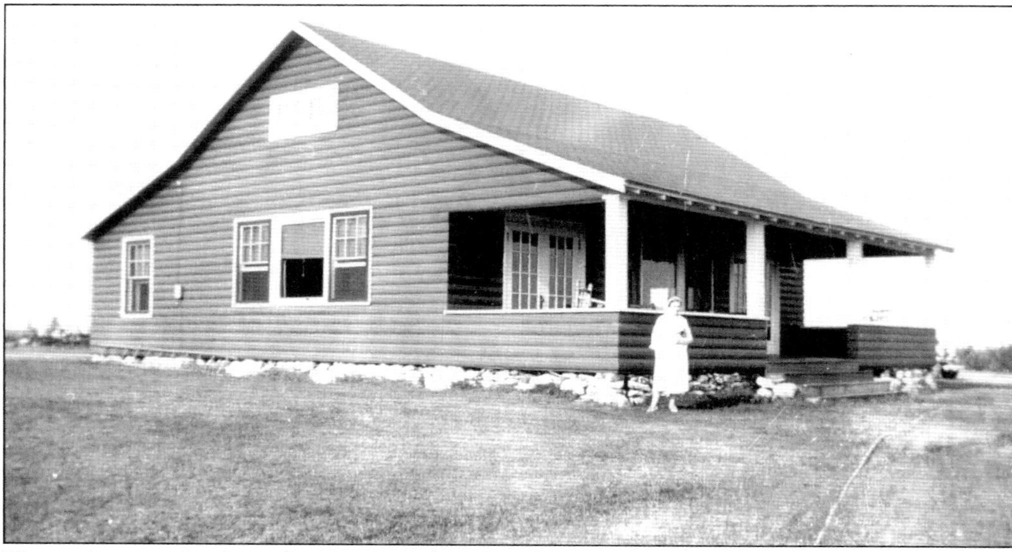

These photographs show the exterior (above) and interior (below) of the Island Country Club, as it appeared in 1935. With the leadership of Stephen B. Knowlton, owner of the Firs and the Felsted, plans for the golf course began in the 1920s. Stock was issued in 1926. Under the name of the Sunset Golf Holding Company of Deer Isle and Stonington, the country club was formed, directors and officers elected, and a schedule of dues and fees adopted. Active members paid annual dues of $15, and golf was an additional $10. These rates included all members of a household. The golf course was laid out by the firm of Stiles and Kleek, golf experts and architects whose services were obtained by Frederick Law Olmsted.

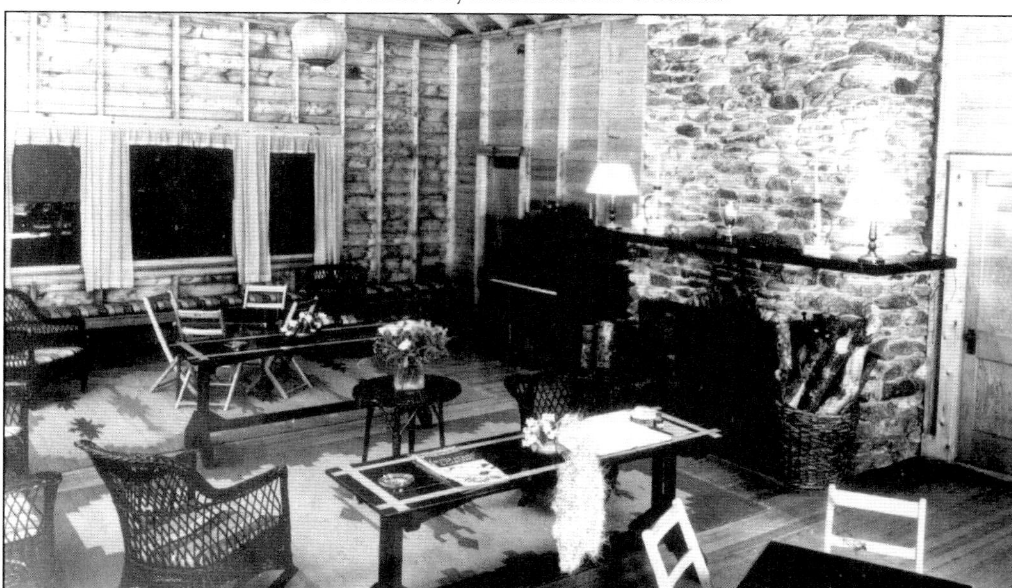

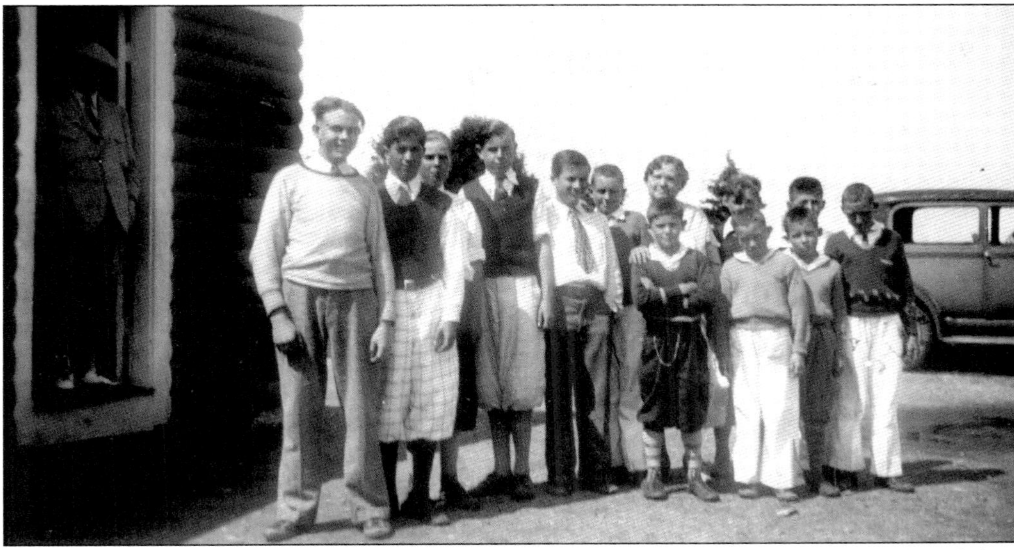

Caddies at the country club pose for a photograph in the early days. Seen here, from left to right, are Martin Snowden, Raymond Haskell, unidentified, Murray Forsythe, unidentified, Willis Snowden, and hostess Mabel "Babe" Powers. The remaining boys are unidentified.

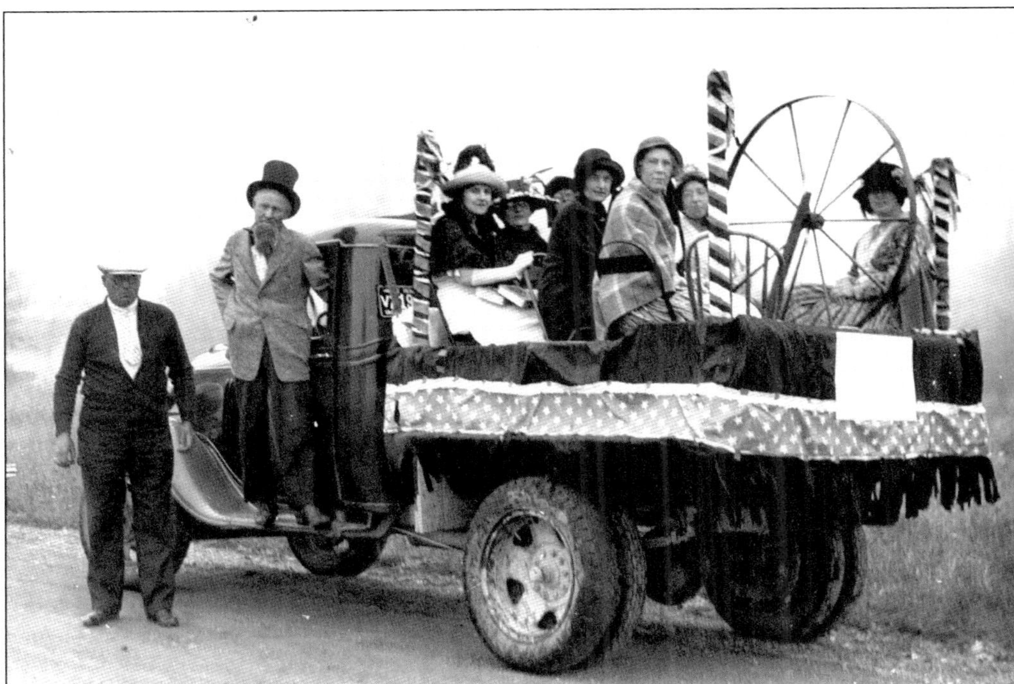

The float in this Fourth of July parade is labeled "Library Sewing Circle, 1934." Those pictured, from left to right, are Ray Lowe, Fred Beck, Pearl Ferguson (the first librarian), Leah Lowe, Minnie Beck, Beatrice Haskell, Adelaide Joyce, Essie Beck, and Bea Marshall. The purpose of the Sewing Circle was to raise money for the library. At the first meeting, in 1928, 25 members attended.

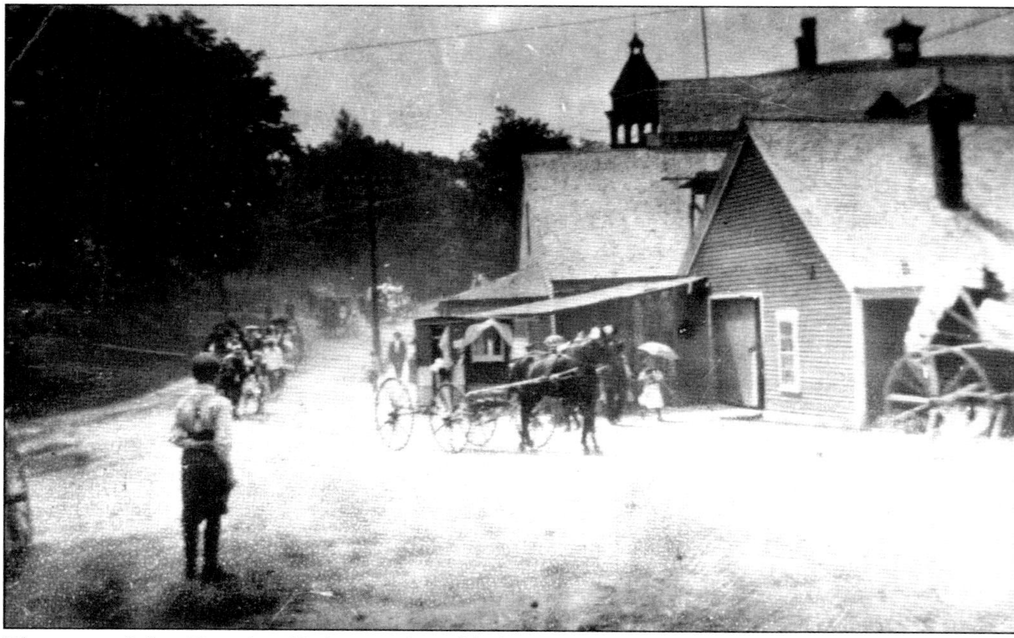

The year of this Fourth of July parade is likely c. 1910. The parade has come down Church Street and is making the turn into Deer Isle Village.

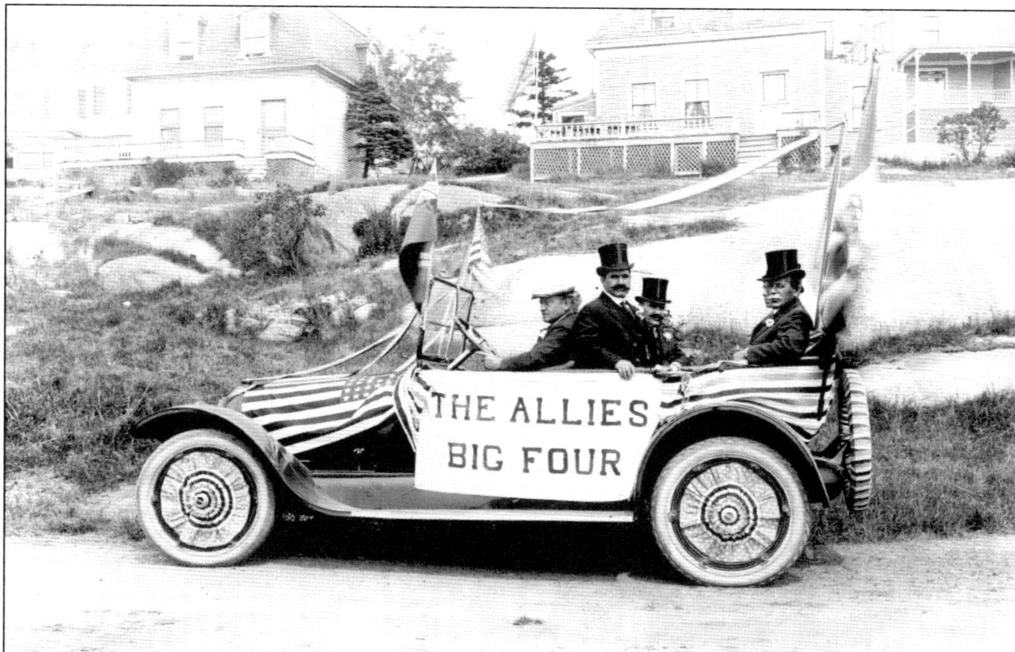

This World War I–era float is driven by Frank McGuire in Stonington's Fourth of July parade. The unidentified gentleman with the black mustache and his hand on the banner represents Italy. Beside him is Arthur Poitras, representing France. Across from Poitras, with only his profile showing, Ernest Coombs represents Woodrow Wilson. Alec Davidson, with the white mustache, portrays the Prime Minister of England.

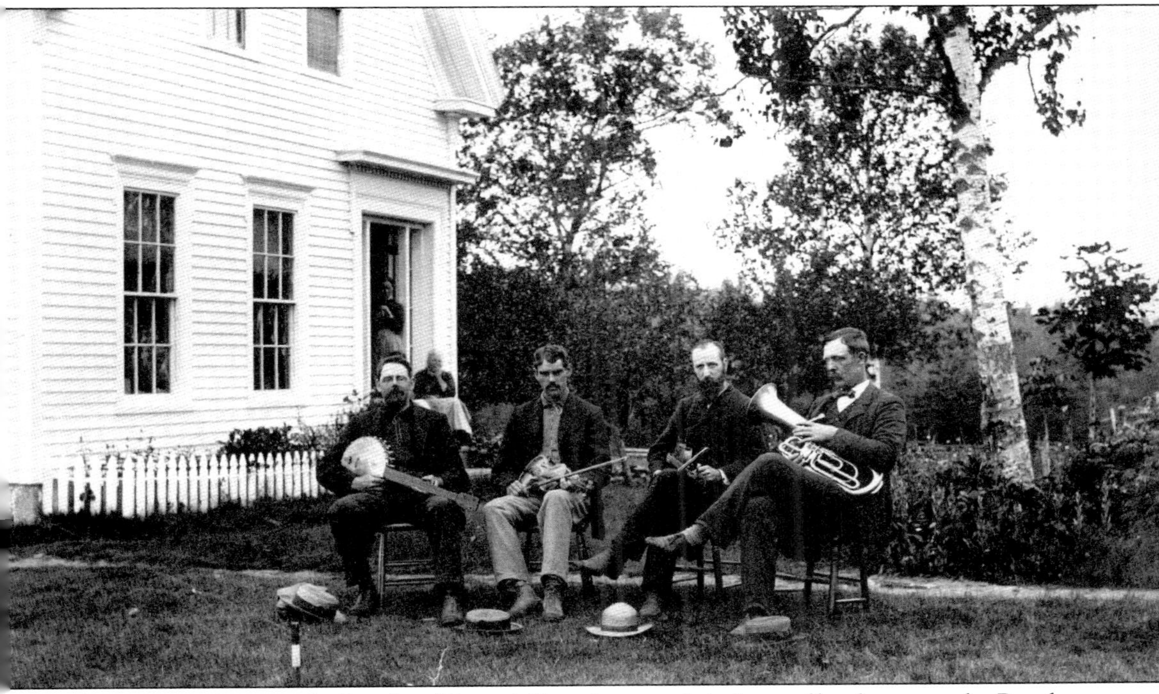

In this c. 1883 photograph, Comfort (Torrey) Greenlaw stands in front of her home on the Reach Road while the Deer Isle Band prepares to strike up music. The members' straw hats are set neatly on the lawn. Comfort was the wife of Capt. Solomon Barbour Greenlaw. The musicians, from left to right, are George W. Fowler, Charles W. Fowler, Ed Adams, and Jim Mann.

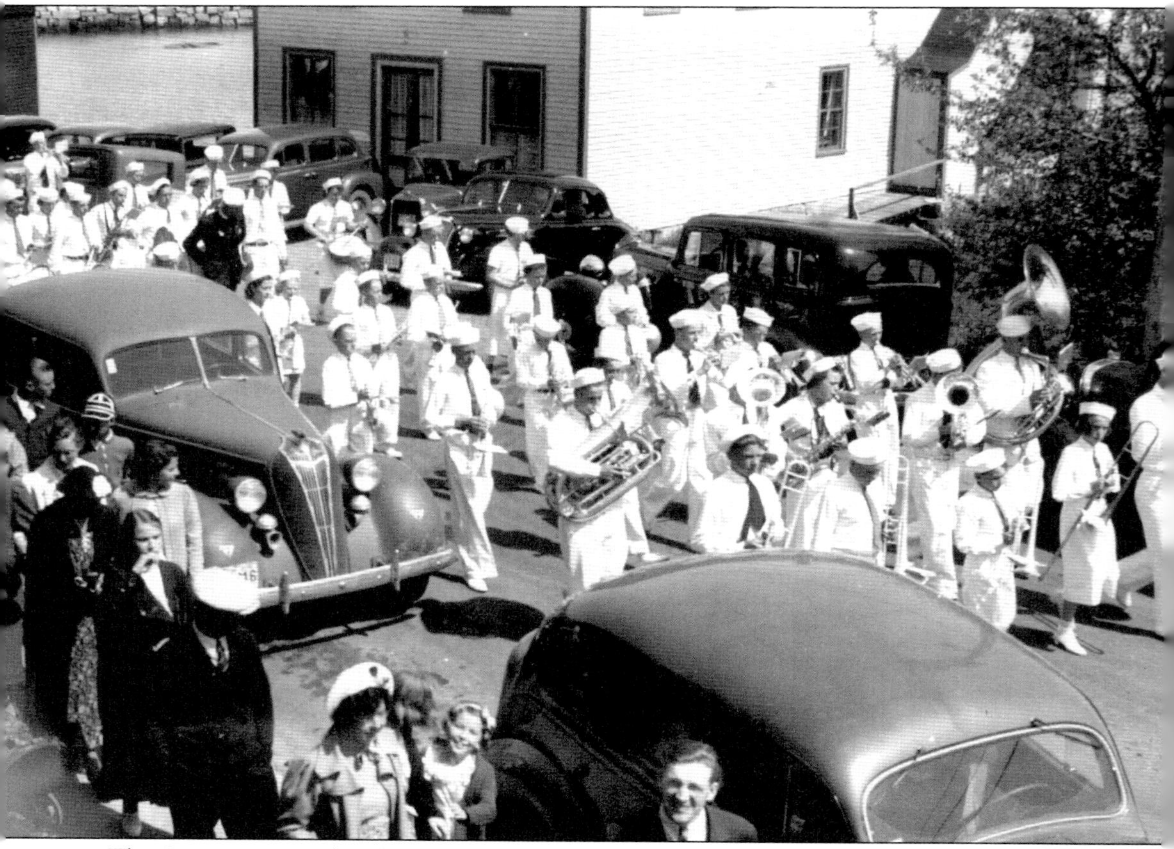

The Stonington High School band marches on Main Street in 1939. The next year, the band acquired new uniforms in black and orange, the school colors, and went to the New York World's Fair. Band members took the steamer SS *White* to Rockland; from there, they went by bus to Providence, Rhode Island, where they took the steamer *Comet* to New York City. They spent two days at the fair and gave two band concerts. A participant reported to Dr. Noyes at Penobscot Bay Archives that "many of their relatives, friends, summer visitors who frequented Deer Isle and Stonington and others identified with the homes of the band members, were coming and going constantly to affiliate with all the band members, and others from Stonington who accompanied them as aides or guides."

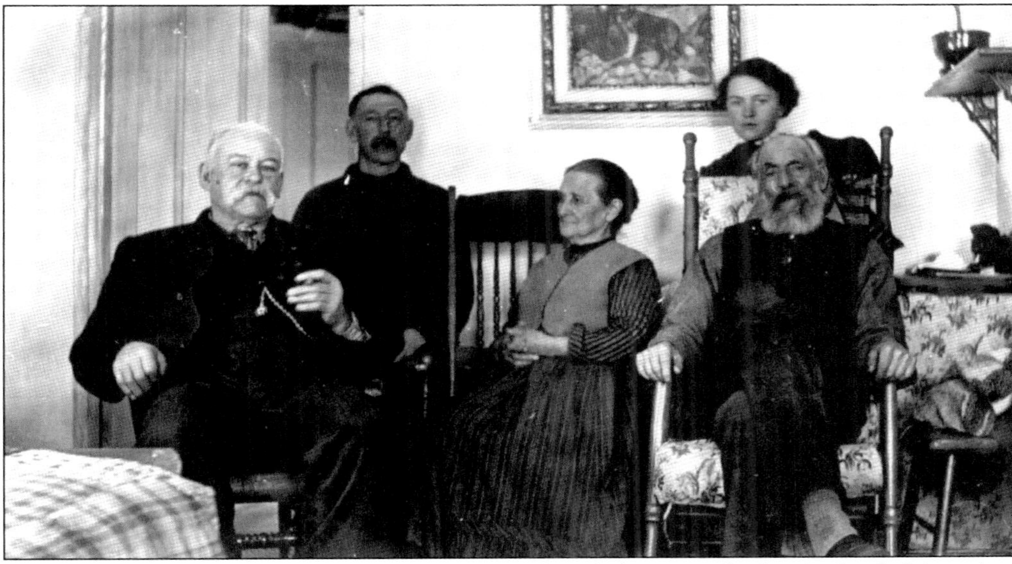

This group includes, from left to right, an unidentified man, Charles Packard, Mary Ann (Cooper) Packard, Rena May Saunders, and Francis Packard. Charlie Packard owned the first "talking machine" on the island, a Victrola, which played cylindrical records. On winter evenings, he took it from home to home, where groups gathered to listen, talk, and enjoy refreshments.

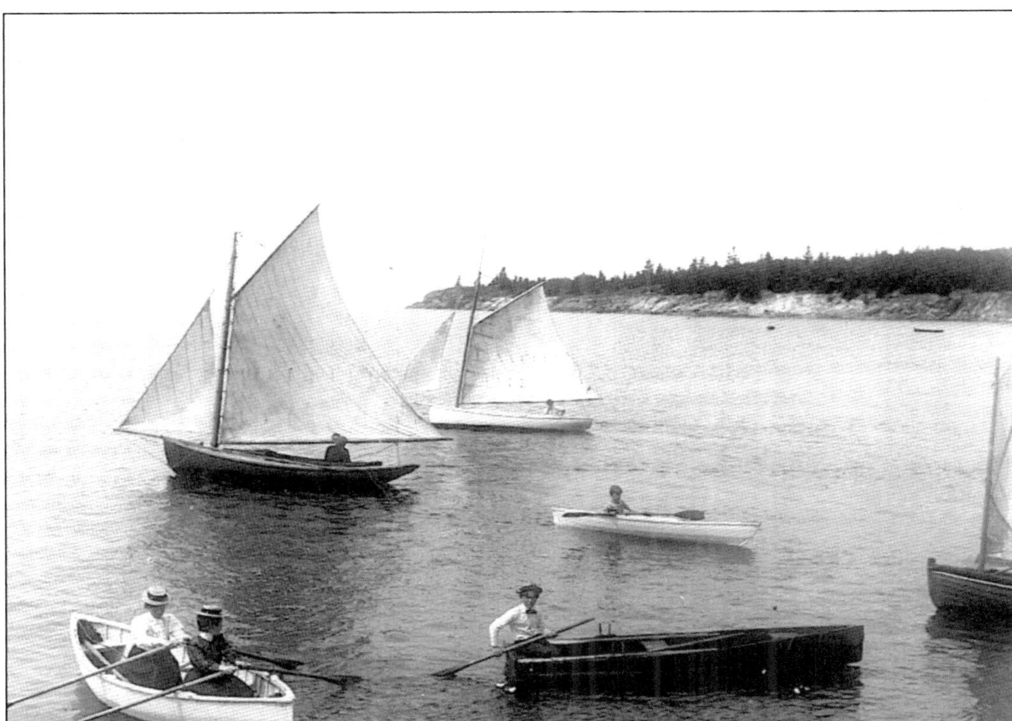

The Southworth family "fleet" appears here c. 1890 off Dunham's Point in Sunset. Members of the Southworth family have spent summers on Deer Isle for 120 years.

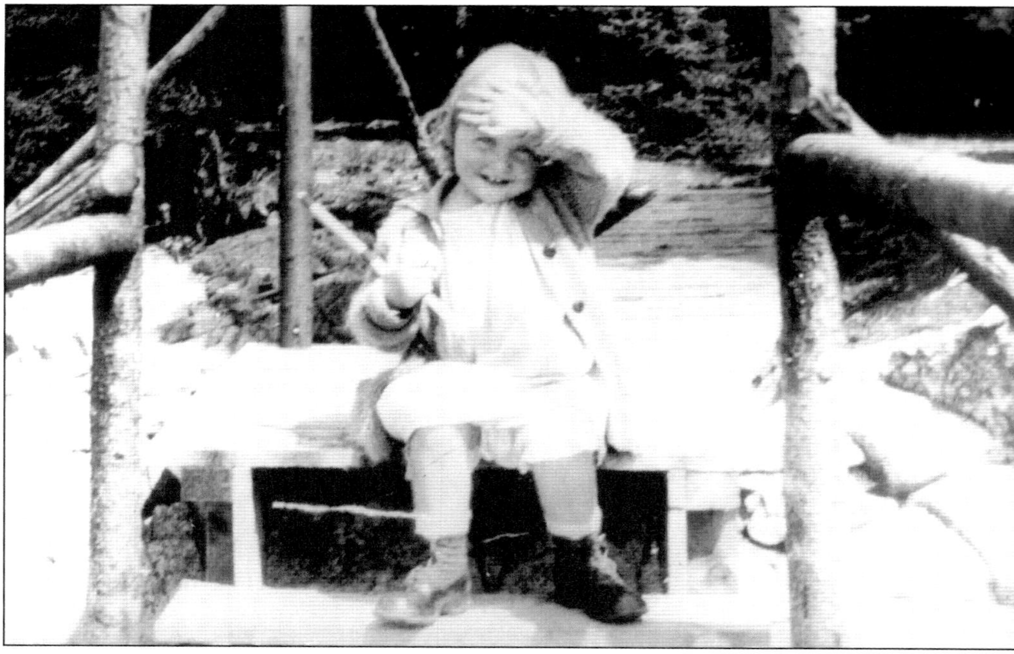

In 1927, Mayotta Southworth Kendrick sits on the first pier built for the Deer Isle Yacht Club.

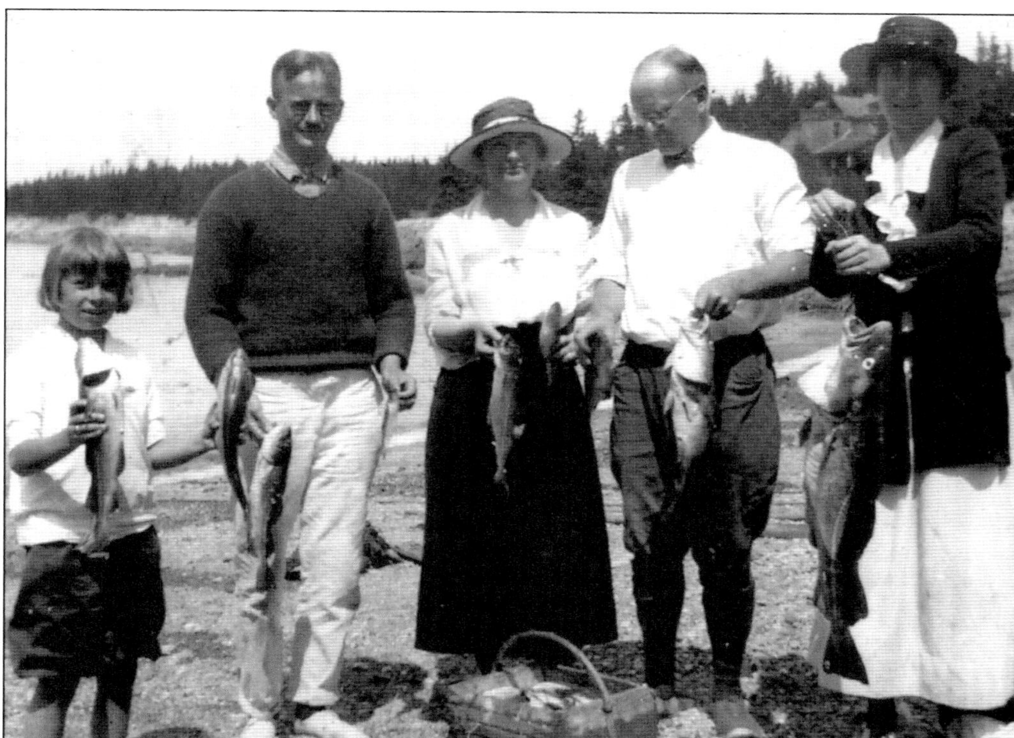

These fishermen are, from left to right, Betty Brown, Dwight Dickinson, Mayotta and Melvin Southworth, and Helen Riley. The photograph was taken *c.* 1922.

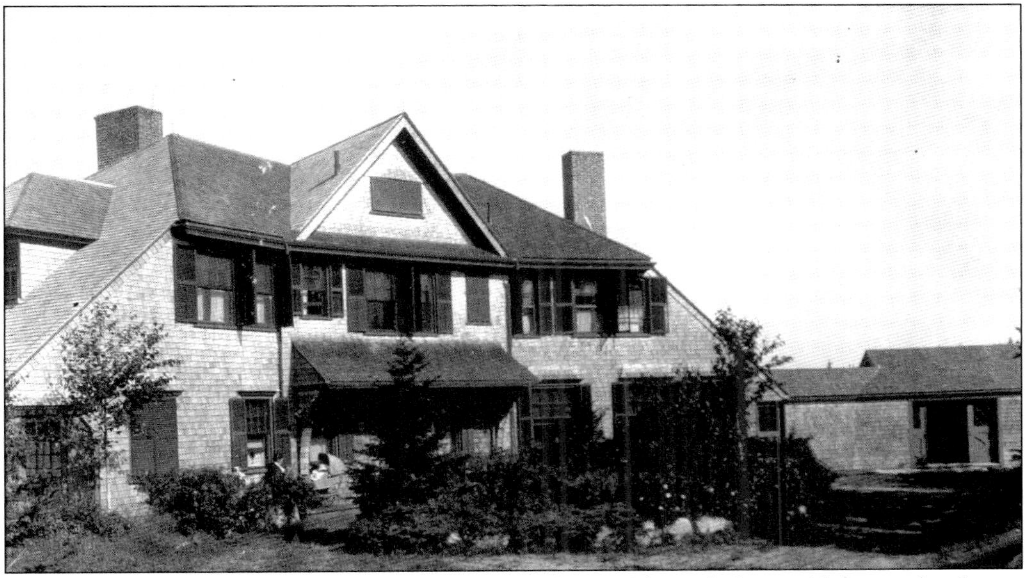

The Felsted was built in 1897 by the wife of Frederick Law Olmsted, the world-famous landscape architect, in the hope that it would help his failing health. He spent only one summer there before he required hospitalization. The house, now a National Historic Site, was designed by William R. Emerson and has been described as "a masterpiece of shingle style design." In the late 1920s, S. B. Knowlton bought the house, added a three-story wing, and converted it to a summer hotel. At the start of World War II, he sold it to people who tore down the wing and restored the house.

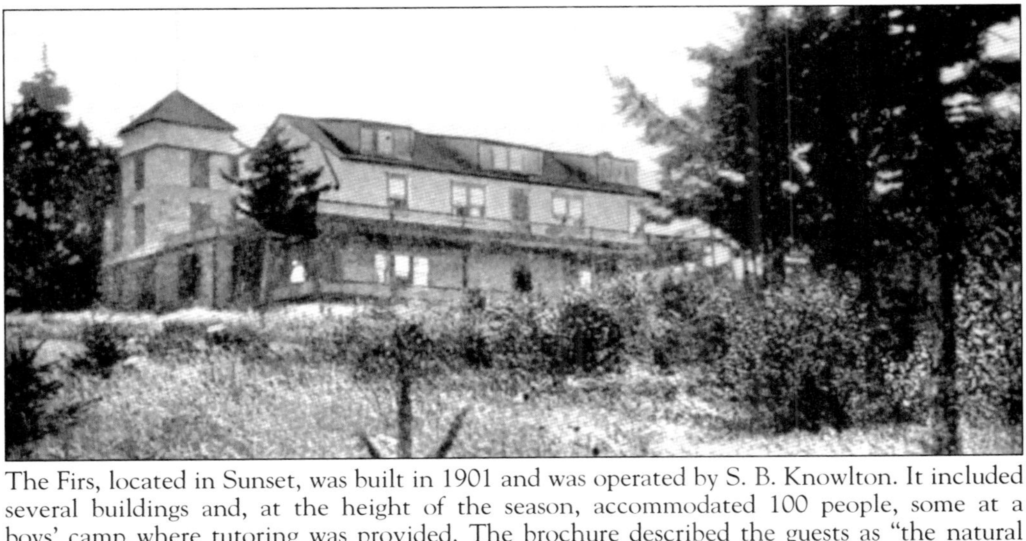

The Firs, located in Sunset, was built in 1901 and was operated by S. B. Knowlton. It included several buildings and, at the height of the season, accommodated 100 people, some at a boys' camp where tutoring was provided. The brochure described the guests as "the natural development of many years of conservative appeal to summer vacationists of the best sort." At the start of World War II, Knowlton, knowing that business would be poor, applied to the selectmen for a tax abatement. When his request was denied, he tore down the hotel.

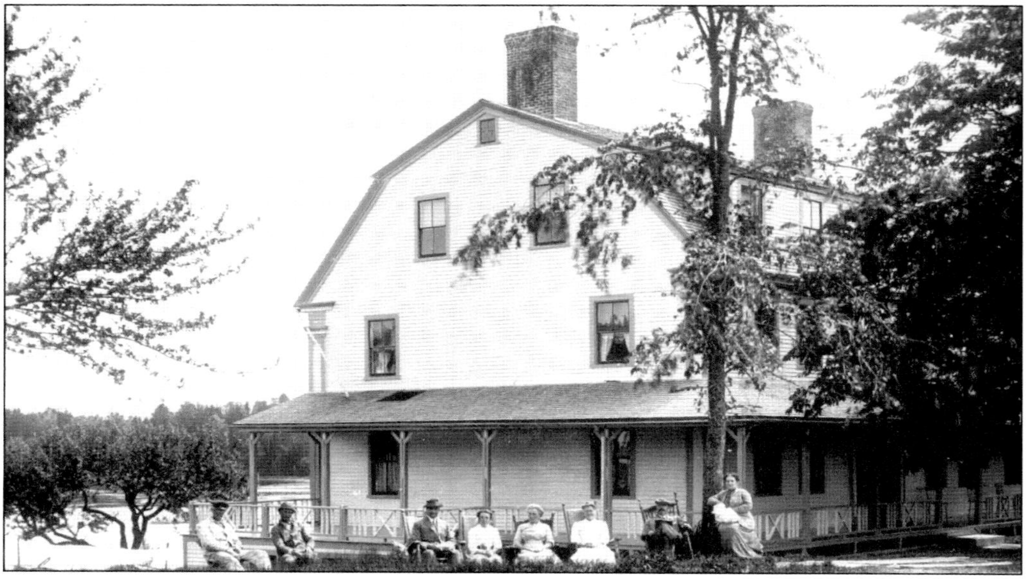

The Ark was built by Capt. Ignatius Haskell in 1793 as a home for his second wife, who wanted a house "like those she was accustomed to in Massachusetts." It remained a private home in the Haskell family until 1915, when William Haskell was lost at sea and his wife, Lizzie, turned her home into a boardinghouse. She added a porch full of long rows of rocking chairs for her guests, added bathrooms, and hung out a sign. Soon travelers began to stop there, returning year after year for her famous cooking. The Ark closed during World War II but later reopened as the Pilgrims Inn.

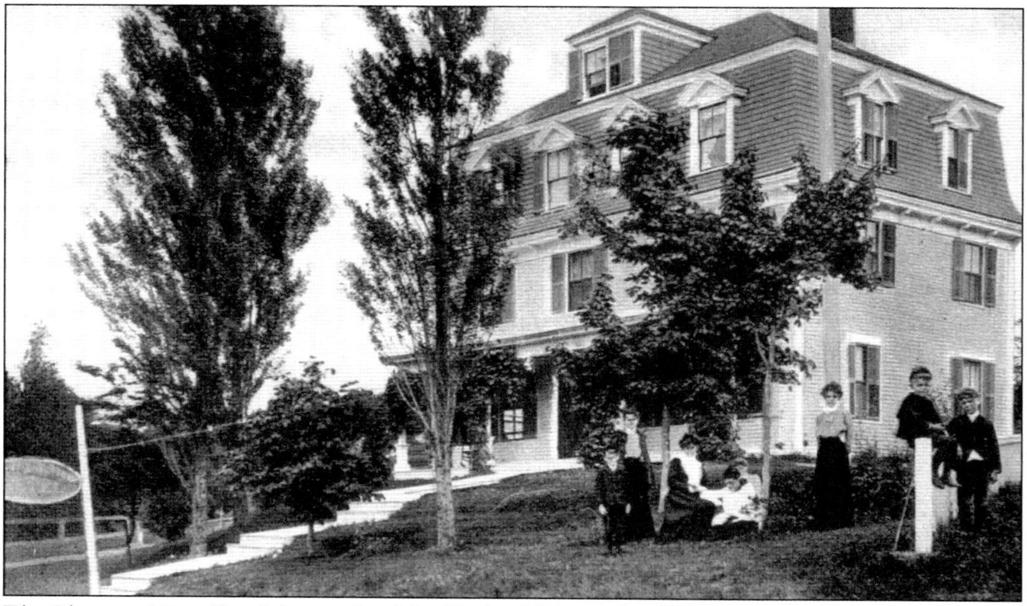

The Pleasant View Hotel, located in "the Harbor" (Deer Isle Village), advertised, "Pleasant View is just as good as it looks and it's certain it wouldn't look so good if it wasn't well patronized, and if it wasn't so well patronized it wouldn't look so good. Write for terms. S.S. Scott, Proprietor." Today, it is a privately owned home.

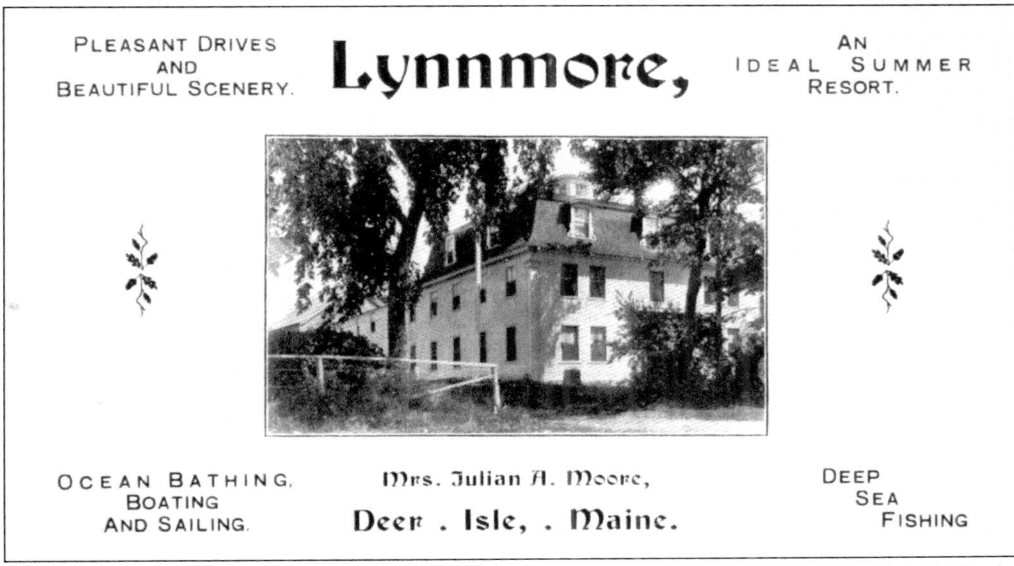

The Lynnmore Hotel was situated at the end of the main street of Deer Isle. In 1915, the *Rockland Courier Gazette* reported that "of the many splendid hotels on the numerous islands of the Penobscot Bay district, none have a wider reputation for fine service." The hotel was closed during the Depression, and part of it was made into a garage. After becoming a warehouse for the Barter Lumber Company, the structure burned down in 1954. Arthur Barter then built a house on the site.

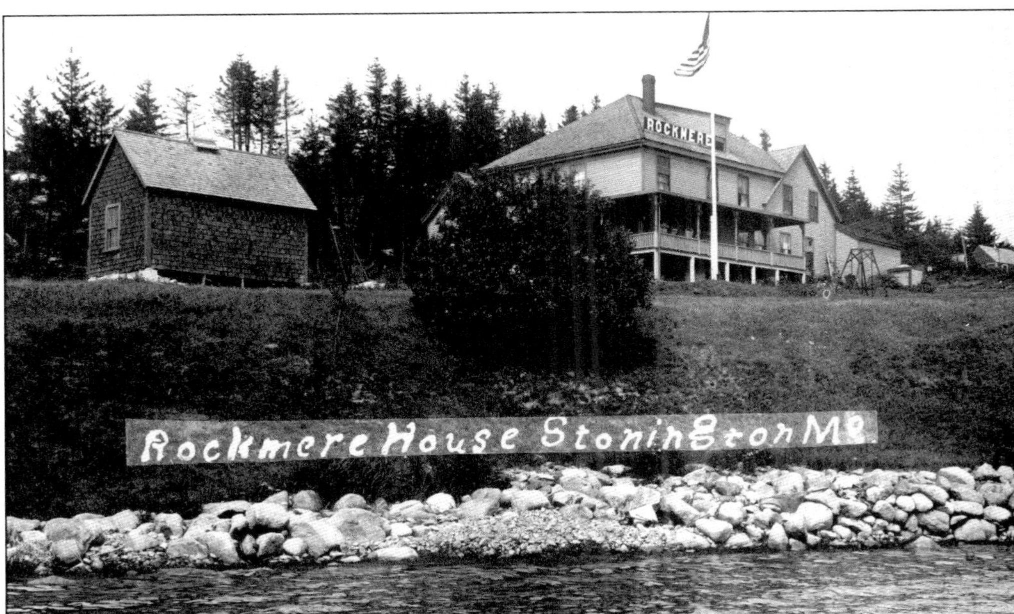

The Rockmere House, operated by Simon and Annie Goss, was located near the present lobster pounds across from Moose Island. It was lost to fire on a January night in 1915. The fire was discovered at 1:00 a.m. by "Mont" Sturdee, who was taking the Sand Beach Road on his way home from courting in the Burnt Cove area.

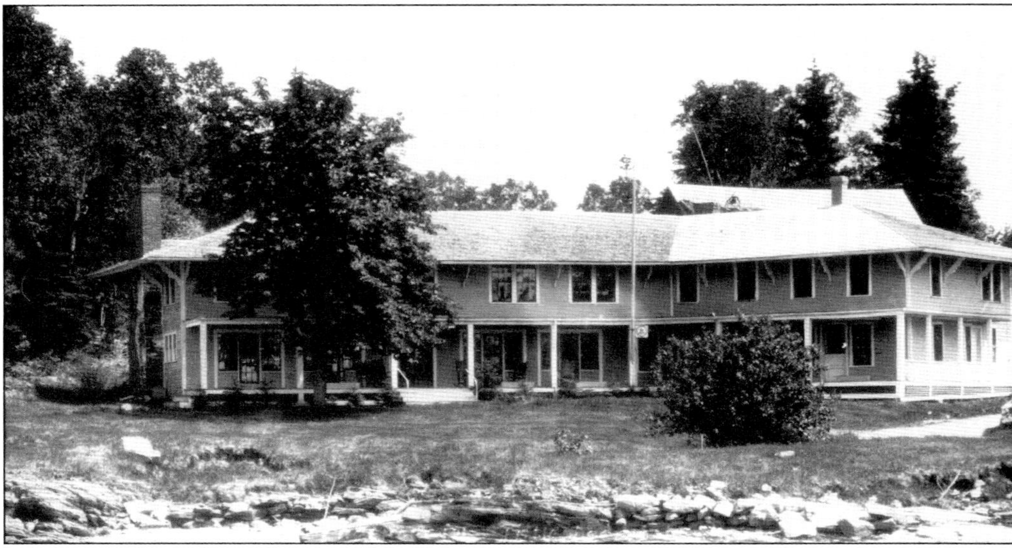

The founding of Babson's Inn marked the beginning of a summer colony on Little Deer Isle not long after the Civil War. Charles Babson was wounded on the battlefield during the war, and his leg was amputated to avoid gangrene. As compensation, the government gave him the position of lighthouse keeper at Pumpkin Island. With so much opportunity to view Indian Cove at Little Deer Isle, he envisioned and built, in 1880, what became known as "the Cookhouse," with cottages surrounding it. A number of people who stayed at Babson's either bought cottages from him or built their own. Seventeen of the original cottages still stand, though the Cookhouse was torn down.

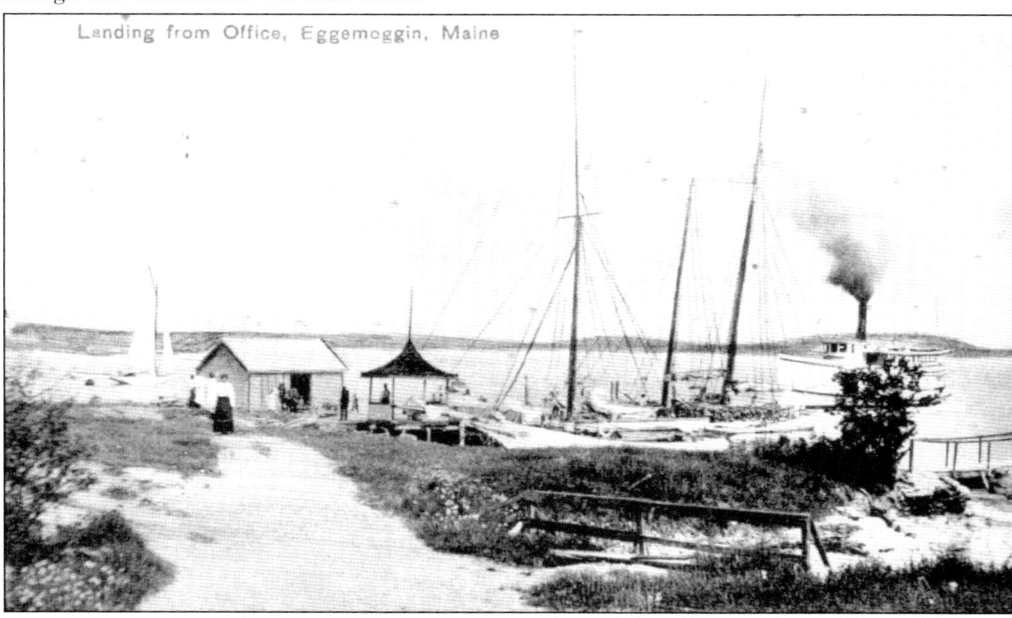

This c. 1908 postcard photograph shows the steamboat landing at Eggemoggin, as it appeared from the office of Babson's Inn. The steamer *Juliette* approaches on the right, and a sloop unloads lumber. The postcard was sent by a woman who had arrived on the *Juliette* from Rockland, where connections were made with steamers from Boston.

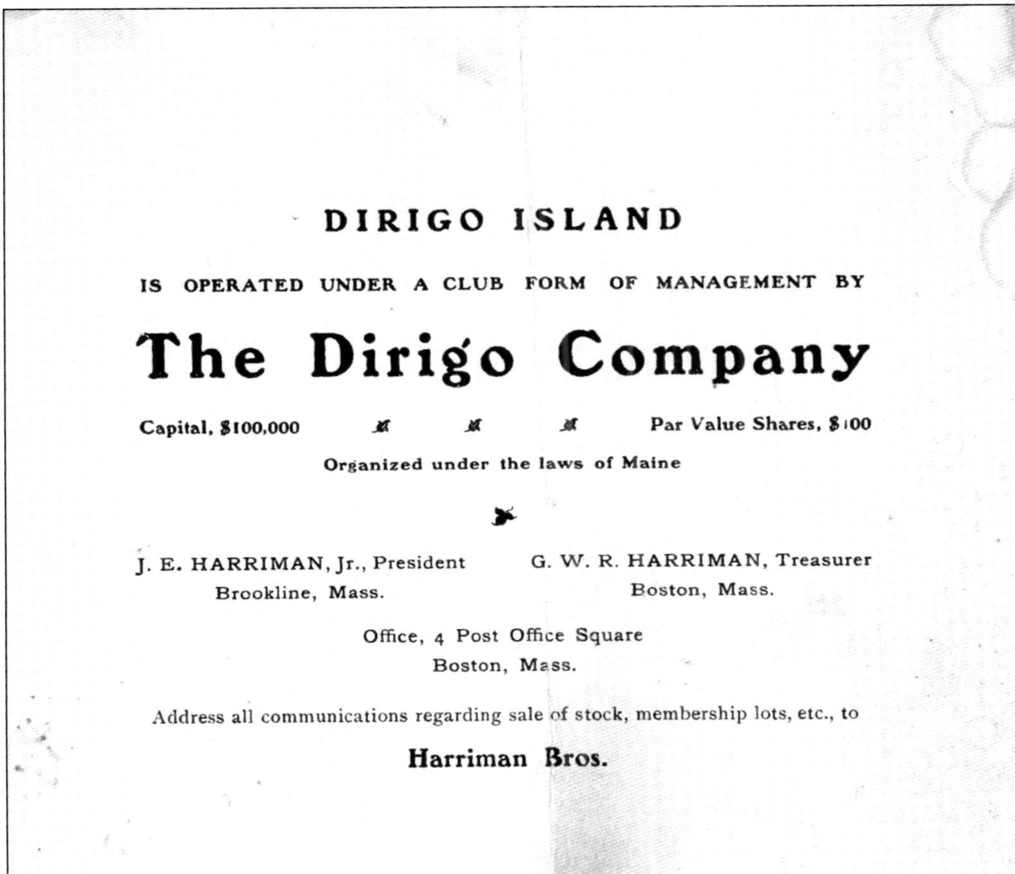

DIRIGO ISLAND

IS OPERATED UNDER A CLUB FORM OF MANAGEMENT BY

The Dirigo Company

Capital, $100,000 — Par Value Shares, $100

Organized under the laws of Maine

J. E. HARRIMAN, Jr., President
Brookline, Mass.

G. W. R. HARRIMAN, Treasurer
Boston, Mass.

Office, 4 Post Office Square
Boston, Mass.

Address all communications regarding sale of stock, membership lots, etc., to

Harriman Bros.

In 1895, brothers George and Emory Harriman purchased Butter Island for the purpose of developing a resort that they envisioned as a village of tents and cottages to be called Dirigo. Existing farm buildings were used as dining and club areas. They hoped to attract "genteel Bostonians" and professionals who would become landowners there. Charles McLane, in *Islands of the Mid-Maine Coast*, reports that in the period from 1905 to 1910, the resort accommodated up to 150 guests, some living in their own cottages but most staying in the central buildings. Dirigo had its own steamboat landing, where regular stops were made. The emphasis was on healthy outdoor living, with lots of hiking and boating. Each August featured a regatta and boat race. World War I brought about the end of the resort; only cellar holes remain.

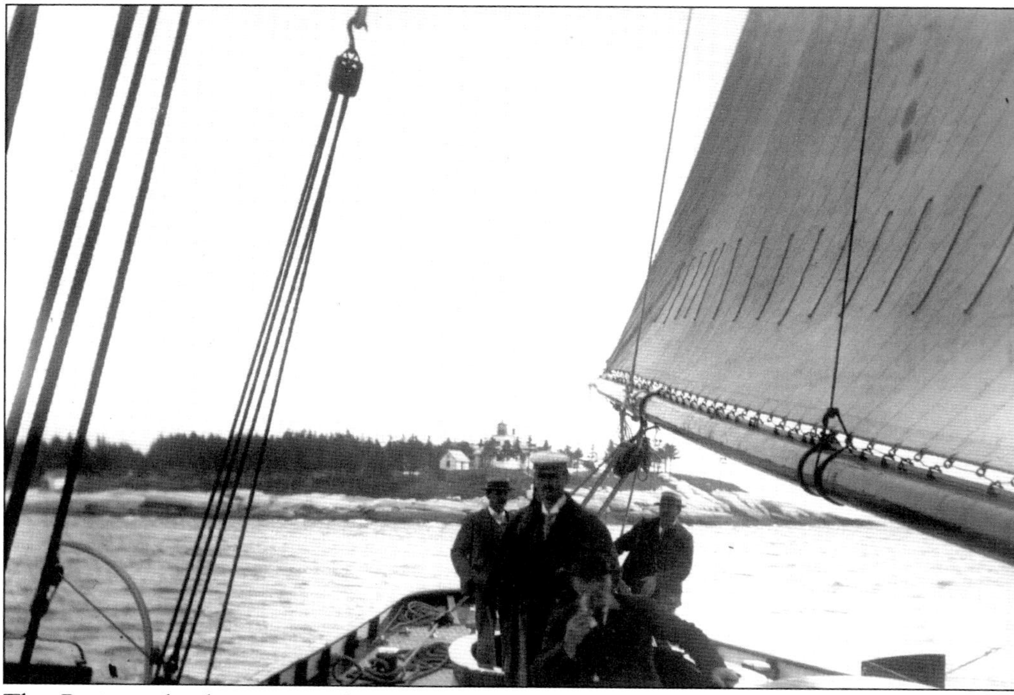

The *Puritan*, also known as "the Boston Bean Boat," belonged to the Eastern Yacht Club syndicate when she successfully defended the America's Cup against England in 1884. That autumn, she was sold to J. Malcolm Forbes of New York, who sailed her both as a sloop and a schooner. Here, as a schooner, she sits off Mark Island Light in 1889.

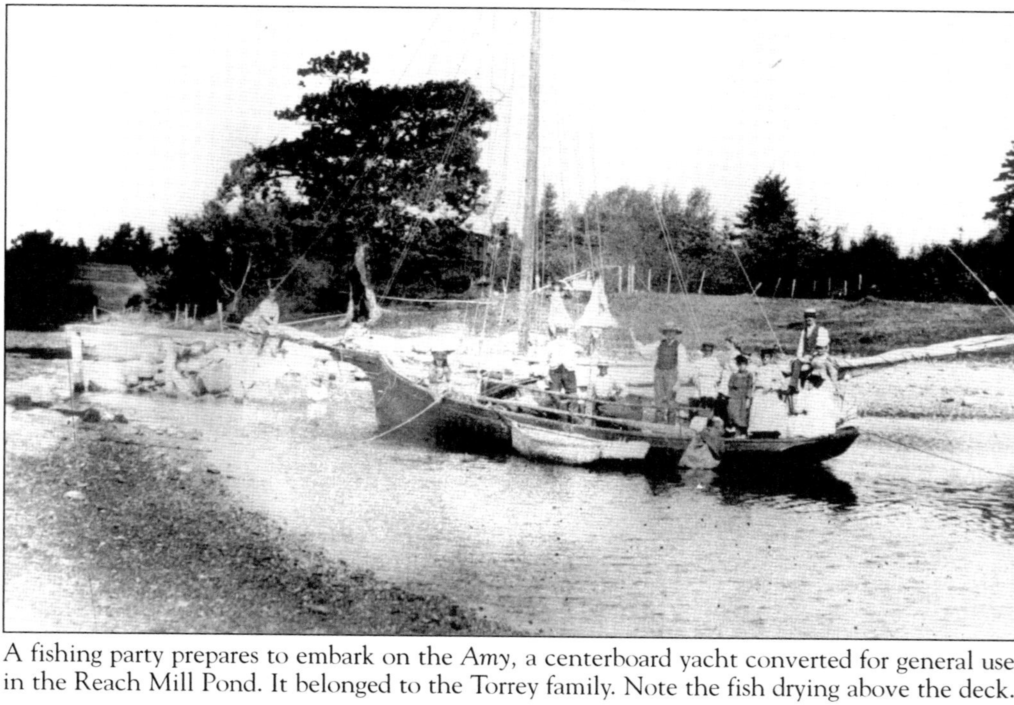

A fishing party prepares to embark on the *Amy*, a centerboard yacht converted for general use, in the Reach Mill Pond. It belonged to the Torrey family. Note the fish drying above the deck.

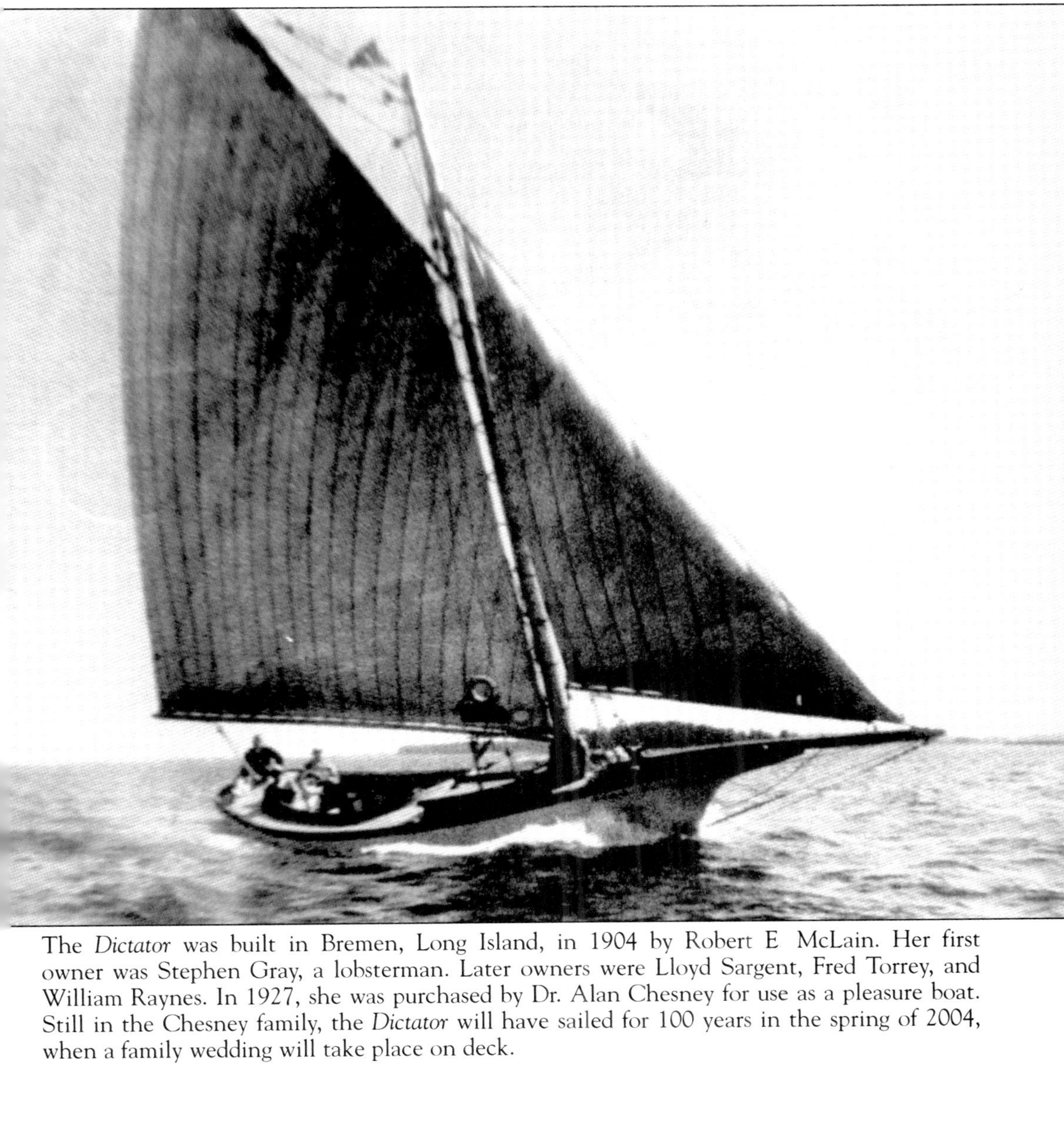

The *Dictator* was built in Bremen, Long Island, in 1904 by Robert E McLain. Her first owner was Stephen Gray, a lobsterman. Later owners were Lloyd Sargent, Fred Torrey, and William Raynes. In 1927, she was purchased by Dr. Alan Chesney for use as a pleasure boat. Still in the Chesney family, the *Dictator* will have sailed for 100 years in the spring of 2004, when a family wedding will take place on deck.

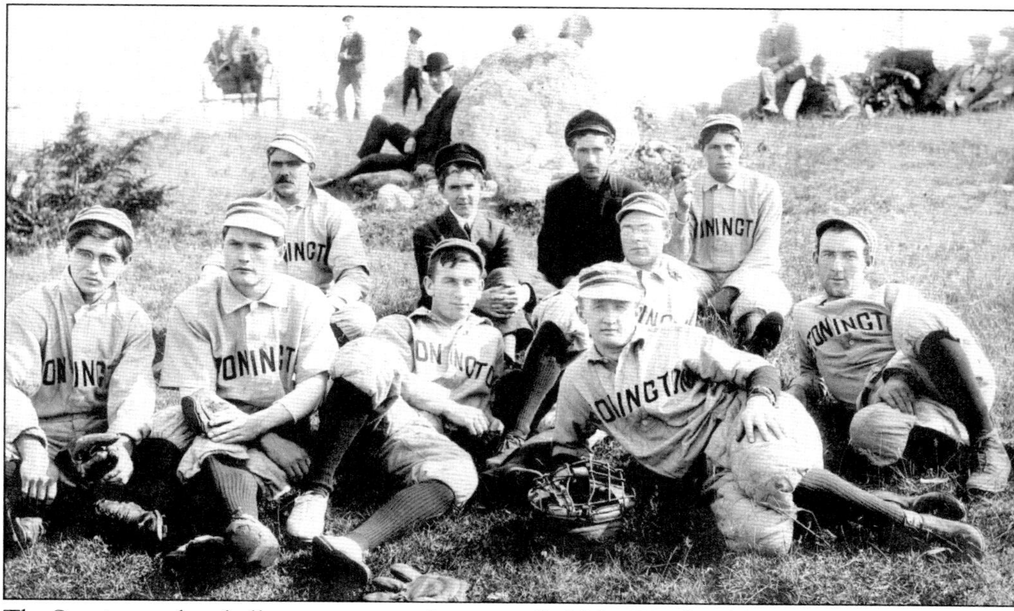

The Stonington baseball team poses in what was called "the Weed Field," c. 1909. Team members, from left to right, are as follows: (first row) Frank Kelley, Howard Cody, James McGuire, David J. White, and Jack Dennan; (second row) John H. Bowen, manager Frank Webb, ? Robinson (a pitcher brought in from Blue Hill), and Malcolm Williams. On the skyline at left, in a gig, are Dr. B. Lake and Linnie Noyes.

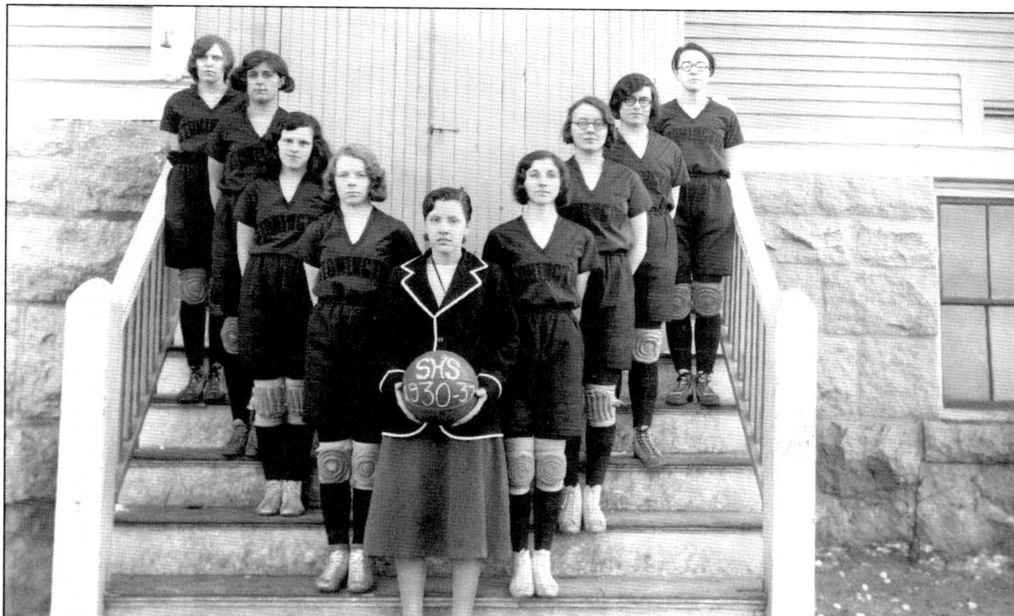

The Stonington High School basketball team of 1930–1931 won the Hancock County girls' championship. Seen here, from left to right, are Eleanor Hardy, Helen Smith Scarci, Gertrude Smith, Veronica McGuire, Helen Cousins, Emily Shepard, Arlene Hendricks, Louise Wallace, and Grace Ethel Faulkingham.

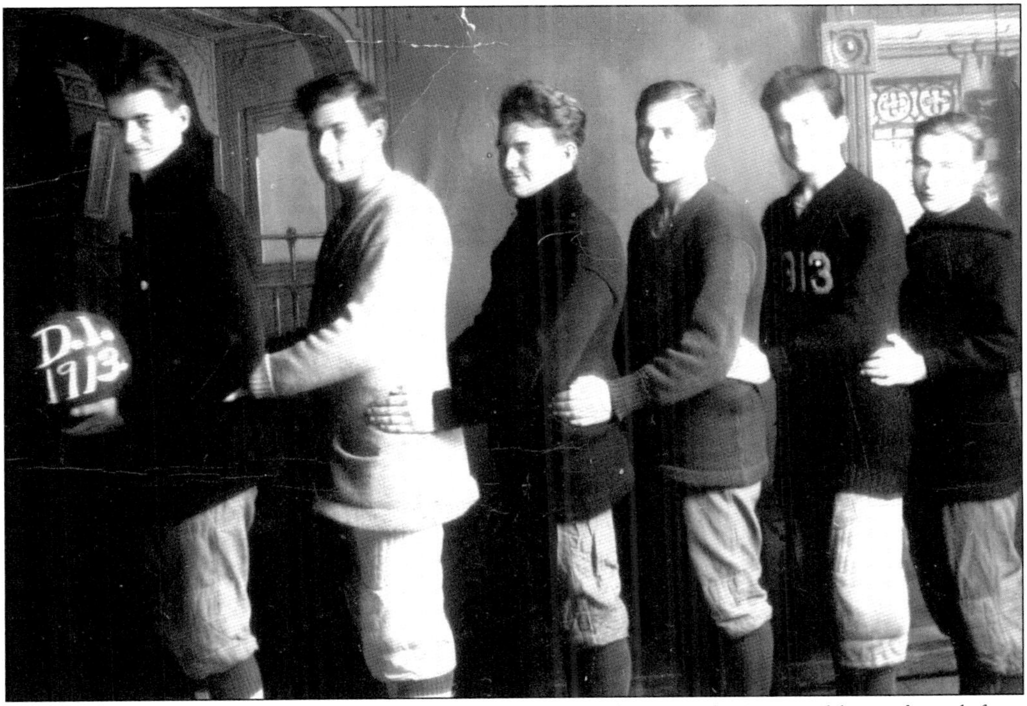

The Deer Isle boys basketball team of 1913 poses for a photograph. Pictured here, from left to right, are Malcolm Carman, Allen Smith, Stacy Haskell, Spofford Thompson, Maurice Gross, and Robert Haskell.

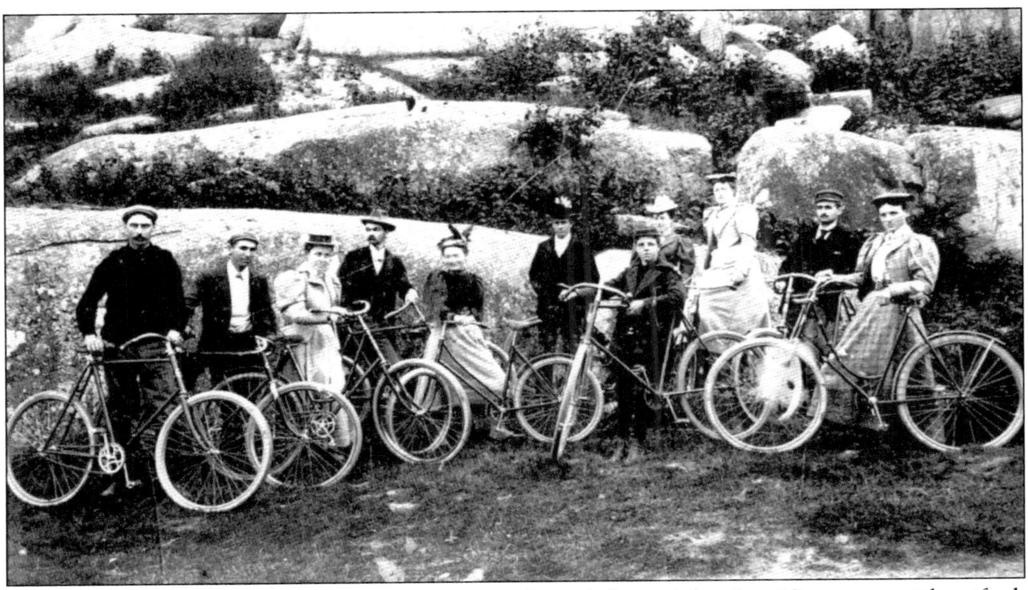

Posing with their bicycles in Stonington are, from left to right, Joe Harmon, unidentified, Annie Thurlow, Dr. B. Lake Noyes, Edith Simpson, James Thurlow, Alice Jones, Madge Small, Lottie Sawyer, Jewett Noyes, and Cora Gray.

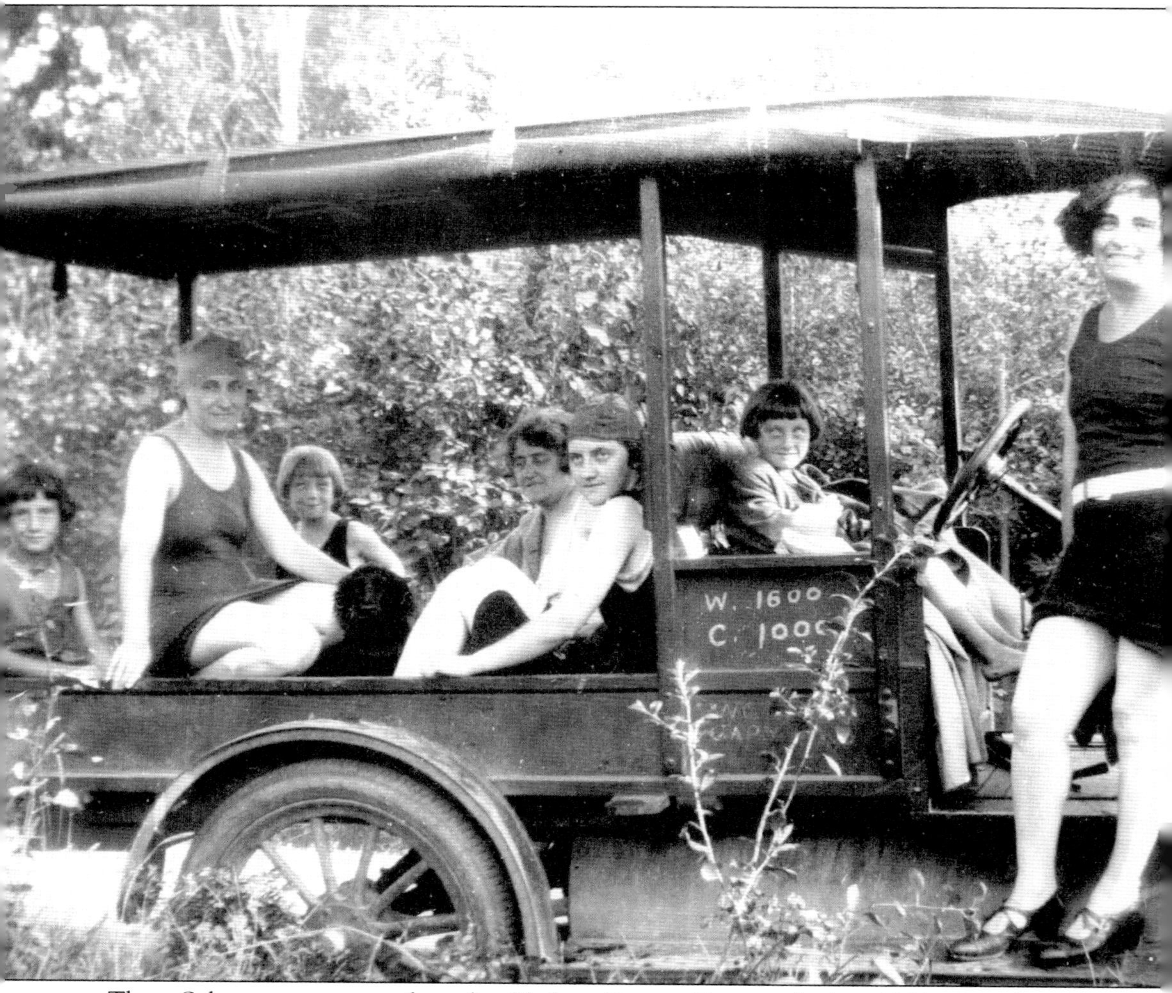

These Sylvester women go for a dip, likely at Pressey Cove in the late 1920s. Seen here, from left to right, are Arlene (Sylvester) Kydd, Carlotta (Green) Brimigion, Norma (Sylvester) Heanssler, Lillian (Green) Sylvester, Dorothy (Sylvester) Carman, Neva (Sylvester) Beck, and Alberta (Sylvester) Reed. They are in Elwyn Sylvester's ice truck.

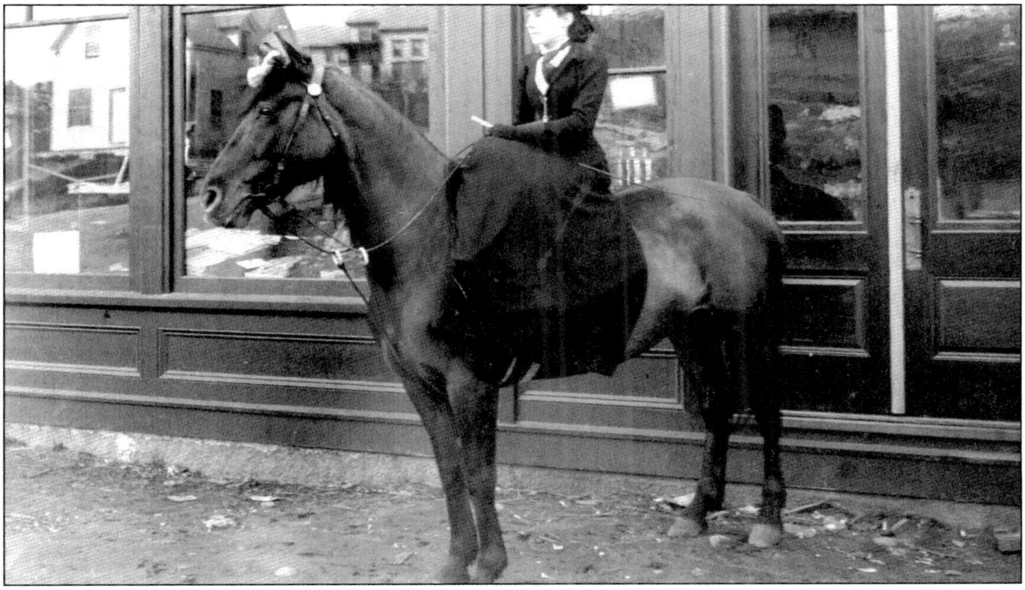

This *c.* 1895 photograph shows Madge (Brimigion) Small atop a horse from her father's stable and livery business. She poses in front of the Stonington Hotel on Main Street. Joseph Brimigion's stable was at the top of Russ's Hill, an area that is reflected in the hotel's windows. Madge was a longtime piano teacher in Stonington.

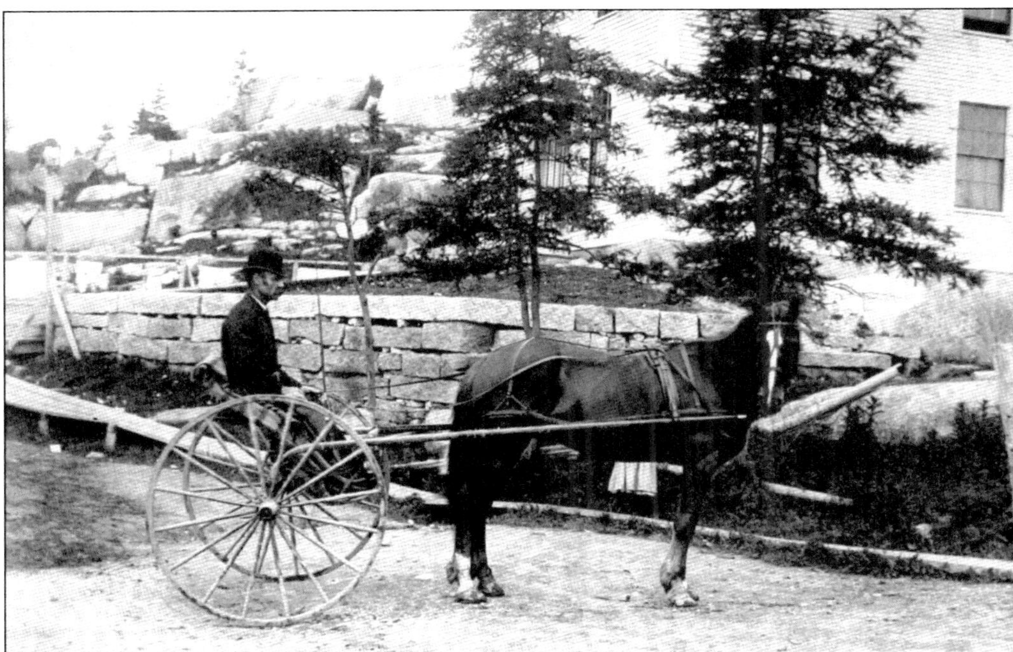

Benjamin Small of South Deer Isle appears with his horse, Bob Knox. They were in many races in Bangor. This photograph was taken in 1891 in front of what is now the town hall in Stonington.

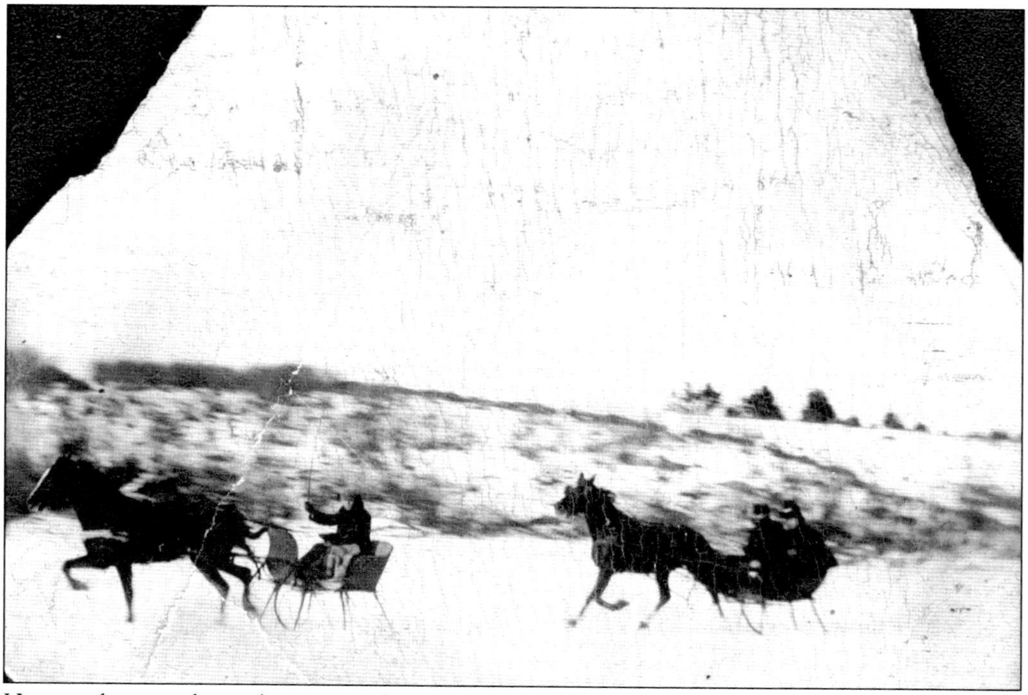

Horses also raced on the ice at the Lily Pond in Deer Isle. Though the horse Bob Knox participated in these races, we do not know if he appears in this photograph.

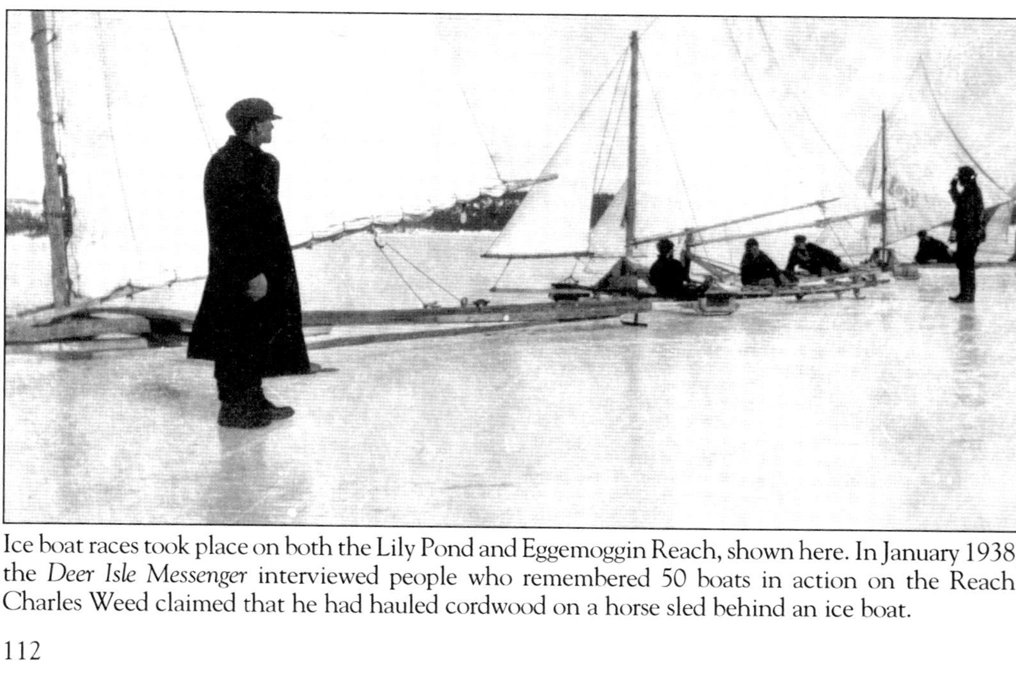

Ice boat races took place on both the Lily Pond and Eggemoggin Reach, shown here. In January 1938, the *Deer Isle Messenger* interviewed people who remembered 50 boats in action on the Reach. Charles Weed claimed that he had hauled cordwood on a horse sled behind an ice boat.

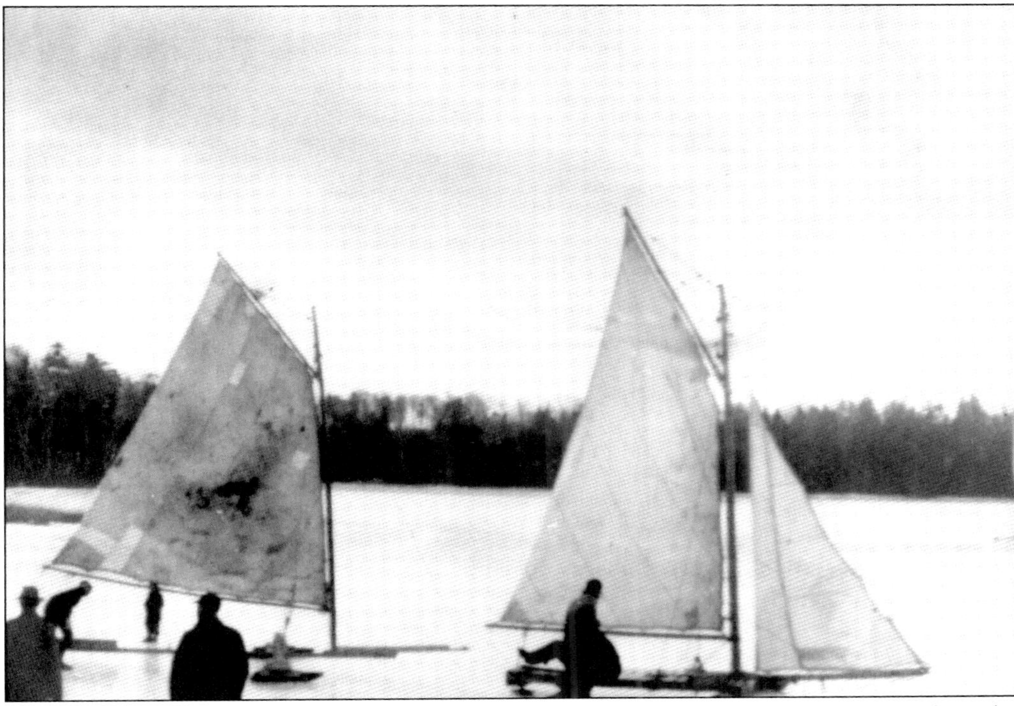

Ice-boating on the Mill Pond was one of the most popular winter sports *c.* 1935, when this photograph was taken. Those standing, from left to right, are Reg Eaton, George Torrey, unidentified, and Orrin Eaton. George Lane Beck is seated. Young and old alike participated in this sport.

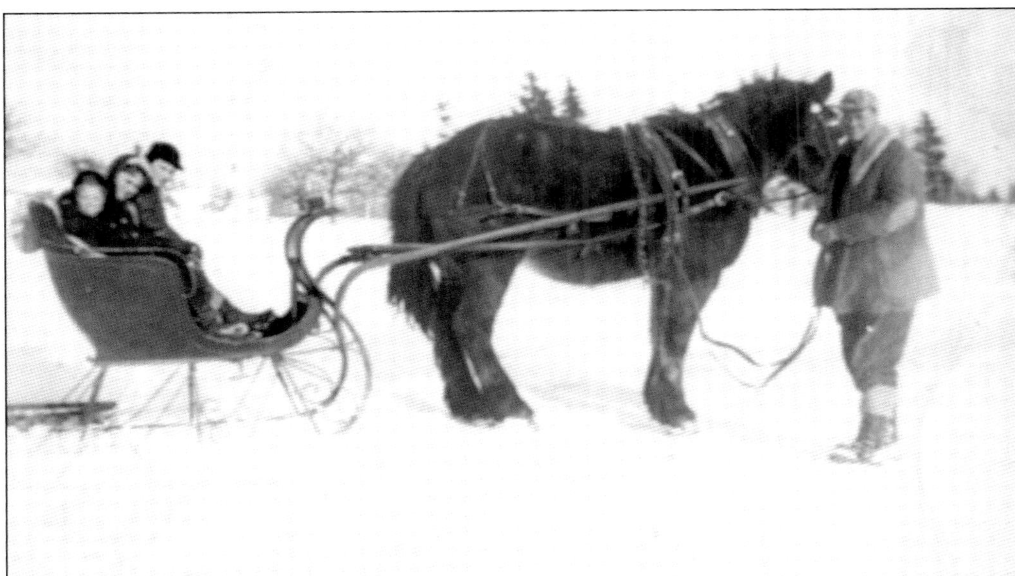

In this *c.* 1946 photograph, Francis "Skinner" Williams takes his children—Elaine, Bobby, and Don—for a sleigh ride with his horse Queen.

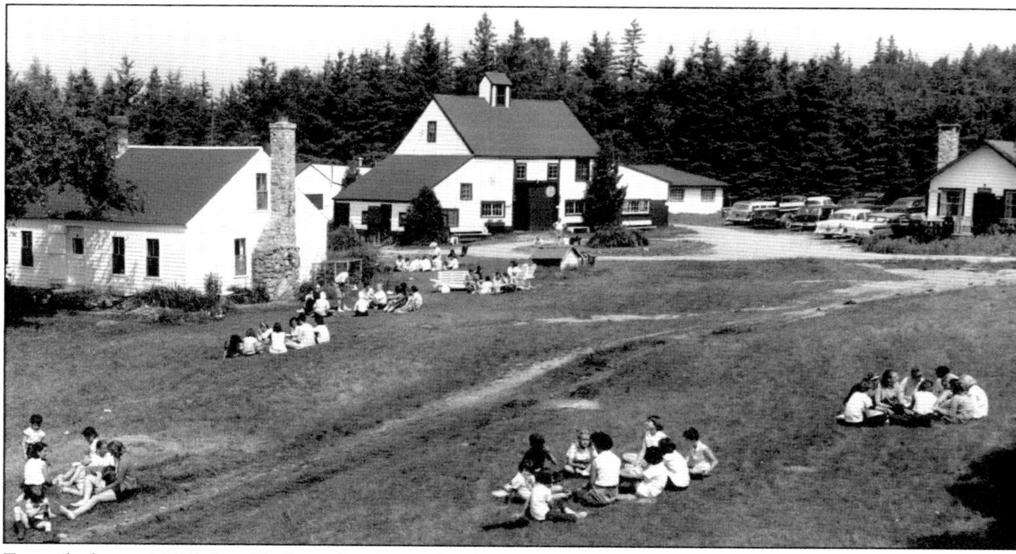

Founded in 1937 by Helma Bush and Elsa (James) Zelley, Les Chalets Francais, known locally as "the French Camp," began with 12 campers on a 97-acre tract of land and grew to 250 campers on 200 acres. The major purpose of the camp was to teach written and spoken French. This photograph shows the girls in a French class. In the center is La Grange, the barn and the center of camp activities. The camp also featured sailing, horseback riding, ballet, and other sports. The camp was sold in 1975. The property has now been divided into several privately owned lots.

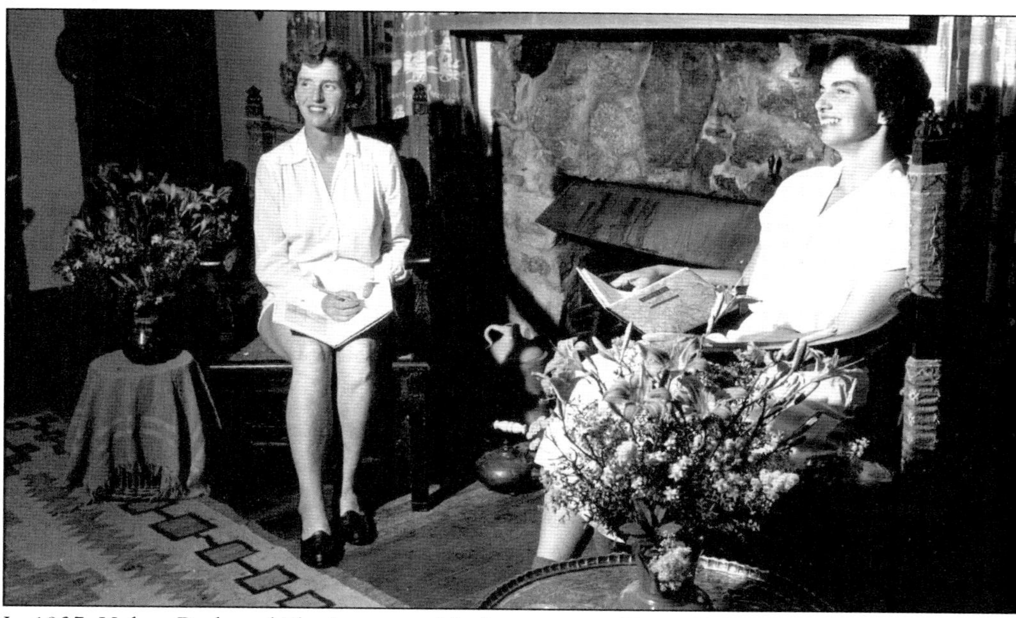

In 1937, Helma Bush and Elsa James—with their parents, Dr. and Mrs. George Nitzsche—came from Princeton, New Jersey, and Philadelphia to purchase property and to found the French Camp. In 1985, Elsa (James) Zelley counted 44 families or individuals who had moved to the island after attending Les Chalets Francais. Former campers continue to move to Deer Isle; some have started businesses here. The sisters both died in 2003.

Six

YACHTING

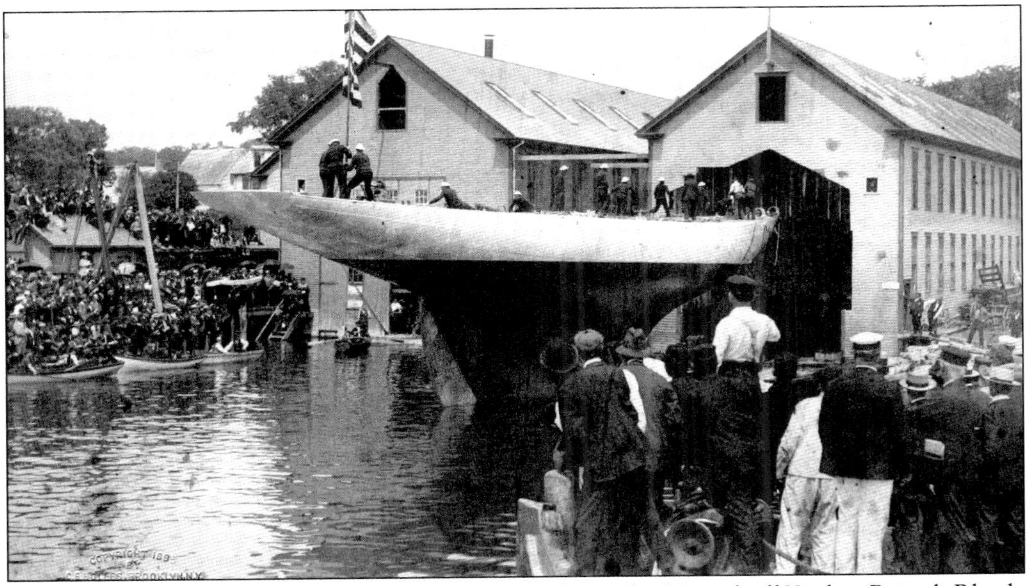

This photograph shows the launching of the *Defender* at the Herreshoff Yard in Bristol, Rhode Island. The year is 1895, and she will soon begin trials for the defense of the America's Cup. It is safe to say that among those watching, there are a number of sailors from Deer Isle. Capt. Hank Haff would have selected the crew already; he was the only crew member not from Deer Isle. Many of the sailors had already participated in Cup races, and most would go on to serve as the crew of the *Columbia*, three years later.

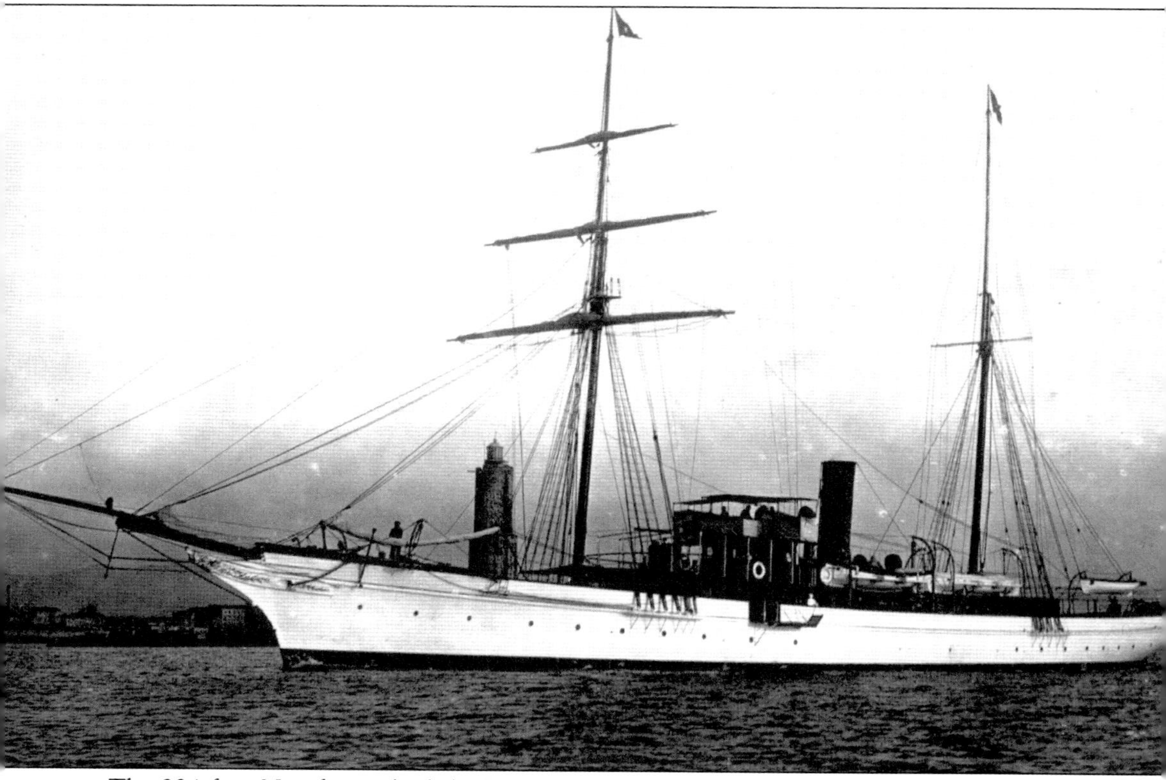

The 224-foot *Narada* was built by Ramage and Ferguson in Scotland in 1889. The owner was Henry Walters of Baltimore, Maryland. Lawrence Gross of Stonington was captain. Randall Haskell of Deer Isle was second mate, George and Frank Trundy of Stonington were seamen, and many other island men were crew members. Capt. Lawrence Gross was the brother of Seth Gross, captain of the large steam yacht *Whileaway*; they had both worked up through the ranks from seamen. *Narada* served as SP 161 during World War I.

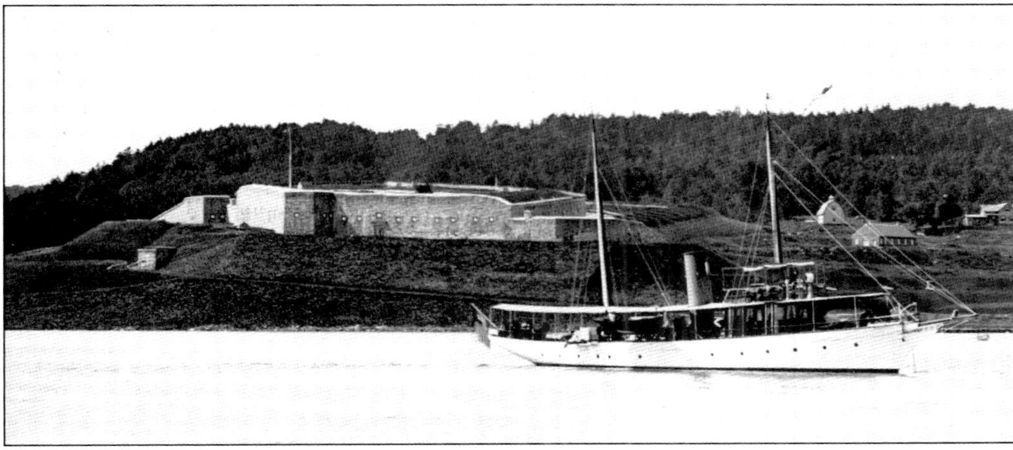

The 92-foot *Akela* was built by the G. E. & P. Seabury Company of Morris Heights, New York, in 1899. The owner was Henry A. Bishop of Bridgeport, Connecticut. Willie Green of Deer Isle was captain, and island men served as crew. Each season when Captain Green brought the yacht to Northwest Harbor at Deer Isle, an Akela Ball was held at the Deer Isle Town Hall. This photograph was taken in Bucksport. Note Fort Knox in the background.

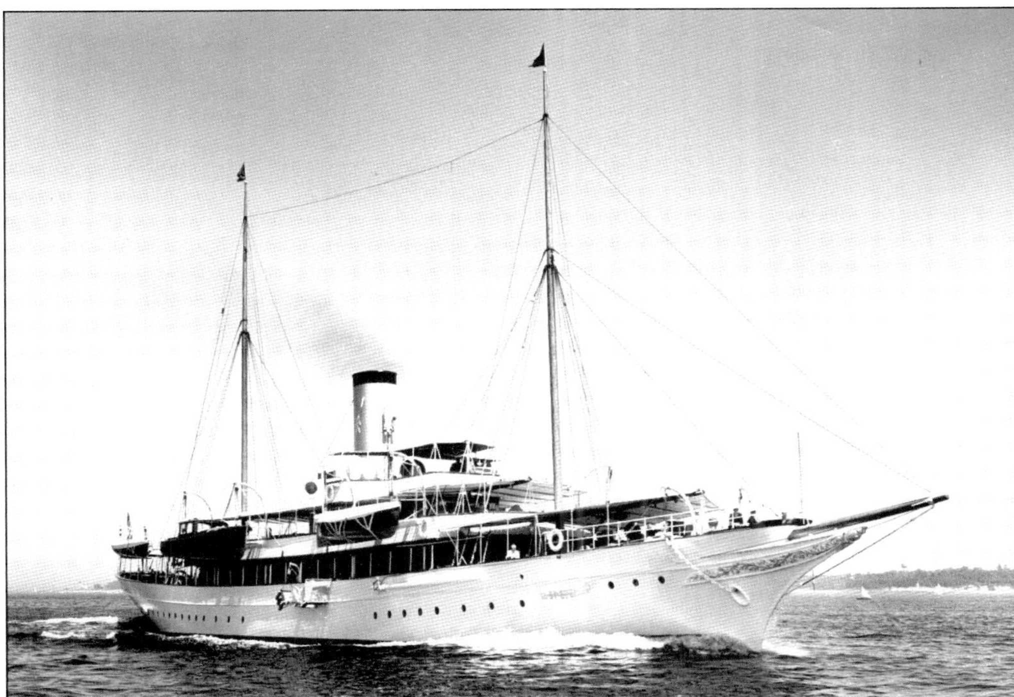

Ramage and Ferguson of Leith, Scotland, built the 179-foot *Cythera* in 1907. Kenneth N. Greenlaw of Deer Isle was second mate. She was owned by Edith H. Harkness of New York, who sold her to the U.S. Navy for $1 in the early days of World War II. The *Cythera*, sailing as the USS *Cythera* (PY 26), was torpedoed and sunk by a German U-boat in 1942. Captain Greenlaw served in the U.S. Merchant Marine and later became captain of several Isthmanian Line freighters.

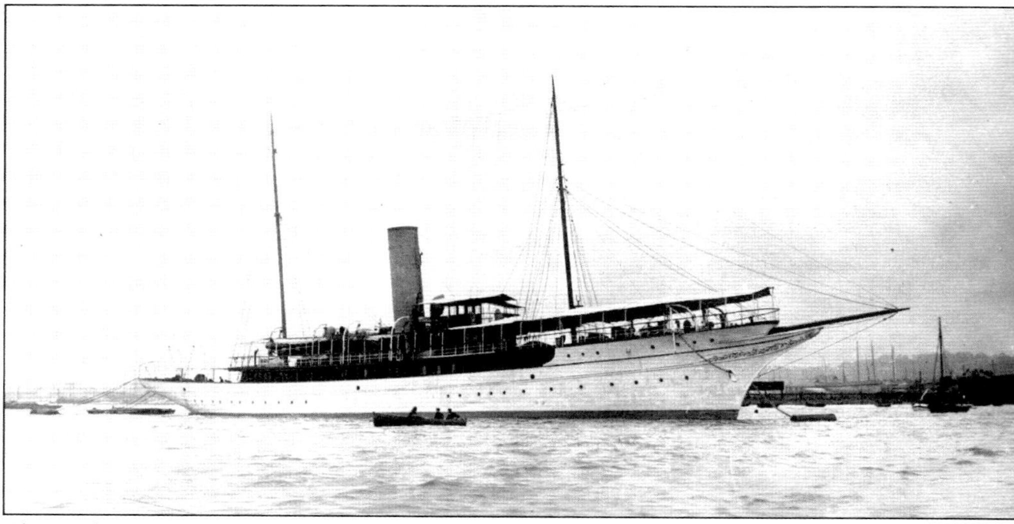

The *Wakiva*, 195 feet long, was also built by Ramage and Ferguson in 1907. The owner was Lamon V. Harkness of New York City. On a voyage to France in 1915, island crew members were Franklin Hardy, Morris Powers, and Alton Torrey. The *Wakiva* served in the U.S. Navy in World War I and was lost on convoy duty in 1918.

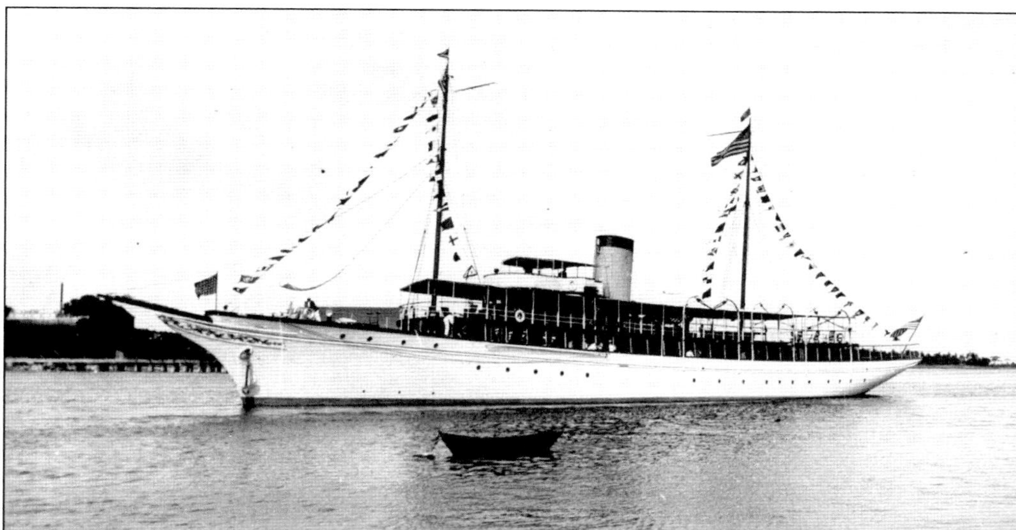

The *Lyndonia* was built by Consolidated Shipbuilding of Morris Heights, New Jersey, in 1920. Cyrus H. K. Curtis of Philadelphia and Camden, Maine, owned the 230-foot yacht. Island crew members were James Coombs and Leslie Conary.

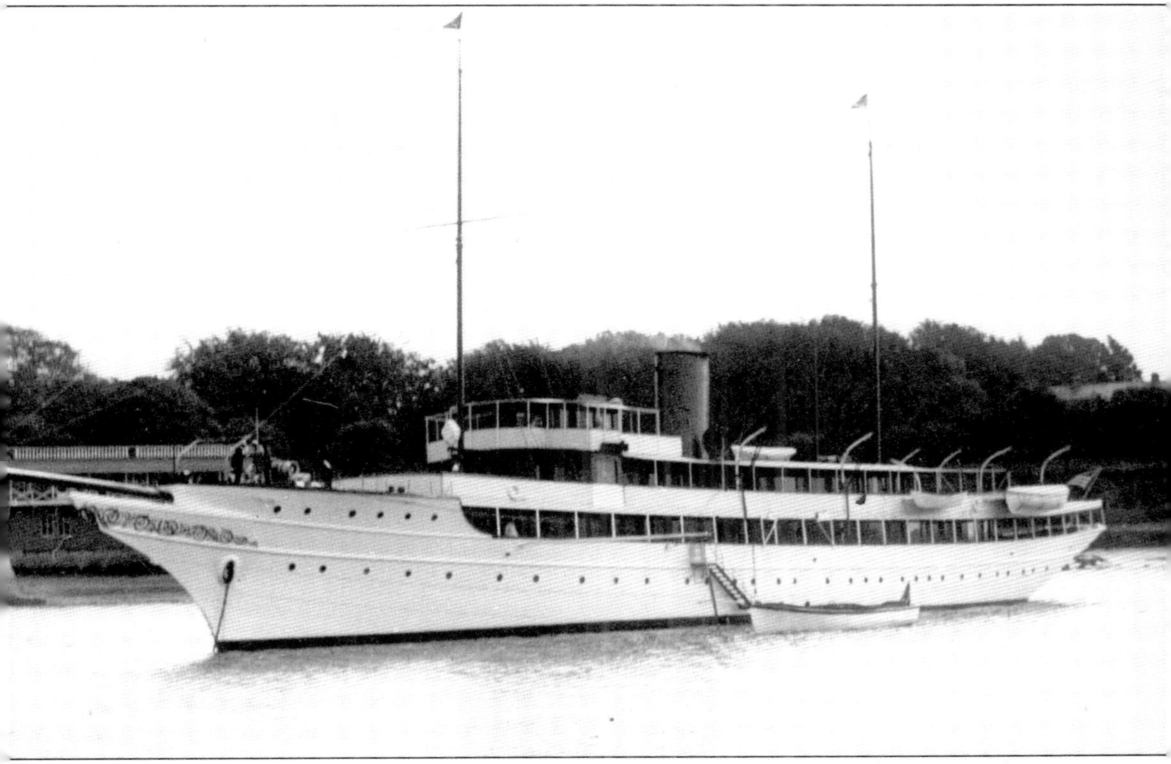

The *Camargo* was built by George Lawley & Sons of Neponset, Massachusetts, and was 221 feet long. She was owned by Julius Fleischmann. Captain was Charles Small, first mate was Merle Greene, and second mate was Norman Gray, all from Deer Isle. The port launch, shown in this photograph, was manned by Harold Turner of Isle Au Haut and later of Stonington. A large percentage of the crew was from the island. In the early 1930s, the *Camargo* made a voyage around the world accompanied by scientists and photographers working for the National Geographic Society. A 1934 issue of *National Geographic* focusing on the South Seas resulted. She was sold in the mid-1930s; her crew delivered her to the Dominican Republic, where she became the personal yacht of the dictator. The *Camargo* was purchased by the U.S. Government at the start of World War II and served as USS *Marcasite* (PY). She was recognized by Arthur "Dud" Haskell in Malta in 1951, though she was much altered.

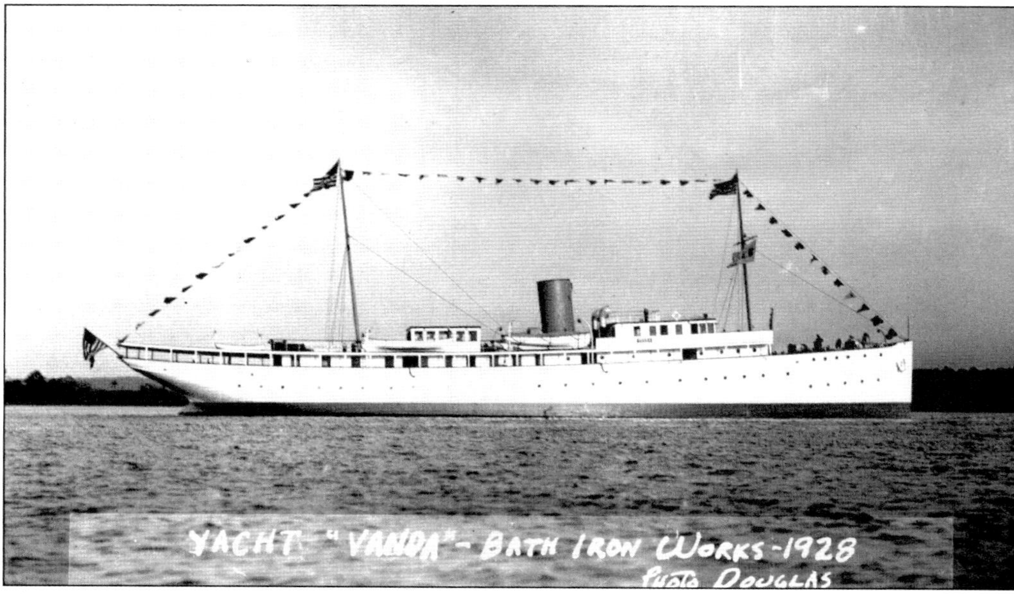

The *Vanda* was built at Bath Iron Works of Bath, Maine, in 1928. She was 240 feet long. The owner was Ernest B. Dane of Brookline, Massachusetts, and Seal Harbor, Maine. The chief mate was Elmer Dow of Deer Isle. Island crewmen were brothers Bradley and Clarence Sawyer of Stonington and George Lane Beck, Kenneth Pickering, and George Barbour of Deer Isle. The *Vanda* served in World War II as USS *San Bernardino* (PG 59).

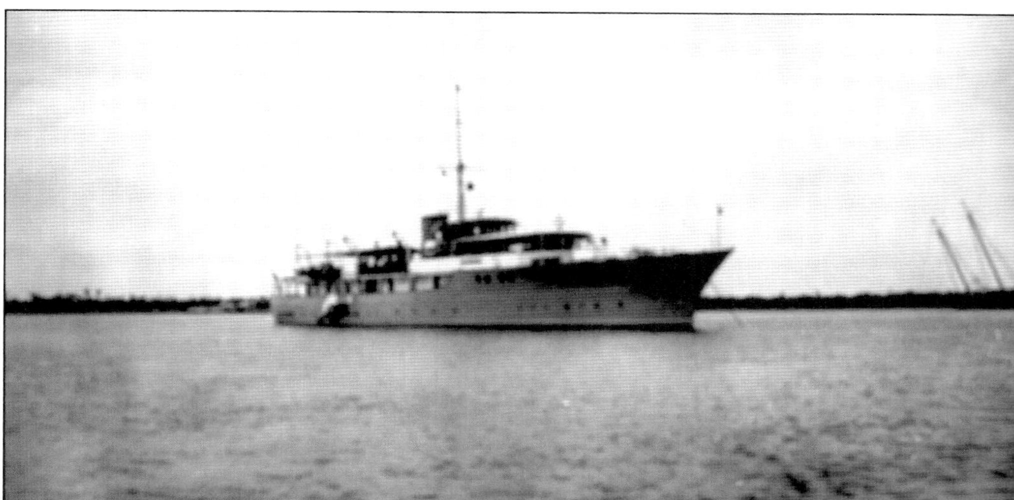

The *Lone Star* was built by Germania Werft of Kiel, Germany, in 1929 and was 161 feet long. Owned by Frederick H. Prince of Boston, she was captained by Robert Haskell of Deer Isle. Island seamen who served on the *Lone Star* were Reginald Greenlaw and Elmer Gross. The yacht served as USS *Moonstone* (PYC 9) in World War II and was lost in a collision in 1943.

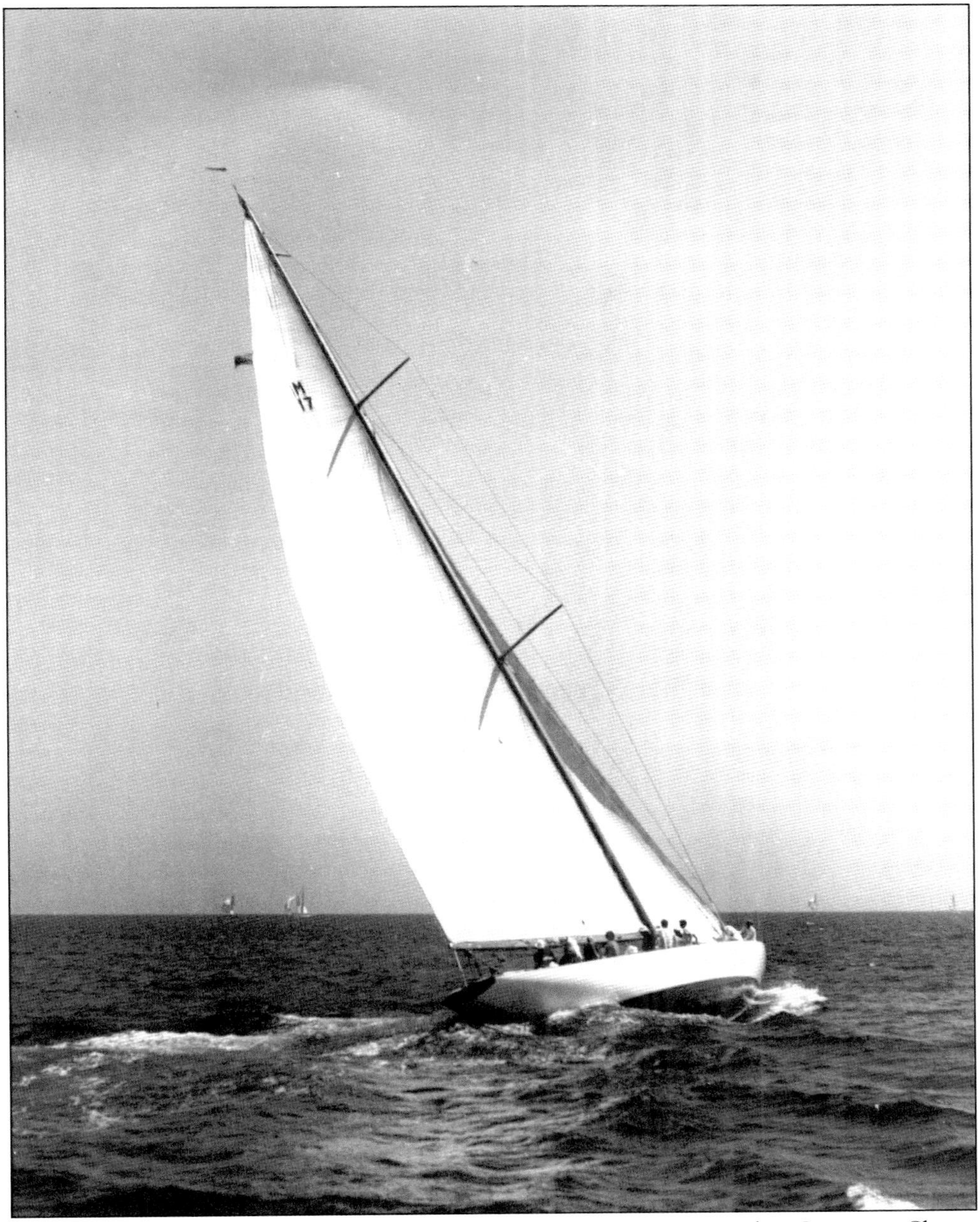

The *Patolita* was built in 1929 by Abeking and Rasmussen of Lemwarder, Germany. She was 53 feet long and was owned by Charles D. Wiman of Santa Barbara, California. Her captain was Fred D. Eaton Sr., and her mate was Fred D. Eaton Jr., both of Little Deer Isle. After racing on the Great Lakes in the early 1930s, the *Patolita* was sailed to California, where she competed in many races from the Santa Barbara area. These races culminated in the setting of the unofficial sailing record from Honolulu to Santa Barbara of 13 days and 15 hours. While racing near Catalina Island, Captain Eaton and deck hand Charles Davis were swept overboard when trimming sails. Captain Eaton was saved, but Davis could not be rescued. Fred Eaton Jr. succeeded his father as captain shortly thereafter.

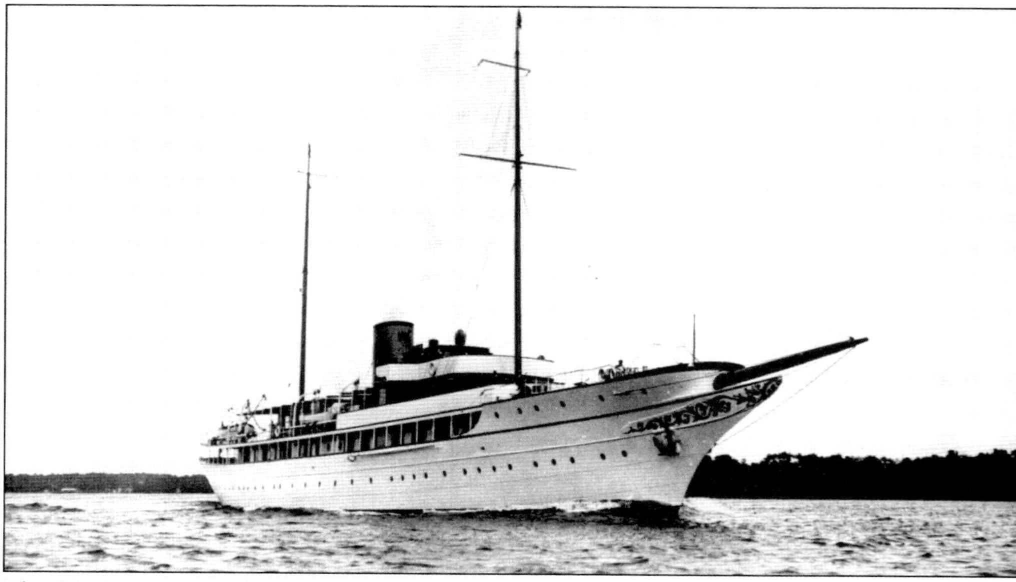

The *Hi-Esmaro*, 266 feet long, was built at Bath Iron Works of Bath, Maine, in 1929. Her owner was H. E. Manville of New York City, and her captain was Grover Small of Deer Isle. She was named for the Manville children: Hiram, Esther, Mary, and Robert. Capt. Grover Small and his brother Charles Small, master of the *Camargo*, worked their way to top command, as did the men of many other island families. A life ring from the *Hi-Esmaro* is on display at Mystic Seaport. She served as USS *Niagara* (PG 52) in World War II.

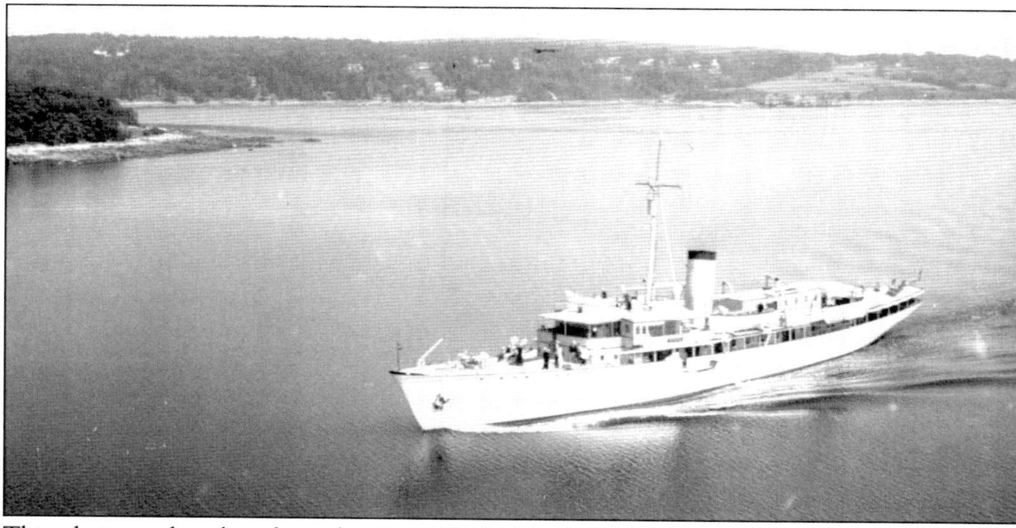

This photograph, taken from the Deer Isle-Sedgwick Bridge, shows the *Elpetal*. The 247-foot yacht was built in Kiel, Germany, in 1930 and was rebuilt from 1947 to 1949 at Bath Iron Works. The owner was Norman B. Woolworth, the first mate was Arthur "Dud" Haskell, the mate was Ernest Smith, the radio officer was Robert Thompson, and the second engineer was Frank Allen. Approximately 15 additional crew members from the island were on the yacht. An emergency appendectomy was performed on Dud Haskell aboard the *Elpetal* while returning from Europe. An intern operated, with the mate and the owner's wife assisting. The *Elpetal* served as USS *Beaumont* during World War II.

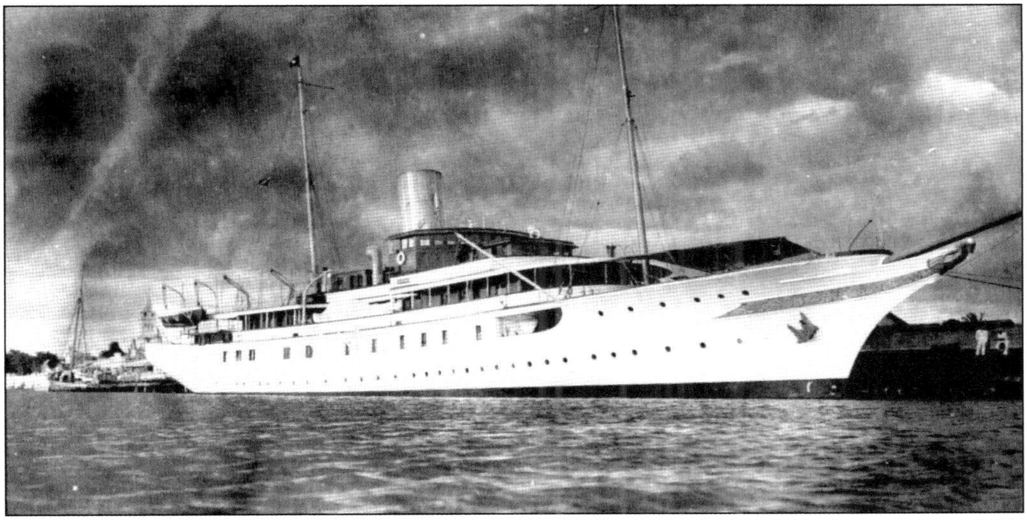

The 272-foot *Viking* was built by Newport News Shipbuilding of Norfolk, Virginia, in 1929; she was owned by George F. Baker Jr. of New York. Her captain was Edwin Thompson of Deer Isle. Also from Deer Isle were Maurice Powers, chief mate; Randall Haskell, second mate; Robert Thompson, radio officer; Allan Smith, second engineer; Percy Joyce, launch man; and approximately 20 other men. The *Viking* served as USS *St. Augustine* (PG 54) in World War II and was lost in a collision.

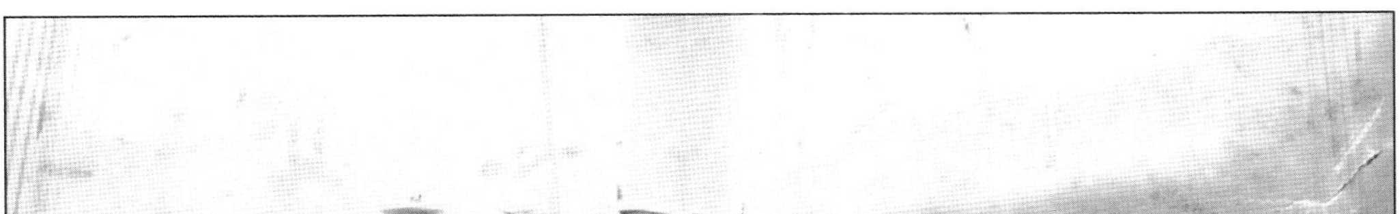

The crew of the *Constitution* poses for a formal photograph. The *Constitution* was built especially for the defense of the 1901 challenge against the *Shamrock II* for the America's Cup. In the preliminary trials, she proved to be a slower yacht than the *Columbia*, representing the United States. A large percentage of the crew was from Deer Isle.

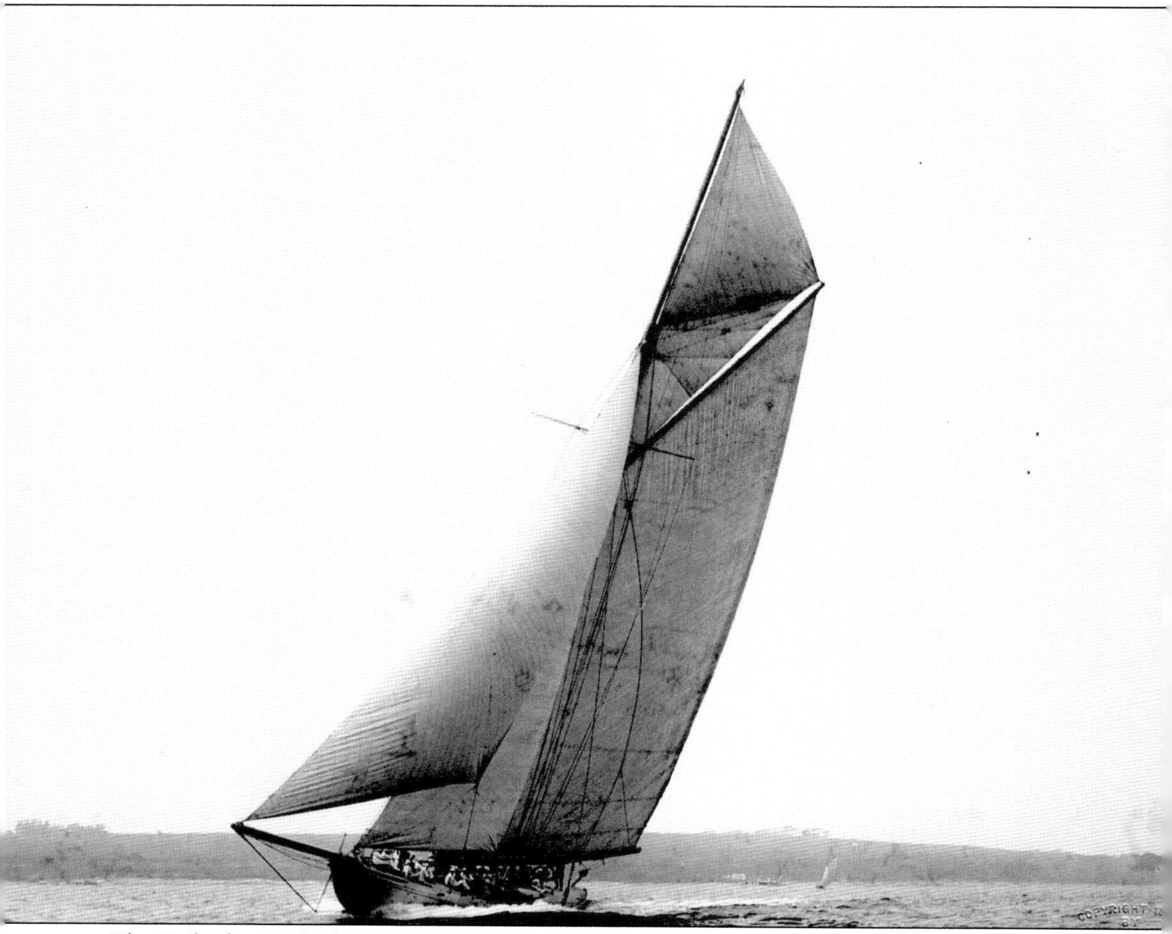

The *Defender* was built by Nathaniel Herreshoff at his shipyard in Bristol, Rhode Island, in 1895. The yacht was built for the New York Yacht Club syndicate, of which William K. Vanderbilt was chairman, for the 1895 defense of the America's Cup race against the British challenger *Valkyrie III*. The *Defender* was victorious.

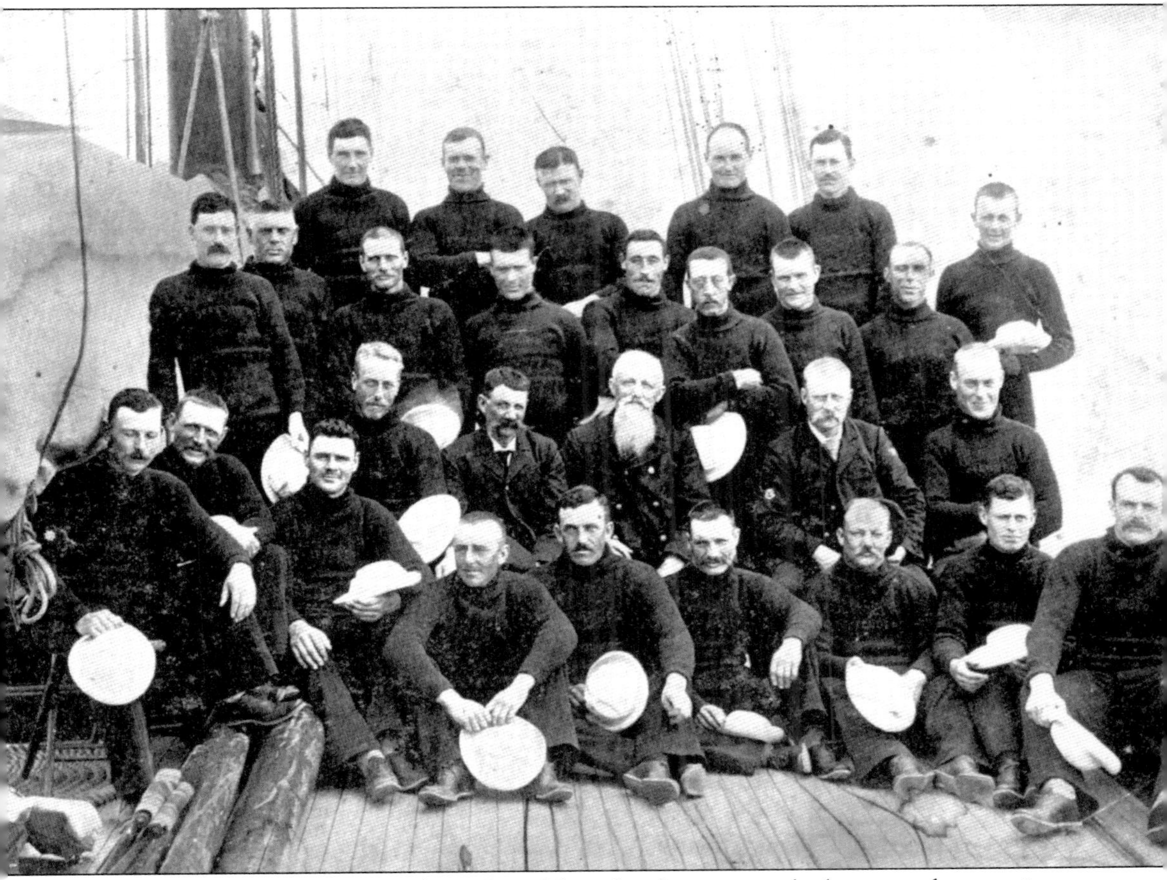

The crew of the *Defender* is shown here. Deer Isle sailors have created a legacy and reputation for seafaring accomplishments over the years. Some island men served on the *Mayflower* in 1886 and the *Volunteer* in 1887. Their reputation was such that C. Oliver Iselin of the New York Yacht Club selected Capt. Fred Weed of Deer Isle to recruit and train an island crew for the *Defender*, to sail under Capt. Hank Haff. At that time, it was the practice of local captains to recruit their crews at town meetings. More than 200 sailors applied to Captain Weed. Because he needed crews for two racing yachts so that trial races could be conducted, Captain Weed selected about 80 men. In the end, fewer than 30 served on the *Defender*.

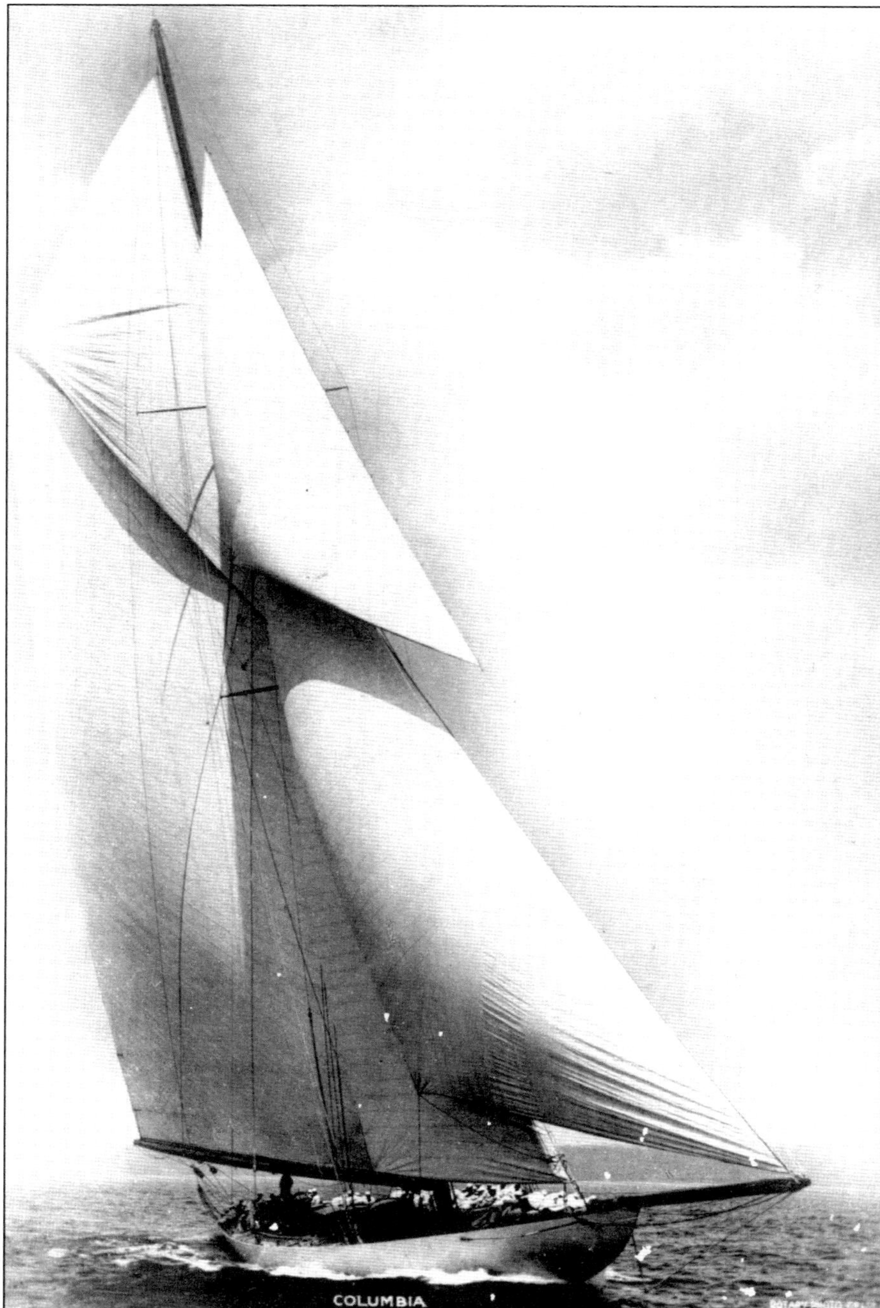

The yacht *Columbia* was built at the Nathaniel Herreshoff Yard in Bristol, Rhode Island, in 1899. She was owned by the New York Yacht Club syndicate during the time that J. P. Morgan was chairman. Capt. Charlie Barr sailed the *Columbia* to three straight victories over the *Shamrock*. Unfortunately for the *Shamrock*, her club topsail was carried away during the second race. Two years later, Captain Barr sailed *Columbia* against the *Shamrock II* and was again victorious in three races.

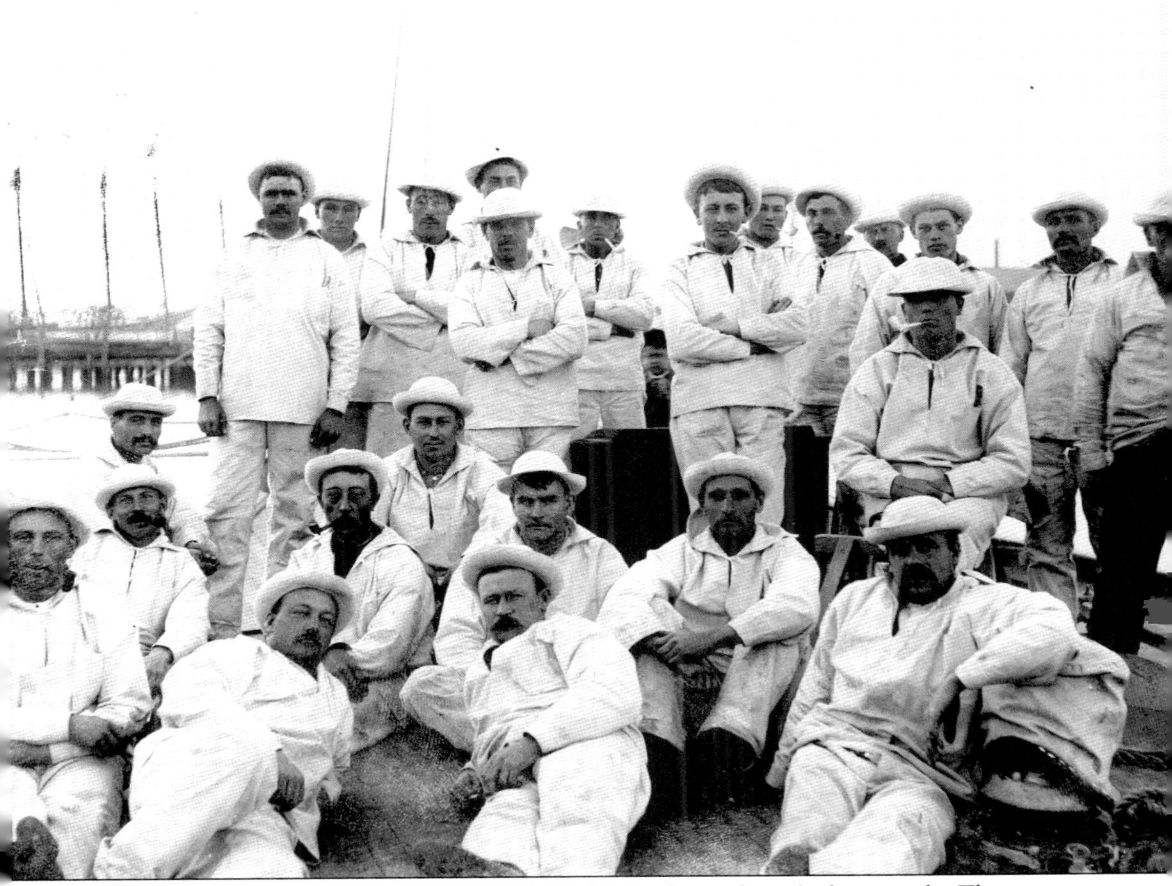

Seen here in 1899, the crew of the *Columbia* relaxes after a formal photograph. The crew members had been training for defense against the challenger, *Shamrock* of the Royal Ulster Yacht Club of Ireland, with a busy schedule of elimination races and activities. The result was another victory. This time about 80 percent of the crew came from Deer Isle and Stonington. Because of the reputation they earned in the Cup races, men from the island were in demand all over the world as yachtsmen.

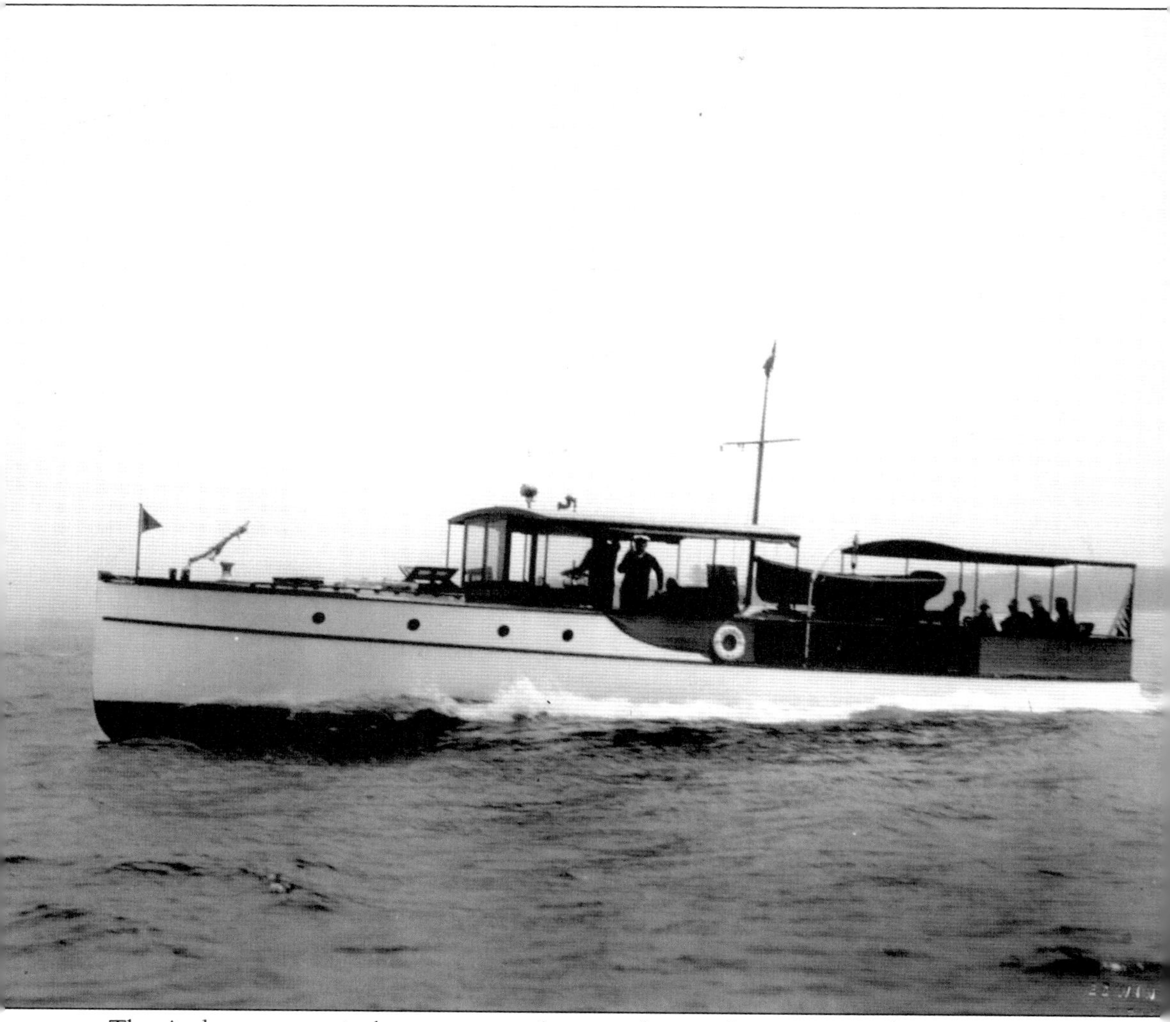

The *Arabus* was a typical commuter yacht, one of many that transported wealthy owners from their estates on Long Island Sound to their offices in Manhattan. Among the island commuter captains were Cleveland and Eugene Eaton of Little Deer Isle, Albert Coombs and Percy Joyce of Stonington, and Harry Annis and Alton Torrey of Deer Isle.